NORTH COUNTRY

NORTH
COUNTRY

Essays on the Upper Midwest
and Regional Identity

Edited by
JON K. LAUCK and GLEAVES WHITNEY

UNIVERSITY OF OKLAHOMA PRESS : NORMAN

Publication of this book is made possible through the generous support of The Gerald R. Ford Presidential Foundation and The McCasland Foundation, Duncan, Oklahoma.

Library of Congress Cataloging-in-Publication Data

Names: Lauck, Jon, 1971– editor. | Whitney, Gleaves, editor.
Title: North country : essays on the upper Midwest and regional identity / edited by Jon K. Lauck and Gleaves Whitney.
Other titles: Essays on the upper Midwest and regional identity
Description: Norman : University of Oklahoma Press, [2023] | Includes bibliographical references and index. | Summary: "Travel north from the upper Midwest's metropolises, and before long you're 'Up North,' a region that defies definition but is nonetheless unmistakable. In North Country, contributing scholars, journalists, and public intellectuals explore the distinctive landscape, culture, and history manifested in the northern margins of the American Midwest"—Provided by publisher.
Identifiers: LCCN 2022044599 | ISBN 978-0-8061-9188-1 (hardcover) | ISBN 978-0-8061-9189-8 (paperback)
Subjects: LCSH: Middle West—History. | Middle West—Ethnic relations—History. | Middle West—Social conditions. | BISAC: HISTORY / United States / State & Local / Midwest (IA, IL, IN, KS, MI, MN, MO, ND, NE, OH, SD, WI) | HISTORY / United States / 20th Century
Classification: LCC F351 .N67 2023 | DDC 977—dc23/eng/20221007
LC record available at https://lccn.loc.gov/2022044599

CONTENTS

INTRODUCTION

Finding the Northern Borderlands
of the American Midwest

On October 1, 2020, I drove northeast out of Sioux Falls, South Dakota, into Minnesota on a family trip. The leaves were turning, and the combine engines of the agricultural Midwest were roaring to the soybean harvest during a dry and cooperative year (the previous fall the ground was soggy and a quagmire for combines). Pheasant season would soon start. The corn harvest would mostly come later. This was the farming Midwest, with dusty chaff from the bean fields swirling around; pumpkins on porches; lines of trucks at grain elevators; and small strips of trees, known as shelterbelts, walling in well-organized farms. So went the drive on Highway 23 through farm fields arranged in a rectangular agrarian grid and through Minnesota towns like Jasper, Pipestone, Holland, Marshall, Hanley Falls, Granite Falls, and Clara City and across the Big Sioux River, Split Rock Creek, the Rock River, and the Redwood River, waterways mostly spent and exhausted and merely trickling this late in the season, long past the spring melt and the summer rains.

Signs of a coming transition appear when entering Spicer, Minnesota, planted next to sprawling Green Lake. In Spicer, the big Cenex farmers' cooperative—Mel's Sport Shop—is more a bait and tackle store than a gas station. Vats of live minnows and chubs and coolers full of nightcrawlers await eager fishermen, and giant faux lures hang on the wall waiting their turn to dangle from the mantle of a Minnesota lake cabin. Past Spicer, one comes to a few more bodies of water like Lake Koronis and towns like Cold Spring and finally enters the famed St. Cloud of Stearns County, the heartland of German Minnesota cleaved in two by the Mississippi River.[1] After a drive around the town's college campus—St. Cloud State University, home of the Huskies (whose mascot is Blizzard the Husky)—we pivot directly north for a half-hour drive to Little Falls, home to Charles Lindbergh, making our way parallel to the Mississippi.

By now, the intensely agrarian rhythms of the traditional Midwest are faint, and we have dialed in a new frequency. Just north of Little Falls we enter one particular gateway to the north, Brainerd, Minnesota, named for Ann Eliza Brainerd Smith, a Vermonter and accomplished author who had to fight off Confederate bandits sneaking into her state from Canada during the Civil War. This is where the world of lakes, forests, and cabins begins. I mean big lakes, like Winnibigoshish (67,000 acres), and big forests, massive stands of trees sprawling over thousands of acres, not mere huddles of trees on a sprawling prairie, seen a hundred miles back, which were planted by farmers during the 1930s to block their houses from the wind. On the north edge of Brainerd sits the Pillsbury State Forest, Minnesota's first (named for Minnesota governor John Pillsbury, of the wheat milling family, who donated the land), and Crow Wing State Forest and other big lakes like Pelican and North Long and Whitefish. The granddaddy of these lakes is Gull Lake, home to famed lodges frequented by those escaping cities for the fresh lake and forest air of the north. These include Grand View Lodge, Cragun's, Madden's, and Whitebirch Resort. Every winter, Gull Lake hosts the world's largest ice fishing tournament, run by the local Jaycees and welcoming 10,000 fishermen to 10,000 pre-augured holes and a city of beer tents—made toasty by warming stoves and propane patio heaters—pitched on the crystalline ice. On our fall trip, we caught the prize ceremony at the Bar Harbor Supper Club on Gull Lake for the Fishing to End Hunger charity tournament, hosted by local celebrity "Walleye Dan" Eigen, a college baseball player–turned–fishing guide, and organized back in 2013 to help needy kids in the Brainerd area.[2] In fifty miles or less, we had made the transition from corn culture to a walleye world, where the amount of corn production has dropped more than 90 percent and people like Walleye Dan are the local celebrities.[3]

The line separating farming Minnesota from northern Minnesota can be drawn across all the Midwest lake states. Instead of turning north to Brainerd, we could have driven from St. Cloud down to Minneapolis and across the bridge over the St. Croix River, once a watercourse swollen with logs and lumber floating toward hungry sawmills, and into Wisconsin, right by Hudson, where the Midwestern History Association was founded.[4] To then proceed East on Highway 12 through Wisconsin is to roughly follow the divide between the state's farming south and the north country. In western Wisconsin, some people place the line slightly north, above Rice Lake and close to Spooner, and prefer the division between north and south created by Highway 8. In central Wisconsin, the north begins above Stevens Point and Appleton, although some would lean toward a line connecting Eau Claire and Wausau, old mill towns that thrived on the northern forests. Some say Portage, home of Frederick Jackson Turner, is a border town and an entry point to the north. While others object that it is too far south, Portage itself declares that it is "where the north begins." Or drive north of the cranberry bogs of greater Warrens in Monroe County, some say, and you will have crossed the line. Whatever the precise threshold, it is clear that Rhinelander, Eagle River, Lake Tomahawk, Hayward, and the glorious and peninsular Door County are in the north, as are the big stands of trees, the Chequamegon-Nicolet National Forest, the Flambeau River State Forest, and the Brule River State Forest.[5] Or, to be obvious: if you are hunkered in a shack outside Hurley on the Michigan line and waiting for a buck to pass by so you can retire to Bear Chasers Lodge Bar & Grill, you are up north.[6] Or, if you are a few counties west, in Douglas County, where Calvin Coolidge fished the Bois Brule River in 1928, and, in 1949, Louis Spray caught the world record muskie out of the Chippewa Flowage and sparked off a battle of fish tales, you are up north.[7]

If you want to avoid Chicago traffic and jump over to find the north-south division in Michigan, drive the hundred miles south from Door County down to Milwaukee and jump on the ferry across Lake Michigan to Muskegon. Then drive north along the big lake until you reach Highway 10 and then turn east. This path east tracks a line that can reasonably be seen as dividing Michigan's agrarian bottom from its wooded top. Others generally agree with the Highway 10 designation but draw a specific line from Pentwater in the west to Pinconning on Saginaw Bay in the east because "South of the line, the land is so flat and farmy—might as well be Ohio."[8] Some locals in Michigan draw the dividing line between Clare and Isabella Counties and between Osceola and Mecosta Counties. Midland County is still farm oriented, which stands to reason from its name, but Lake County, by a similar logic, is above the line where the woods and lakes begin. Above Mt. Pleasant and the city of Mecosta is definitely north. Of course the *Upper* Peninsula is by definition the north country and so different that some Yoopers want to break away entirely from the lower parts of the Michigan mitten.[9]

All this is to say that the North Country is a unique and identifiable subregion of the Midwest. Its identity is so strong that a few think, mostly jestingly and largely to market their stocking caps, it should separate itself from the overall Midwest and instead declare itself "The North."[10] It all speaks to the power of place and the recognition, as D.H. Lawrence said, that "different places on the face of the earth have different vital effluence, different vibration, different chemical exhalation, different polarity with different stars."[11] More Native American reservations are located in the North Country, for example, and their northern orientation contributes to the area's complexity and sense of separation from the south.[12] There are also more French names—Cloquet, Eau Claire, Fond du Lac, Grand Marais, Grosse Pointe, Isle Royale, LaCrosse, Presque Isle—because New France and its traders and explorers and black robes arrived early.[13] The biome is distinct, featuring lots of pine and birch, and it is colder, so corn will not grow, creating a critical distinction with the more southerly Midwest.[14] Native Americans long knew that to grow corn one must live far enough south to have a safe 160-day growing season (140-day was possible, but risky) and if one lived above that line, it was best to focus on hunting and fishing.[15] The colder climate above the line fosters activities such as ice fishing, skiing, snowmobiling, ice hockey (which defines the lives of many Northwoods families—see the recent documentary *Hockeyland*), and even ice yachting.[16] The massive stands of timber led to a lumber industry that left a deep imprint on the region (much like the open prairies of the southern Midwest made it rectangular farm country). People still know about cruisers, sawyers, swampers, and river pigs and carry on the tradition of big checked woolen shirts (to get in the spirit, mark the summer lumberjack festival in Wolverine, Michigan, on your calendar).[17] The great historian of the north woods, Agnes Larsen, called these enduring flannels the product of the "red-shirted Garibaldians of the pineries."[18] Place-names include Logging Creek, Logger Lake, Lumberjack

Lake, Two Axe Lake, Bootjack Lake, and Paul Bunyan Punch Bowl.[19] The lumberjacks also sang songs:

> On its banks and right before me
> Stood a pine in stately glory.
> The forest king he seemed to be.
> He was a noble Big Pine Tree.
> I gazed upon his form gigantic.
> Thoughts ran through my head romantic.
> These were my musings as I stood
> And viewed that monarch of the wood.[20]

The topography also facilitates a walleye fishing culture that sustains many guides, outfitters, and boat dealers (think Hemingway and the Two-Hearted River); the culture of hunting and rifles is strong in a land of deer, moose, and bear; and hunting cabins (called "camps" in Wisconsin and Michigan) dot the Northwoods (which were, appropriately, the home of Charlton Heston).[21] Wolves and mountain lions roam the northern reaches of the region. This is also where the Algonkians hunted elk, moose, and woodland caribou.[22] Viking lore hovers, not just because of the Minnesota football team, but because of lingering legends of early Norse explorers in the region whose veracity continues to stir debate.[23]

Across the Great Lakes is Canada, making the North Country more connected to and conscious of our northern neighbor, which is largely forgotten by other Americans.[24] The Great Lakes are perhaps the most powerful unifying force for the region. Besides creating a nexus with Canada, the lakes support a large-scale shipping industry and sustain ports such as Duluth, Marquette, and Two Harbors and a retinue of lock managers and, in decades past, lighthouse keepers.[25] The lakes connect mines in the north to factories in the south via impressively large ore haulers slogging their cargos across the lakes.[26] The mystique of the big boats lives on, and not just in the form of the *Edmund Fitzgerald*, but in the recognition of the arduousness of life on the lakers; the cold suffering of the dead who were swallowed during the "Season of the Witch" by the notorious storms over the deep waters, especially Superior; and the "human need to honor, grieve, and remember."[27]

The need to remember and to find and describe particular places of special meaning are driving forces behind this volume, which is designed to explore many of the varied corners and legacies of the North Country as part of the effort to revive the study of the Midwest.[28] The Midwest is a "lost region," at least in the historiography of the United States.[29] Its history has been woefully neglected in comparison to other American regions, and it deserves more attention. This volume focuses on the northern reaches of the Midwest and attempts to draw the historical gaze to this subregion's particularities. It resists the flattening effects of national histories and the erasure of regional distinctions and recognizes that place matters.[30]

The story of the Midwest's northern borderlands obviously begins with the Native American experience. The story of one Anishinaabe family, as told by Theodore Karamanski in his chapter, illustrates the creative blend of persistence and accommodation that was required of people caught up north on what became the American-Canadian line. Karamanski demonstrates how one Native family, divided by the border but sharing a similar northern Midwest heritage, attempted to blunt assimilationist and removal policies by forming an alliance with the Roman Catholic Church, a European institution that was outside state control and anxious to undertake independent missionary outreach. By creating Native Catholic communities, tribal leaders preserved their people's place in the northern Midwest, giving the region added uniqueness by way of a persisting Native presence.

In his chapter, Peter DeCarlo moves the story from the Anishinaabeg to the Dakhóta. Few texts have focused on the movement of Dakhóta people onto the Northern Plains after their wars with the Anishinaabeg and the U.S.-Dakhóta War of 1862. The borderland that the Dakhóta migrated into—the Upper Red River Valley between Pembina, North Dakota, in northeastern Dakota Territory and Fort Garry in Winnipeg—is largely uncharted in the literature. DeCarlo's chapter presents the Upper Red River Valley not only as a colonial borderland, claimed by the United States and Hudson's Bay Company, but an Indigenous one in which the Ojibwe, Métis, and Dakhóta asserted their sovereignty and shaped the culture and history of the northern Midwest. It also contributes to the history of the U.S.-Dakhóta War, reframing the Dakhóta's movement north as a political and economic decision within a longer colonial struggle instead of a forlorn retreat from state violence. Dakhóta leaders Šákpedan and Wakȟáŋ Ožaŋžáŋ are reinterpreted as sophisticated leaders who used the borderland and colonial law to resist oppression and put their stamp on the region.

Another distinctive population of the northern Midwest stems from the Finnish immigration stream to the region, which flowed, in particular, into the Upper Peninsula of Michigan. The Upper Midwest's Northwoods region, Hilary-Joy Virtanen explains in her chapter, is identifiable by its abundant forests and lakes; a cold and harsh climate; a labor history centered on mining, logging, and commercial fishing; and a mostly rural cultural community consisting of Indigenous woodland peoples and the descendants of immigrants from Eastern and Southern Europe and the Nordic countries. These factors have contributed to the development of stereotypes, many of which support the notion that inhabitants of the Northwoods are hardy, self-sufficient, and stoic people, who may on the one hand be suspicious of newcomers and social change but on the other hand be generous and kind to total strangers in need. In Virtanen's chapter, the role of gender and ethnicity in the development of stereotypes will be explored through the case of the Finns, whose cultural presence has had an immense impact on the Upper Midwest, and particularly on Michigan's Upper Peninsula, northern Wisconsin and Minnesota, and southwestern Ontario. Gendered stereotypes of Finns draw from and are retold through many sources, including jokes, stories, songs, and even epic poetry and internet memes that serve to define the upper reaches of the Midwest as a particular place.

While the Finns were moving into the Upper Midwest during the nineteenth century, the region was becoming increasingly identifiable as a particular place in part due to its natural landscape and associated economy. Outlining the Midwest and its subregions with greater accuracy, Gregory Rose argues, requires discarding state borders and instead identifying regional boundaries that deviate from political or legal lines and that consider the margins of the Midwest as transition zones rather than sharp demarcations. Rose finds the approximate edge between a traditional Midwest and a northern-oriented subregion, and this edge roughly approximates the northern line of the Corn Belt. If the Corn Belt is considered the core of the Midwest, then most of northern Michigan, Wisconsin, and Minnesota is beyond the overall region's corn-dominated core. The Dairy Belt, the agricultural zone immediately north of the Corn Belt, has a climate less conducive to the production of corn as grain. At the northern edge of the Dairy Belt a vegetative transition zone occurs where prairie or deciduous forests merge into predominately coniferous forests. Rose also notes that immigration by non-Indigenous peoples to the northern areas of Michigan, Wisconsin, and Minnesota occurred later and that the mix of populations was different and included proportionally more New Englanders, New Yorkers, and foreign natives, notably from Canada, Germany, and Scandinavia.

If cropping patterns, topography, and demography are too abstract to advance the project of understanding regional identity in the North Country, consider some of the specific experiences of particular people, like the freelance reporter

John Bartlow Martin. Inspired by a honeymoon visit, Martin, an Indiana native who had established his writing base in Chicago, convinced the noted publisher Alfred Knopf Sr. to take a chance and agree to publish his book on the history and people of the Upper Peninsula of Michigan, an intellectual journey described in Ray Boomhower's chapter. Published on May 15, 1944, Martin's book *Call It North Country: The Story of Upper Michigan* captured not only the region's wild beauty but the character of those who lived there—people "among the finest and friendliest on earth," who, Martin said, "when they know you and like you, there is absolutely nothing they will not do for you. But this takes time, you must not push, they have to find out about you." Fascinating, often larger-than-life characters populate *Call It North Country*, from trappers and surveyors to ore miners, lumberjacks, and prostitutes, all in a wild wilderness region isolated from state government in Lansing, Michigan, and which, by all logic, should have been part of Wisconsin. Martin also included famous names in his book, such as William Austin Burt, who painstakingly surveyed the region and discovered the first iron deposits, as well as the Detroit automotive magnate Henry Ford, who at one time owned a million acres in the Upper Peninsula. The discovery of iron and copper set a pattern for the region, which Martin described as "boom-and-bust country, mineral land, timberland. Yet it always had remained wilderness country."

The balance and battles between mining and nature, between industry and wilderness, is what concerned Sigurd F. Olson of Minnesota, one of the foremost American environmentalists of the twentieth century. In his chapter, Jacob Bruggeman explains how Olson served as vice president and president of the Wilderness Society and as a member and president of the National Parks Association's board of trustees and remains the only individual to have received each of the highest honors from the Sierra Club, Izaak Walton League, Wilderness Society, and National Wildlife Federation, along with the John Burroughs Medal for nature writing. Bruggeman argues that Olson's involvement in the conservation movement was guided by an environmental ethic firmly rooted in regional identity and especially its historical components as embodied by Minnesota's lineage of woodsmen and the French "voyageurs" who once called the Quetico Superior wilderness their homes. Olson thought that his region's historical and natural heritage was so precious that he devoted his life to protecting and writing about it, producing several best-selling volumes and countless essays on the region's history and wilderness. More than his conservation activism, it was these writings that marshaled public support for wilderness protection. In reemphasizing the centrality of regional identity in Olson's writings, Bruggeman resituates his environmental ethic in the growing scholarship on the Midwest's history and argues that Olson's popular appeal was made possible by its cultivation of an accessible, reasonably coherent concept of the region's environmental and cultural history.

In a personal and more contemporary consideration, and one with echoes of Sigurd Anderson, Christopher Vondracek recalls how, as a southern Minnesotan, the North Country held a mystical, unknowable quality for him and always captured his imagination on trips up Highway 169 or 71 for cross-country meets or to enjoy his family's cabin outside Itasca State Park. Far from the taconite-pellet-in-hand musings of a grandfatherly poet, or the foreboding stories about union busting, or even the canoe trips into a pristine, pine-sheltered lake for a ghost story about the Windigo, a boy from Wells and Kiester, Minnesota, knew the flat horizons of farm country and the taciturn crank of combines far more than he ever knew of Grand Marais or Warroad. But a commonality existed among rural folk, who understood the psyche of "out-staters," often defined and diminished by the hot glare of the Twin Cities. Stuck associating with the quieter, less romantic reaches of a land so often identified with its northern forests and legendary wildlife, Vondracek delves into his own ambivalence about marketing fights over the "Bold North" and seeks to mend that incongruous divide: what can the soybean farmer from Faribault County along the Iowa border say to the miner up in Eveleth?

The line between north and south was also at work in the mind of the intellectual Michigander Russell Kirk (1918–94), who, by his midthirties, had become a towering figure in the world of letters. Little appreciated is the extent to which Kirk's imagination and philosophical sensibilities were formed in a childhood divided between two very different Michigan places—one in the growing city of Plymouth, a leafy suburb of Detroit; the other in the fading village of Mecosta, in a glaciated sand county "up north." Even though both of these communities are in Michigan's Lower Peninsula, in Kirk's mind, the two hundred miles separating them might as well have been continents apart. For Kirk internalized two dramatically different perspectives in Plymouth and Mecosta. The former gave him the sense of communal New England solidarity that hearkened back to John Adams's virtuous republic; life there was civil and earnest. The latter gave him a sense of nature's abiding ruggedness in the "stump country" frontier up north;

life there was harder and less polite. In Kirk's writings, there is a stark boundary between the two different places. One way to interpret Kirk's many works of fiction and nonfiction is to see the New England influence in Plymouth in fierce tension with the raw stump country up north. This geographic and cultural polarity would inform a variety of Kirk's works—from his philosophical conservatism to his gothic fiction to his autobiographical writings. In his chapter, Gleaves Whitney looks at the forging of this polarity between Plymouth and Mecosta in Kirk's childhood, as laid out in his autobiographical writings.

In another personal reflection, and one in the vein of Vondracek and Kirk, that contemplates the passage from the agrarian Midwest to the Northwoods, Kevin Koch takes a multifaceted look at Lake Itasca and connects it topically as well as personally to his downriver home along the Mississippi in Iowa in the Midwest Driftless Area. Koch traces the rush among Euro-American explorers to "discover" the headwaters of the Mississippi River, culminating in Henry Schoolcraft's 1832 locating and renaming of Omushkos (or Elk Lake) as Lake Itasca, the "true head." The Ojibwe found this obsession with the headwaters confounding because it raised one tributary above all others in the formation of the great river. They thought the river and its tributaries were all one thing and realized that ecosystems by their very nature are multilayered and interconnected. Koch discusses the glacial geological forces that formed Itasca, investigates the expansive modern-day forest surrounding the lake and the logging industry that nearly decimated the old-growth timber, and reports on animal populations such as the return of wolf packs, icons of the North Country.

The deep ecology of Lake Itasca considered by Koch also figures in the story advanced by Hank Meijer in his chapter about a lost mastodon and the Mason-Quimby Line. The unlikely odyssey of one of the most complete mastodon skeletons ever found offers a lens through which to take a fresh look at the upper limits of what we think of as the Midwest. Natural history merges with nineteenth-century notions of popular entertainment in this account of what happened to the remains of a great beast once common to the region that would become the Old Northwest. Enterprising promoters endeavored to wring profit from the bones discovered in southern Ontario, and their traveling show bounced around small towns, often along the routes of the Great Northern Railway, the line that brought immigrant settlers to the frontier. The westward journey came to a stop in North Dakota. There the bones, after evading repatriation, disappeared for decades before reemerging at the end of the twentieth century.

Why they languished so long remains a mystery, but their trail quite coincidentally follows another line, one that predated the Great Northern route. This was
a line mapped out by a pair of archaeologists named Quimby and Mason, who
traced the northward extent of the mastodon migration as the glaciers receded.
The Mason-Quimby Line is a new way to think about where the upper stretches
of the Midwest begin.

The riddle of the mastodon and the northern mystique described by Vondracek both speak to a certain sense of mystery that pervades the literature of the
region, as Zachary Michael Jack explains in his chapter. Readers often associate
the iconic settings of English literature with the word "gothic," conjuring places
such as the Yorkshire moors of Emily Brontë's *Wuthering Heights* or the haunting Dartmoor of Arthur Conan Doyle's *The Hound of the Baskervilles*. But while
the genre emanates from the United Kingdom and northern Europe, it refuses
to be confined to old-world locations. Instead, its trademark dark, wild, and
brooding landscapes can and do occur in analogous climates and topographies
around the world. The heavily wooded and windswept shores of Michigan and
Wisconsin, in particular, make them perfect for the development of a new world
fatalism as cultural aesthetic. In fact, a twenty-year run of Great Lakes Gothic hits
begins with the publication of Michigander John Voelker's *New York Times* best-
selling novel of 1956, *Anatomy of a Murder*; gathers momentum with Wisconsin
resident Robert Bloch's 1959 novel *Psycho*; and culminates in the darker notes,
the duende, of Gordon Lightfoot's chart-topping single of 1976, "The Wreck of
the Edmund Fitzgerald." While coastal critics too often failed to connect the
dots, the pronounced literary and cinematic interest in the region across two
decades heralded a Great Lakes Gothic phenomenon that continued well into
the 1980s and beyond in the "Dark Lutheranism" and "Prairie Gothic" of Minnesotans Garrison Keillor and filmmakers Joel and Ethan Coen, among others.

Beyond the mystique and the mystery and the underlying current of darkness in the literary culture is a generally happier and much more tangible aspect
of contemporary life in the North Country: tourist fishing. As Tim Frandy
explains in his chapter, the Upper Midwest has branded itself as an outdoors
tourist destination. Beginning in the early twentieth century, resorts sprang
up to accommodate ever-growing numbers of tourists who traveled north
to swim, fish, boat, and partake in other outdoor recreational activities. For
long-term residents of the region, traditions of subsistence fishing were now
mixed with their ability to sell their services as guides to tourists. The impacts

of this tourism on the region were complex, in particular as it called attention to pronounced cultural differences between insiders and outsiders and intensified these distinctions through the mid-twentieth century. This intensification was crucial in the evolution of a distinct Northwoods identity, rooted both in its own tradition as well as in dialogue with tourists. This fieldwork-based chapter looks at a sampling of the enduring narratives of fishing guides and tourists that continue to be told three-quarters of a century later. These stories—rich in humor, in insider-outsider themes, in coded messages suggesting how to conduct oneself outdoors—reflect how identity was constructed through this discourse between locals and tourists.

The emerging fishing economy also collided with ascendant demands of Native Americans and led to extensive litigation. From the mid-1980s through the early 1990s, as Adam Mertz explains, federal court decisions recognizing Ojibwe nations' rights to hunt, fish, and gather off their reservations embroiled Wisconsin in controversy. The conflict grew especially confrontational and violent in the northern third of the state, where the Ojibwe exercised these rights. While some Wisconsinites supported Native Americans as a civil rights issue, critics of treaty rights charged that these "special" rights for Native Americans undermined the state's increasingly significant tourism industry. Rural white residents in northern Wisconsin were particularly dependent on the tourism industry, and they worried that Native Americans' increased ability to exercise treaty rights—especially Ojibwe rights to spear walleyes in public lakes—would reduce the number of annual tourists, thereby threatening the livelihood of those involved in tourism. Since northern Wisconsin residents already harbored hostility toward the more-populous southern part of the state, the fishing controversy fueled north-south tensions and tapped a deep vein of animosity against state government agencies headquartered in the south.

Lastly, words of thanks are in order for all of those who made this multifaceted look at the North Country possible. This project began with an extensive panel discussion at the Midwestern History Association conference in Michigan in 2018, and all of us involved in this book thank the organizers for their strong support and for giving us a platform. At that conference, Gleaves Whitney and I finalized the plans for this project, which would not have been possible without the MHA; the Hauenstein Center, which hosted the conference; and the many scholars who joined this effort to understand the deeper meanings of regional identity in the United States. Special thanks are extended to Joe Schiller, acquisitions editor at the University of Oklahoma Press and a proud son of Detroit Lakes, Minnesota, who has more than enough hockey injuries to prove his North Country bona fides.

NOTES

1. See Kathleen Neils Conzen, *Making Their Own America: Assimilation Theory and the German Peasant Pioneer* (Washington, DC: German Historical Institute, 1990).

2. Daniel Huss, "Walleye Dan First Dropped Anchor in Eden Prairie," *Southwest News Media* (Savage, MN), April 12, 2017; "Fishing to End Hunger Attracts More Than 100 Anglers," *Pine and Lakes Echo* (Brainerd, MN), October 12, 2019.

3. In far southwest Minnesota, in Rock County, 136,000 acres are devoted to corn production. In Crow Wing County, home of Brainerd, 6,500 acres are devoted to corn production. *Census of Agriculture* (U.S. Department of Agriculture, 2017).

4. Bill Glauber, "A Bar Full of Academics, a Few Old-Fashioneds, and Donald Trump Spur Midwest History Resurgence," *Milwaukee Journal Sentinel*, July 25, 2017.

5. Barry Adams, "Up North, Not on a Map but a Prolific Wisconsin Place," *Wisconsin State Journal*, May 24, 2014.

6. See Travis Dewitz, *Blaze Orange: Whitetail Deer Hunting in Wisconsin* (Madison: Wisconsin State Historical Society Press, 2014).

7. See Dennis Anderson, "A Fishy Record-Chasing Tale Involving Bud Grant," *Star Tribune*, July 11, 2019.

8. Peter Gavrilovich, "Where Does Up North Even Begin, Anyway?," *Detroit Free Press*, August 4, 2013.

9. Camden Burd, "A New 'State of Superior': Political Fracture and Anti-environmentalism in the Upper Midwest," in *The Conservative Heartland: A Political History of the Postwar American Midwest*, eds. Jon K. Lauck and Catherine McNichol Stock (Lawrence: University Press of Kansas, 2020), 153–70.

10. Steve Marsh, "What Is North?" *Minneapolis-St. Paul Magazine*, November 19, 2015.

11. D. H. Lawrence, *Studies in Classic American Literature* (London: Heinemann, 1964), 5–6.

12. Joseph D. Schiller, "Hiawatha and Leatherstocking, from Native Borderlands to Regional Border," in *The Interior Borderlands: Regional Identity in the Midwest and Great Plains*, ed. Jon K. Lauck (Sioux Falls: Center for Western Studies, 2019), 201–14.

13. Robert Michael Morrissey, "The French Midwest," in *The Oxford History of the American Midwest*, ed. Jon K. Lauck (New York: Oxford University Press, forthcoming).

14. Howard G. Roepke, "Changes in Corn Production on the Northern Margin of the Corn Belt," *Agricultural History* 33, no. 3 (July 1959): 126–32.

15. Richard White, *The Middle Ground: Indians, Empires, and Republics in the Great Lakes Region, 1650–1815* (New York: Cambridge University Press, 1991), 43 (placing the line around Green Bay, or about thirty miles north of Highway 10); Michael A. McDonnell, *Masters of Empire: Great Lakes Indians and the Making of America* (New York: Hill and Wang, 2015), 27 (noting that the Huron "lived close to the 120-frost-free-day line that marked the northern limit of maize cultivation").

16. Dave Caldwell, "Hockeyland: The Minnesota Towns Where High School Players Are Stars," *The Guardian*, November 23, 2021; Charlotte Peterson, "When Water Freezes Over," *Sailing Magazine*, March 1, 2017.

17. Ruth Stoveken, "The Pine Lumberjacks in Wisconsin," *Wisconsin Magazine of History* 30, no. 3 (March 1947): 322–23; George B. Engberg, "Lumber and Labor in the Lake States," *Minnesota History* 36, no. 5 (March 1959): 157; Moira F. Harris, "Echoes from the Woods: Legacies of Logging in Minnesota," *Minnesota History* 63, no. 5 (Spring 2013): 204.

18. Agnes M. Larsen, "When Logs and Lumber Ruled Stillwater," *Minnesota History* 18, no. 2 (June 1937): 166. For Larsen's classic treatment, see Agnes M. Larsen, *History of the White Pine Industry in Minnesota* (Minneapolis: University of Minnesota Press, 1949).

19. Randall E. Rohe, "Place-names: Relics of the Great Lakes Lumber Era," *Journal of Forest History* 28, no. 3 (July 1984): 126–28.

20. Shan T. Boy, "Ye Noble Big Pine Tree," in *Pinery Boys: Songs and Songcatching in the Lumberjack Era*, eds. Franz Rickaby, Gretchen Dykstra, and James P. Leary (Madison: University of Wisconsin Press, 2017), 165.

21. John J. Miller, "Northern Michigan People: Charlton Heston's Northwoods Boyhood," *My North*, November 14, 2012.

22. Harold Hickerson, "The Feast of the Dead among the Seventeenth-Century Algonkians of the Upper Great Lakes," *American Anthropologist* 62, no. 1 (February 1960): 83.

23. David M. Krueger, *Myths of the Rune Stone: Viking Martyrs and the Birthplace of America* (Minneapolis: University of Minnesota Press, 2015); Douglas Hunter, *Beardmore: The Viking Hoax That Rewrote History* (Montreal: McGill-Queen's University Press, 2018).

24. See John J. Bukowczyk, Nora Faires, David R. Smith, and Randy Widdis, eds., *Permeable Border: The Great Lakes Basin as Transnational Region, 1650–1990* (Pittsburgh: University of Pittsburgh Press, 2005).

25. Theodore J. Karamanski, *Mastering the Inland Seas: How Lighthouses, Navigational Aids, and Harbors Transformed the Great Lakes and America* (Madison: University of Wisconsin Press, 2020).

26. Frank Boles, *Sailing into History: Great Lakes Bulk Carriers of the Twentieth Century and the Crews Who Sailed Them* (East Lansing: Michigan State University Press, 2017); Bruce Bowlus, "Bold Experiments: The Evolution of the Great Lakes Ore Carrier," *Michigan Historical Review* 22, no. 1 (Spring 1996): 1–17; Jeffrey T. Manuel, *Taconite Dreams: The Struggle to Sustain Mining on Minnesota's Iron Range, 1915–2000* (Minneapolis: University of Minnesota Press, 2015).

27. Michael Schumacher, *Torn in Two: The Sinking of the* Daniel J. Morrell *and One Man's Survival on the Open Sea* (Minneapolis: University of Minnesota Press, 2016), 10 (witch); Jacqueline Justice, "Classical Tragedy and the Wreck of the *Edmund Fitzgerald*: Why the Legend Lives On," *Journal of American Culture* 36, no. 2 (June 2013): 89 (human). See also Victoria Brehm, ed., *White Squall: Sailing the Great Lakes* (Detroit: Wayne State University Press, 2018).

28. Jon K. Lauck, "The Origins and Progress of the Midwestern History Association, 2013–2016," *Studies in Midwestern History* 2, no. 11 (October 2016): 139–49.

29. Jon K. Lauck, *The Lost Region: Toward a Revival of Midwestern History* (Iowa City: University of Iowa Press, 2013).

30. Wilfred M. McClay and Ted V. McAllister, eds., *Why Place Matters: Geography, Identity, and Civic Life in Modern America* (New York: Encounter Books, 2014).

FOUNDING FATHERS AND SONS

One Anishinaabe Family's Multigenerational
Struggle to Resist Settler Colonialism in the
Great Lakes Borderland

Great Britain spawned two powerful settler colonial states in North America,
the United States and the Dominion of Canada. Each imposed themselves on
indigenous polities and for generations used policy and history to all but erase
Native presence. The borderland between the settler colonial states posed unique
challenges to the numerous indigenous nations whose homeland was sundered
by the U.S.-Canada political frontier. The territory of the Wabenaki, Iroquois,
Blackfeet, and Ojibwe nations were all disrupted by the artificial line.[1] Invasion
and division posed unique challenges to the Native people of the northern border region. The story of one Anishinaabe family illustrates the creative blend of
persistence and accommodation that was required for people caught between
the tectonic plates of settler colonial states. Their experience also illustrates
the striking similarities between British-Canadian First Nation policy and the
Indian policy of the United States. Although these settler colonial states started
with very different approaches to indigenous people by the mid-nineteenth

century, the Anishinaabeg both north and south of the line found themselves with a similar challenge to survivance.[2]

Where Lake Michigan and Lake Huron come together is the traditional homeland of the Odawa people. It is one of the historic crossroads of the Midwest region that has long been the locus of trade and transportation. The very name "Odawa" means "to trade" in the Algonquin language the Odawa share with their Anishinaabe cousins and neighbors, the Ojibwe and Potawatomi. Since time immemorial it has been a region where east-west and north-south trade routes came together. But historically, waterways have served to both divide as well as unite peoples. Division was the decision made by British and American negotiators at the conclusion of the American Revolution when the Great Lakes became a blue-water boundary between the new nation and Great Britain's Canadian colonies. The Odawa had not been parties to the negotiation that sundered their homeland, and they did not accept it meekly.

Two Odawa brothers born on the shores of Lake Michigan initially chose to ignore the artificial line. Although we do not know the exact date Assiginack and Mackadepenessy were born, it is likely they were adolescents when the Treaty of Paris was signed. Both of their names derived from an Odawa variation on the words "Blackbird" and "Blackhawk." The boundary did not prevent the boys born at the L'Arbre Croche village in what is now northern Michigan from going to Canada to receive a European education from Sulpician priests at the Lac-des-Deux-Montagnes mission school. They were likely recruited because they were the grandsons of Pungowish, one of the leading war chiefs of the Odawa. Tribal elders may have selected the boys to be trained as interlocutors with the European Americans. In Canada, they were tutored in the Catholic faith and gained some familiarity with the language and customs of the French and English. Their school was located on the canoe route west from Montreal, and Mackadepenessy, likely the older of the two boys, at some point gave up his studies and joined one of the fur trade brigades bound for adventure in the northwest. For nearly twenty years he lived with Odawa trappers in Manitoba. During this time, his contact with the avarice of European traders and voyageurs taught him to have a healthy suspicion of the white man. Meanwhile, his brother Assiginack seems to have been more receptive of their school experience, and under the priest's tutelage, he became a devout Catholic.[3]

The brothers reunited in Michigan on the eve of the War of 1812, which they perceived as a chance to drive the Americans from their homeland. Assiginack participated in the capture of the U.S. troops at Fort Mackinac and later led warriors in support of British attacks as far west as Prairie du Chien and as far east as Niagara. This aggressive role was in contrast to the stance of an older brother, Ningegon, who headed an Odawa band near the straits that refused to take up arms against the Americans. Assiginack and many other Anishinaabeg trusted that the British alliance would protect their homeland. Late in the war, both Assiginack and Mackadepenessy participated in a raid that penetrated deep into the Indiana Territory in which they killed nine American soldiers and brought back one as a prisoner. However, when they returned, British officers told them that in Europe a peace had been agreed to, and the British would withdraw to their side of the lake border, leaving the Odawa at L'Arbre Croche to the tender mercies of the Americans. This reinstatement of the international boundary divided the brothers. Assiginack cast his lot with the British and was given the position as the interpreter at His Majesty's new fort at Drummond Island. Mackadepenessy remained at L'Arbre Croche, but every summer he and many of his people took their canoes to Drummond Island to receive "gifts" from their British "father." In this way, Odawa families divided by the border remained connected.[4]

Mackadepenessy accepted British gifts, but, like many other Odawa, he was disillusioned by what they took to be betrayal by the British. At the same time, he also had no illusions as to the challenge to his people posed by the return of American sovereignty. His low opinion of all white men was conveyed to his son. "He told us to beware of them, as they all were after one great object, namely to grasp the world's wealth." To secure this end, they would "lie, steal, rob and murder." Yet, Mackadepenessy understood that his people faced a crisis that could only be managed by some type of accommodation to the growth of European American power on the lake frontier. The two brothers divided by an imaginary line nonetheless cooperated on a strategy that could accommodate the settler states pressing in on First Nation country and still preserve autonomy for the Odawa. At the heart of this strategy was the embrace of Christianity to increase their access to sacred power and build alliances with factions within the settler states. They studiously rejected the Protestant missionaries sent by the U.S. government to Mackinac Island and instead reached out to the Catholic Church. This was a conservative path to cultural change, one that reinforced their bonds with the Odawa-French mixed-blood fur traders who were critical to the economy of the region, and with a Church that had long resided among the Odawa during the French regime. The Jesuits had based missionaries in the straits region from the time of Father Jacques Marquette in the 1670s to the British conquest of Canada in 1763. Their harvest of converts was meager, and their presence had not disrupted Odawa lifeways, which made them seem a safe option.[5]

The strategy the two brothers worked out with other Odawa leaders[6] is revealed in a series of petitions that were sent from L'Arbre Croche to the seats of European and European American power. The first was to President James Monroe in 1823 and requested U.S. government assistance in their conversion to "civilization," which essentially meant settlement in agricultural villages and instruction in Christianity. "Trusting in your paternal goodness, we claim liberty of conscience, and beg you grant us a master or minister of the gospel belonging to the same society as members of the Catholic Society of St. Ignatius." The careful claim of "liberty of conscience" indicates the degree to which the Odawa appreciated the marginal status of Catholicism within the halls of the American government, which openly used federal funds to promote Protestant missions to the Indians. Such a phrase also reveals the fingerprints of the Odawa's white interlocutors. In particular, this was Father Gabriel Richard, the only priest in the Michigan Territory and a savvy political operative who in 1823 served as the territorial delegate to Congress. Richard had visited L'Arbre Croche several times and was a logical conduit to get their petition to Washington, D.C. Four months later, a second petition was sent to President Monroe. This missive, likely at Richard's instigation, was also reprinted in the *Annales de l'Association de la Propagation de la Foi,* a Paris-based publication series designed to promote Catholic overseas missions.[7]

While the Monroe administration did not respond to either overture, they did elicit a response from the Catholic Church, which in 1825 sent a visiting priest, Vincent Badin, to L'Arbre Croche. What he found there surprised and impressed him. Arriving by canoe, he was escorted to a bark chapel erected by the Odawa, where he was greeted by hymn singing "uplifting his soul" and rivaling anything he had ever heard in Europe. This was followed by a long queue of Odawa awaiting formal baptism. This impressive showing was largely the handiwork of Andowish, an Odawa who had studied Catholicism in Canada, and Mackadepenessy. The former returned to his home village, where he took on the role of lay minister and directed the building of the chapel and taught Catholic hymns and prayers. Mackadepenessy set up an impromptu school in his lodge, where he taught what he remembered of a written version of the Algonquin language that he had learned years before at Lake of the Two Mountains. He also presented Father Badin with yet another petition, this one to the

Superior General of the Jesuits and the king of France. It emphasized social and economic problems such as alcohol abuse and requested "a French priest to teach us temperance and the way to salvation."[8]

The petition to the king of France revealed the degree to which the Anishinaabeg and the Catholic Church ignored the legalities of international borders. Before Badin returned to Detroit, he crossed the border to meet with Assiginack on Drummond Island. The missionary regarded Assiginack as "*les grand chef*" of the Odawa, and he wanted his influence as an orator, which was widely acknowledged, and his knowledge of Catholicism available to fortify the budding Catholic movement at L'Arbre Croche. Assiginack accepted this responsibility, and armed with Catholic hymnals and missals, he resigned from the British Indian service and returned to his home village. His nephew later recalled: "Every Sunday he preached to his people and taught them how to pray to God and the Virgin Mary and all the saints and angels in heaven."[9] Through the work of Andowish, Mackadepenessy, and Assiginack, the Odawa had shown remarkable initiative in adopting what European Americans called the path of "civilization." To follow such a path, however, required more than Odawa initiative. Adapting to a more commercial economy required access to European American tools and livestock. As early as 1816 the L'Arbre Croche Odawa had petitioned the United States for such assistance, but none was provided. The British gave gifts each summer and pledged friendship, but they had provided no practical assistance. At the same time, the leaders at L'Arbre Croche were unsettled by news of land cessions forced by the Americans on the Grand River Odawa in central Michigan. Five years of silence followed their petition to President Monroe requesting a Catholic mission and agricultural assistance, so the Odawa elected to make an overture to the British to see if a better fate could be found north of the border.

In the summer of 1828, the Anishinaabeg again showed their flexible response to the border. Mackadepenessy and Assiginack sent a request to Colonel William McKay of the British Indian Department that the brothers wanted to lead a delegation of Odawa chiefs across the "great salt lake" to London to confer personally with the king's ministers. This request was a desperate attempt to cut through the layers of imperial administration and determine if the Odawa faced a better future in Upper Canada than in Michigan. It was also a fact-finding mission to see up-close the European American manner of living. Mackadepenessy even proposed to "come back thro' the Big Knives [American] Settlements. I wish to see and hear all." British officials seized the opportunity to bind the Odawa to their side and approved the delegation's travel "in a Public Vessel next year." The London mission, however, was destined never to happen. By the spring of 1829, the Odawa civilization program in Michigan suddenly began to bear fruit.[10]

Odawa attention swung back to the American side of the border when the L'Arbre Croche was finally assigned a resident priest, who arrived in the company of Bishop Edward Fenwick. Even if the Odawa petitions to Washington had gone unanswered, they clearly had succeeded in engaging the Catholic Church at a high level. The presence of the bishop was part of a significant commitment by the Church in the Odawa mission. In short order, a school was established to give literacy to Odawa youths, and a new, entirely Catholic village was founded. Named New L'Arbre Croche, the settlement was located on the shore of Little Traverse Bay. Here European American log houses were built around a new church, rectory, and school.[11]

The move of the Catholic Odawa to a new village was an indication of a growing division among the people of the L'Arbre Croche coast. Mackadepenessy, Assiginack, and a handful of other leaders had elected to adjust to the growth of European American power through cultural change, a change that included a new source of spiritual power and literacy. Yet to fully embrace Catholicism meant breaking with many traditional Odawa beliefs. This inevitably frayed the ties that bound the Odawa to one another. In European American societies, the adoption of a new religion was often met with violence—as Mormons in America would discover in the next decade. Anishinaabe society had no tradition of compulsive social control. Chiefs could not determine individual behavior, and fundamental divisions in a community were resolved peacefully by the voluntary removal of people to a new village. The Odawa who had earlier been split by the artificial international boundary now became further fractured by a spiritual schism.

For Mackadepenessy and several of the other men who made the move, it was more than a change of location. Embracing "civilization" meant becoming more sedentary by abandoning the traditional winter retreat to inland hunting camps, thereby greatly reducing their involvement in the fur trade. Instead, they focused more on farming and producing maple sugar and fish for the market on Mackinac Island. More personally disruptive changes followed for Mackadepenessy. A year after the founding of the new village, his wife was horribly burned while making maple sugar and died after several painful days. In 1833, he was further devastated by news that his son William Blackbird had died. The lively and intelligent boy was the family's hope for the future. He had been sent to Cincinnati to study with Bishop Fenwick and he had done so well that he matriculated at a college in Rome, where he studied for the priesthood. Then in the summer of 1833, Mackadepenessy received a letter announcing William's death from complications resulting from an accident. This news immediately spawned suspicion and wild theories at New L'Arbre Croche that the young man had been murdered. Mackadepenessy's trust in the Church of Rome was shaken. When they asked if he would agree to let his youngest son, Andrew Blackbird, go to Rome to take his brother's place, the old chief replied, "They have killed one of my sons . . . and they will kill another."[12]

In the early 1830s, the brothers were once more divided by the border when Assiginack left L'Arbre Croche and returned to British Canada. The Odawa on both sides of the border were being pressured by their respective settler states to cede territory. While Assiginack was attached to the Catholic community he had created with his brother, he had a deep antipathy for the American government and a reservoir of loyalty to British military officials flowing from the many battles fought at their side during the War of 1812. He had no desire to negotiate with the Americans, whom he reviled as "big knives" or "people with hats." The British Indian Department tried to lure him with the offer of the title Grand Chief of the Western Indians, which he wisely refused. The offer of British government help in making a Christian Odawa agricultural settlement was more enticing. In Assiginack's mind, north of the border were Odawa friends who needed his leadership and white men he could trust. When he crossed the international line, he may have been accompanied by as many as two hundred Odawa canoes abandoning Michigan for Upper Canada.[13]

In 1836, Mackadepenessy and Assiginack were both drawn into treaty negotiations on their respective sides of the Great Lakes border. Mackadepenessy was a leading figure in an Odawa delegation to Washington, D.C. He was aided by Augustin Hamlin, a young Odawa-French mixed-blood nephew who had studied in Rome with William Blackbird. Traveling through the United States and dwelling in the American capital was an illuminating experience, but the negotiations were frustrating. President Andrew Jackson appointed Henry Rowe Schoolcraft to represent the United States. Mackadepenessy knew him well, as he was the Indian agent at Mackinac, and the Odawa had gone to Washington in part to get away from middlemen and form a bond of trust with the nation's leaders. They were afforded only the briefest audience with President Jackson. Schoolcraft made the negotiations difficult by trying to undermine Augustin Hamlin. The young man had been recruited by the Catholic bishop of Detroit to be a spokesman for the Odawa because of his fluency in English, but Schoolcraft resented him as a potential rival. The Odawa delegation was also harassed by a swarm of Michigan fur traders who also came east to ensure the eventual treaty would include payments to them.[14]

The final Treaty of Washington was a major land cession that gave to the United States all of northwest Michigan and the eastern Upper Peninsula, almost 14 million acres. In return, the Odawa and Ojibwe were to share $600,000 in annuities as well as educational and economic assistance to transform their mode of life. Critically, the Odawa were promised a 50,000-acre reservation at Little Traverse, but after Mackadepenessy left Washington, the U.S. Senate amended the agreement. The large reservation was no longer guaranteed in perpetuity but rather for a mere five years preliminary to removal to a trans-Mississippi reservation. This was insufferable because avoiding removal had been the Odawa's principal goal in entering the treaty process. Feeling betrayed but fearing rumors of imminent removal by U.S. troops, Mackadepenessy was among the chiefs who agreed to the altered document. However, in doing so, the Odawa had a plan to outflank the Americans—they would use the annuity money to purchase land and then rely on private property rights to avoid removal.[15]

North of the border there was even less of a negotiation before a treaty was imposed on the Odawa. While Assiginack had been in Michigan, British Indian policy had undergone a change. Previously the government saw Indian allies as a key part of the defense of Upper Canada (today's Ontario) from feared American attack. Indeed, Indian allies had played a major role in stopping American invasions between 1812 and 1814. But now the British treasury wished to stop annual gifts and limit expenditures to what was needed for missions and an Anglo education. The new Lieutenant Governor of Upper Canada, Sir Francis Bond Head, was dubious about the efficacy of even that aid. In August 1836, he visited Manitoulin Island to undertake the annual distribution of gifts and on the spot elected to negotiate a land cession treaty with the Odawa and Ojibwa. In return, he promised to make Manitoulin Island a refuge for Canadian Indians displaced by white settlers. According to a memorandum he drew up, the Indians would cede a considerable amount of land along Lake Huron while the Manitoulin Island archipelago would become "the Property (under your Great Father's Control) of all Indians whom he shall allow to reside on them." Such was Assiginack's blind faith in the trustworthiness of British officials that he agreed to sign this unilateral document and helped convince other chiefs to do the same, thereby giving their consent.[16]

Manitoulin Island had an important place in Odawa identity. It was often referred to as Ottawa Island (Odawa Minising), and many Odawa regarded it as their people's place of origin. Assiginack had no attachment to the lands on the Bruce Peninsula surrendered as part of the 1836 treaty. Securing the right to settle Odawa on Manitoulin suited his purposes both for the people he previously had led on Drummond Island as well as for his kinsmen in American territory. He believed Manitoulin Island could be a refuge for all the Odawa people as well as their Three Fires allies, the Ojibwe and Potawatomi. In the wake of the Treaty of Washington, a considerable number of Catholic Odawa abandoned L'Arbre Croche and joined Assiginack on Manitoulin Island. There, with the help of Jesuit missionaries, they formed the nucleus of a Catholic Odawa community.[17]

Britain's Sir Francis Bond Head and America's Henry Rowe Schoolcraft were attempting to placate the multiplying hordes of white settlers that swelled the population of the Great Lakes region and demanded more land for farms. Sounding a bit like the great remover—Andrew Jackson—Head predicted that the Native people of the Great Lakes were doomed "to vanish before us like grass in the progress of the forest flames . . . melting like snow before the sun." In the face of such thinking, Assiginack and Mackadepenessy were playing a high-stakes game with few winning cards. The best they could hope to win was time. In this they were successful. Settler pressure to take Odawa land lessened in the decade after the 1836 treaties. In 1837, the United States was stricken with one of the worst financial panics of its history, which destroyed the previously soaring market in western lands and brought frontier expansion to a virtual halt. Across the border, Britain's Canadian colonies were rocked by revolutions against the oligarchic administrations installed by London. Rather than "melt like snow," the Odawa remained deeply rooted in their divided homeland. However, the treaties for the first time bound the Odawa to the emerging settler states through annuities and other guarantees. Those ties to European American states weakened cross-border connections to Odawa kinfolk.[18]

The Treaty of Washington was Mackadepenessy's last act as an Odawa leader. Like Assiginack, his influence was based on communal respect for his prowess as a hunter, warrior, and councilor. Yet for the rising generation of Odawa, both the way of the warrior and the way of the hunter were no longer open. Leaders for the new generation would need to know the ways of the settler states that encompassed Odawa villages. The brothers both had sons who would follow their fathers' lead and strive to obtain the education necessary to play that role. The challenge of the fathers had been to resist the first stage of settler colonialism—the alienation of indigenous land. The sons would be burdened with trying to ward off the settlers' attempts to erase their culture and history.

Mackadepenessy's youngest son, Andrew Jackson Blackbird, was every bit as adventurous as the Odawa warriors of old. As a teenager, he spent more than a decade navigating the Great Lakes region working in the white world as a sailor, harvest hand, and blacksmith. He went on to secure an education at the Twinsburg Institute in Ohio and the Michigan State Normal School. This gave him the skill to talk back to the representatives of the settler state. Between 1850 and 1855, he played a key role in enabling the Odawa to be recognized as citizens of Michigan through appeals to the governor, state legislature, and State Supreme Court justices. He was the youngest of the Odawa leaders who signed the 1855 treaty that ended the threat of removal and entitled them to allotments of land for their permanent home. He would continue to be an advocate for the Odawa when he served as an interpreter in the Office of Indian Affairs.[19]

Assiginack's son Francis, the third of his eight children, also embarked on a career that made him a mediator between the settler state and his people. As young student, he sometimes signed his school papers "A Warrior of the Odah-wahs." He eventually received an advanced education at Upper Canada College (the future University of Toronto). His tuition was supported by the British Indian Department, yet when he applied to advance to medical school, he was brusquely denied. They saw no value in an Odawa with medical knowledge. He then devoted the rest of his life to either teaching at the government Indian school on Manitoulin Island or working as a clerk and occasional interpreter for the Indian Department based in Toronto. It must have been dispiriting to work on treaties and policies that marginalized Canada's First Nations. In reaction to policies of erasure, Francis published three essays on Odawa language and culture in the *Canadian Journal of Industry, Science, and Art*. His literary ambitions, however, were cut short by consumption, and he died in 1863.[20]

In Michigan, Mackadepenessy's son Andrew also took up the pen after attending the Michigan State Normal College (the future Eastern Michigan University). In 1900, he published a pamphlet critiquing U.S. Indian policy. In *The Indian Problem from the Indian's Standpoint*, Blackbird focused on the failure of government boarding schools to do more than train Indians for menial tasks. Blackbird referred to his advocacy for Indian education as his "war song." He did not oppose the concept of boarding schools but felt that such institutions should provide a well-rounded liberal arts education to fit Indian youths for leadership roles in a democratic society. He was best known, however, for the book *A History of the Ottawa and Chippewa Indians of Michigan*, which he published in 1887. The volume is at once a collection of Anishinaabe legends and a memoir of his personal and family history. He defended his endeavor by noting that his "account of the Ottawa and Chippewa Indians" is as important as the "histories of nations as that of any other people." Both Andrew Blackbird and his cousin Francis Assiginack fought against the settler colonialism's trope of the disappearing Indian. One of the final acts of settler conquest was erasure of the culture that had come before. While Francis was in school struggling to learn English, he was inspired by the dream that his work was to preserve for "mankind the story of the valour and beauty and poetry that had always echoed round the campfires of the Algonquins." Similarly, Blackbird was spurred to write out of a fear that his people's traditions would be lost amid the influx of European Americans who swamped the Odawa homeland. Perhaps some whites saw their writings as exotic curiosities of a vanished race. Yet Blackbird closed his history on a note of enduring defiance. "When the white man took every foot of my inheritance, he thought to himself I should be a slave. Ah, never, never." However, the two cousins, who shared a similar background and literary goals, had no documented contact with each other after their families were split by the 1836 treaties. Their fathers had crossed and recrossed the border as they saw fit, but for the sons, the border was less permeable, and the Odawa people tied to annuities and later allotments were effectively divided by the legal status of the treaties.[21]

For a time, the independent Odawa communities founded by Mackadepenessy and Assiginack were a bulwark against the settler colonial states. Catholic missionaries did not work to integrate the Odawa into the settler societies; rather they focused on creating parish-centered cocoons that isolated and sheltered their converts. This suited many Odawa, as the parish community buffered the pace of cultural and economic change. In 1849, the flourishing Catholic Odawa community on Manitoulin husbanded the resources to erect a new large stone church. Their fishing enterprises flourished. In Michigan, the L'Arbre Croche Odawa took full advantage of the path to state citizenship that Andrew Blackbird's lobbying had earned. By 1856, young, educated Odawa took over the administration of Emmet County, Michigan. They served as justices of the peace, deputy sheriffs, recorders of deeds, and township administrators. In both Canada and the United States, their alliance with the Catholic Church, notwithstanding occasional conflicts with patriarchal priests, proved useful in their relations with their respective settler governments. Unfortunately, this freedom to control their land and government was eventually eclipsed by land-hungry European Americans.[22]

Manitowaning, the Manitoulin Island settlement that Assiginack had helped found as an Anishinaabe refuge from American expansion, was the first to fall. In 1862, the Canadian colonial administrators forced on the Odawa a treaty that ended Manitoulin Island's special status as an indigenous refuge and opened most of the archipelago to white settlers. Sadly, Assiginack, then over ninety years old, argued that it was his duty to Queen Victoria to sign his assent. His misplaced sense of honor and loyalty to the colonizers split his family, with his son Amable supporting the father while the eldest son Sampson Assiginack (b. 1820), aka Itawashkash, led the opposition to the cession. Caught in the middle was Francis, acting as interpreter for British negotiators. Flattered by colonial authorities and proud of his splendid blue uniform and meritorious decorations J. B. Assiginack was dismayed by the violent rejection of his leadership by the majority of the Odawa. Yet, despite that, Crown officials succeeded in securing a sordid cession, likely through the use of alcohol and bribery. Persistent attempts by Sampson Assiginack to have the fraudulent treaty annulled failed. J. B. Assiginack died four years later, his life of leadership tarnished by his support for the 1862 Manitoulin Island Treaty.[23]

New L'Arbre Croche, the town the brothers helped found in 1830, became Harbor Springs, Michigan, whose white merchants and realtors in the 1880s worked assiduously to defraud the original Odawa inhabitants of their small landholdings. In the wake of the Civil War, Odawa officeholders in Emmet County were all voted out by white newcomers. By that time, Mackadepenessy was dead, but his son Andrew Blackbird labored to defend Odawa landowners, eventually securing a federal investigation of the rampant abuse. When this failed to intimidate the local "land sharks," Blackbird lobbied to be named Superintendent of Indian Affairs for Michigan. Yet, rather than allow an Indian to occupy that key post, his opponents in Congress withdrew funding for the position, effectively severing further federal interference in Odawa affairs. Both at Manitoulin and in northern Michigan, the pine forests of the Great Lakes borderland were too valuable a source of high-quality lumber for would-be white lumber barons to leave in Odawa control.[24]

Mackadepenessy, Assiginack, Andrew Blackbird, and Francis Assiginack were in many ways founding fathers and sons of a new Odawa world in which they would live as a beleaguered minority in their own homeland. It was through the efforts of that special family's fathers and sons—and a handful of other insightful Native leaders—that the Odawa were able to endure in that Great Lakes homeland. Their embrace of Christianity, especially the Catholic Church, provided access to a new source of spiritual power and afforded an alliance with a powerful nongovernment institution that supported Odawa autonomy. When the respect and opportunity promised by the democratic settler states proved illusory, the Catholic Church's parish-centered structure helped sustain Odawa identity in isolated Native communities. Of course, this, too, came at a cost paid in an erosion of traditional practices and often abusive boarding schools. In 1836, the fathers were obliged to cede Odawa control of the lakes region for restricted reservations. Their sons embraced the chance for an education, and though Francis Assiginack and Andrew Blackbird even went on to college, they were both frustrated in their desire to become doctors. Their education made them middlemen between their people and the settler state. More than any of the great warrior chiefs lauded in American national memory, the sons, Andrew and Francis, who secured schooling and learned the ways of the colonizers, were the predecessors for the Odawa "legal warriors" of the twentieth century. In the 1970s and 1980s, it was educated Odawa who used the treaties made by Assiginack and Mackadepenessy to reassert government-to-government relations with the settler state and to regain some control over their natural resources. The brothers Mackadepenessy and Assiginack, together with their sons, were not heroic figures. They were pivotal if flawed transitional figures in the painful process by which the Odawa on both sides of the Great Lakes boundary found a balance between the intrusive order of the settler states and the trusted traditions of their tribe.

NOTES

1. Philip C. Bellfry, "Division and Unity, Dispersal and Permanence: The Anishinabeg of the Lake Huron Borderlands" (PhD diss., English/American Studies, Michigan State University, East Lansing, MI, 1995), 18–19.

2. "Anishinaabe" can be translated to mean "the good people." Susan E. Gray, "Emerging Borderlands," *Michigan Historical Review* 34, no. 1, Emerging Borderlands (Spring 2008): 1–24; John J. Bukowczyk et al., *Permeable Border: The Great Lakes Basin as Transborder Region, 1650–1990* (Pittsburgh: University of Pittsburgh Press, 2005).

3. Douglas Leighton, "Francis Assiginack," *Dictionary of Canadian Biography* (Toronto: University of Toronto Press, 1976), 9:10–11; Andrew J. Blackbird, *History of the Ottawa and Chippewa Indians of Michigan, and Grammar of Their Language* (Ypsilanti, MI: The Ypsilantian Job Printing House, 1887), 9, 26–27. Assignack also perfected his linguistic skills further by serving as a translator for the Rev. David Bacon,

a Presbyterian missionary briefly stationed at Mackinac between 1802 and 1803. For more, see Cecil O. King, *Balancing Two Worlds: Jean-Baptiste Assiginack and the Odawa Nation, 1768–1866* (Saskatoon, SK: Saskatoon Fastprint, 2013), 62–65.

4. Blackbird, *History of the Ottawa and Chippewa*, 26–29; J. Garth Taylor, "Assiginack's Canoe: Memories of Indian Warfare on the Great Lakes," *The Beaver* (October–November, 1986), 50–52; Lieut. Col. Robert McDonall to Capt. A. Bulger, May 2, 1815, *Michigan Pioneer and Historical Collections* (Lansing, MI: Michigan Pioneer and Historical Society), 23:512–13.

5. Blackbird, *History of the Ottawa and Chippewa*, 89–90; Theodore J. Karamanski, *Blackbird's Song: Andrew J. Blackbird and the Odawa People* (East Lansing: Michigan State University Press, 2012), 39–47.

6. Throughout this chapter, I focus on the leadership of Mackadepenessy and Assiginack. While they were key leaders, they were allied with other chiefs such as Apokisigan, Wakezoo, and others who will not be named. Odawa leadership was based on consensus building, and working with others was key to what the brothers were able to achieve.

7. Petition of the Chiefs of the Ottawa Indians, Arbre Croche, August 12, 1823, Chronological File, Manuscripts Division, Wisconsin Historical Society; *Annales de l'Association de la Propagation de la Foi* (Paris: La Libraririe Ecclesiastique DeRusand, 1826), 9:121–35.

8. *Annales de l'Association de la Propagation de la Foi* (1826), 9:121–35; Blackbird, *History of the Ottawa and Chippewa*, 46–47.

9. Blackbird, *History of the Ottawa and Chippewa*, 47.

10. Jean Baptist Assiginack to Thomas Anderson, September 22, 1827, *Michigan Pioneer and Historical Collections*, 23:140; Thomas Anderson to Col. William McKay, July 22, 1828, *Michigan Pioneer and Historical Collections*, 23:150–51; Anderson to McKay, November 29, 1828, *Michigan Pioneer and Historical Collection*, 23:156.

11. Blackbird, *History of the Ottawa and Chippewa*, 47–48; Karamanski, *Blackbird's Song*, 54–55.

12. Blackbird, *History of the Ottawa and Chippewa*, 38–41; Cardinal Carlo Pedicini to Bishop Frederick Rese, July 13, 1833, and April 3, 1836, Diocese of Detroit Papers, University of Notre Dame Archive, South Bend, IN.

13. Alan Corbiere, "Jean Baptiste Assiginack / The Starling (aka Blackbird): Anishinaabeg in the War of 1812," https://earlycanadianhistory.ca/2017/02/06/jean-baptiste-assiginack-the-starling-aka-blackbird-anishnaabeg-in-the-war-of-1812/, accessed August 2021.

14. Speech of Augustin Hamlin reported by Chabwawee, Bubenesu, and Baubewegeick, November 24, 1835, National Archives, Letters Received by the Office of Indian Affairs, Michigan Superintendency, RG 75, M-1, R01172, frames 159–60; Father Simon Saendrel to Bishop Rese, July 20, 1835, Diocese of Detroit Papers, Notre Dame Archives; Records of a Treaty concluded with the Ottawa and Chippewa Nations at Washington, D.C., March 28, 1836, Papers of Henry Rowe Schoolcraft, Library of Congress, Washington, D.C.

15. Henry Rowe Schoolcraft, *Personal Memoirs of a Residence of Thirty Years with the Indian Tribes of the American Frontiers* (Philadelphia, PA: Lippincott, Grambo, 1851),

534–38; Fr. John DeBruyn to Bishop Rese, June 17, 1836, Diocese of Detroit Papers, Notre Dame Archives; Karamanski, *Blackbird's Song*, 77–90.

16. Robert J. Surtees, *The Manitoulin Island Treaties* (Ottawa: Treaties and Historical Research Centre, Indian and Northern Affairs Canada, 1986), https://www.rcaanc-cirnac.gc.ca/eng/1100100028959/1564583230395, accessed August 2020; John Sheridan Milloy, "The Era of Civilization: British Policy for the Indians of Canada, 1830–1860" (DPhil diss., Oxford University, 1978), 168–80.

17. Fr. Francois Pierz to Bishop Lefevere, January 2, 1843, and July 9, 1845, Diocese of Detroit Papers, Notre Dame Archives; Ruth Bleasdale, "Manitowaning: An Experiment in Indian Settlement," *Ontario History* 66 (1974): 147–57.

18. Sir Francis Bond Head to Lord Glenelg, November 10, 1836, quoted in Milloy, "The Era of Civilization," 182.

19. Blackbird, *History of the Ottawa and Chippewa*, 55–62.

20. H. G. Tucker, "A Warrior of the Odahwahs," *Papers and Records of the Ontario Historical Society* 18 (1920): 32–36; Leighton, "Francis Assikinack," in *Dictionary of Canadian Biography*, 9:10–11.

21. Andrew Jackson Blackbird, *The Indian Problem from the Standpoint of the Indian* (Ypsilanti, MI: Scharf, Tag, Label, and Box, 1900); Tucker, "A Warrior of the Odahwahs," 33; Blackbird, *History of the Ottawa and Chippewa*, 102; Karamanski, *Blackbird's Song*, 222.

22. Emmet County Supervisors Journal, 1859–1863, and Statement of Votes, 1855–1869, Office of Emmet County Clerk, Petoskey, MI.

23. Cecil King, "J. B. Assiginack: Arbiter of Two Worlds," *Ontario History* 88, no. 1 (March 1994): 46; Shelley J. Pearen, *Four Voices: The Great Manitoulin Island Treaty of 1862* (N.p.: Shelley J. Pearen, 2012), 25–54.

24. Karamanski, *Blackbird's Song*, 198–207; Bleasdale, "Manitowaning," 55–57; Corbiere, "Jean Baptiste Assiginack."

PETER J. DECARLO

2

BORDERLAND TO BORDERED LAND

Colonial Struggles between the Bdewákhaŋthuŋwaŋ
Dakhóta, the U.S. Army, and the Hudson's Bay Company
at the Forty-Ninth Parallel, 1863–1865

In the middle of the night of January 17, 1864, two sleds flew southward across the snowy trail between the Hudson's Bay Company's (HBC) Red River Settlement and Pembina, Dakota Territory. Tensions in the borderland were high, and the drivers moved their teams with urgency. Their cargo was central to the refugee crisis at the Red River Settlement and to the war between some of the Dakhóta bands of the Očhéthi Šakówiŋ (Seven Council Fires, commonly called the Sioux) and the United States, which had engulfed the lands south of the forty-ninth parallel. Driving one of the sleds and heading the operation was John H. McKenzie. McKenzie had lived his life on both sides of the border: born in Canada, naturalized in the United States, a farmer in Hutchinson, Minnesota, a supplier for the U.S. Army, and now, a trader outside of British Fort Garry. The other driver, Onsiume Giguere, was a French-Canadian interpreter who worked in the fur trade.[1]

Their cargo was human. McKenzie and others had manipulated two Bdewákhaŋthuŋwaŋ Dakhóta leaders into leaving their people. Then they got them intoxicated, drugged them with chloroform, and strapped them to sleighs. Their object: deliver them to U.S. Army Major Edwin Hatch, whose battalion was stationed at Pembina, just across the border. Tied to one sled was Šákpedan (Little Six, also known as Shakopee). Restrained on the other was Wakȟáŋ Ožaŋžáŋ (Medicine Bottle, also known as Sacred Light). Hunted by the U.S. military since the U.S.-Dakhóta War of 1862, the two men had led their people north to British territory, knowing the colonial border would afford them some kind of protection. Now they were being brought back across that border against their will. Yet, it is likely that on that cold January night, the sled drivers and the Bdewákhaŋthuŋwaŋ leaders didn't know exactly when they crossed the border. The forty-ninth parallel existed in colonial law but was almost completely unmarked on the ground. Even local U.S. and British officials were unsure where the line lay. For the indigenous peoples of the region, primarily the Ojibwe, Métis, and Dakhóta, the border that cut through their traditional territories had even less meaning as their trade networks and buffalo hunts moved them back and forth across the invisible line. This borderland was a surviving vestige of a multicultural fur trade society that had existed for two hundred years in the North Country. It was in this particular place, where the Northwoods met the plains and the Red River flowed across the border, that war would bring much of that society to a sudden end and begin decades of war to the west.[2]

The crisis that swirled around the two men tied to the sleighs shifted the region from a borderland to a bordered land as colonial governments, threatened by Native resistance, strained to enforce their claims to sovereignty. The forty-ninth parallel, which had been imagined by far-off imperial officials and was mostly ignored by local inhabitants, became real as both the Dakhóta and the United States used it to their advantage. Though war made the border real, it was not rigid, as U.S. soldiers and British citizens on the ground ignored it to fulfill their goal of controlling indigenous peoples. The combination of groups struggling to assert sovereignty in the region set it apart as a subregion of the North Country: several indigenous nations who called both the woods and the plains home, including the Métis, who were unique to the borderland; the specialized Hudson's Bay Company government; and the expansionist United States.

The roots of the borderland crisis lay hundreds of miles to the south deep in the homeland of the Santee (eastern) Dakhóta. When the U.S.-Dakhóta War began, both Šákpedan and Wakȟáŋ Ožaŋžáŋ were living on the Dakhóta reservation along the Minnesota River. Šákpedan had recently risen to leadership upon his father's death. Wakȟáŋ Ožaŋžáŋ served his people as a *wičháša wakȟáŋ* (medicine man). The onslaught of U.S. colonialism and starvation convinced some Dakhóta that the time to fight had come. The push for war originated in the soldiers' lodge of which Šákpedan was a part. Both men led warriors at various battles, and evidence suggests, but does not prove, that Šákpedan and Wakȟáŋ Ožaŋžáŋ may have taken part in the killing of civilians. As the war continued, the tide turned against the Dakhóta, culminating in the Battle of Wood Lake on September 23, 1862. After the battle, many Dakhóta moved westward onto the plains to live with their Očhéthi Šakówiŋ relatives.[3]

The exact movements of Šákpedan, Wakȟáŋ Ožaŋžáŋ, and their people over the next year is unknown, but some things can be postulated. Like other Santee Dakhóta, they moved west and north, joining the villages of other Očhéthi Šakówiŋ people, and at other times, traveling on their own. As early as December 1862, Dakhóta bands visited the Red River Settlement to treat with the Hudson's Bay Company, Ojibwe, and Métis of the Red River. They sought refuge and a renewal of fur trade–era alliances with mixed results. Beginning decades of warfare on the Great Plains, the U.S. Army invaded Očhéthi Šakówiŋ lands to hunt down as many Dakhóta people as possible in the spring of 1863. The invasion ended with the Massacre of White Stone Hill. In September of 1863, U.S. troops assaulted an Očhéthi Šakówiŋ village, killing men, women, and children indiscriminately. When the Native people fled, the U.S. Army burned their lodges and destroyed their possessions and all of their food.[4]

After the violence of 1863, and with winter approaching, Dakhóta people sought protection farther north. Some went to Devil's Lake, then to Turtle Mountain, a stronghold of the Ojibwe. Ohíye S'a (Always Wins, also known as Charles Eastman) was a child at the time of the Dakhóta diaspora. He moved north into British lands with his band and recounted the experience as an adult:[5] "In the long night marches to get away from the soldiers, we suffered from loss of sleep and insufficient food. . . . Now we were compelled to trespass upon the country of hostile tribes and were harassed by them almost daily and nightly. Only the strictest vigilance saved us."[6]

Pursued by the U.S. military and stalked by cold and hunger, more Dakhóta journeyed north to the Red River Settlement, throwing the borderland society there into chaos. Though some Dakhóta claimed an "ancient right" to the land, in 1863 the Ojibwe were the primary power in the area and regarded the Dakhóta with suspicion. For decades, Métis and Ojibwe people had ranged southwest onto the plains for the annual buffalo hunt. As herds dwindled in number, they were forced to venture deeper into Očhéthi Šakówiŋ territory, and thus conflict between indigenous peoples escalated. Ojibwe and Métis lands abutted those of the Iháŋkthuŋwaŋna (Yanktonai) Dakhóta to the west. As kin to the Iháŋkthuŋwaŋna, the Santee Dakhóta were seen as unwelcome visitors. The Dakhóta and Ojibwe regarded the lands just west of the Red River as their boundary—one that was frequently contested.[7]

The Dakhóta were aware that they were crossing a colonial border and entering lands claimed by Great Britain or, more specifically, the British HBC. They crossed the border for economic and political reasons, but also because they knew the border could keep the U.S. Army from following them. The Dakhóta were using the border as the "medicine line," a term Native people would use for the boundary in the 1870s because of its ability to keep the U.S. Army at bay. The Dakhóta also knew the Red River Settlement operated politically and economically as a center of the fur trade, not as a settler state, like Minnesota. The HBC's claim to the area dated back to 1670 when the British government granted the company a monopoly on the fur trade in the region. The land granted to the company was named Rupert's Land. The Red River Settlement was established on ceded Ojibwe land and had been governed by the HBC since 1836. The settlement was administered as part of the District of Assiniboia, and when the Dakhóta arrived, it consisted of a European American trader community, Upper and Lower Fort Garry, and about fifty Métis settlements along the Red and Assiniboine Rivers.[8]

In the late summer and fall of 1863, the U.S. Army forces that had pursued the Dakhóta onto the plains returned south. In their place, the U.S. government dispatched a specialized unit to prosecute the war into the winter and onto its frontier. A battalion of cavalry, under Major Edwin Hatch, was recruited at Fort Snelling, Minnesota, and sent north to the border in October 1863. The unit was meant "to hold in check the hostile Sioux who had retreated for safety into her Majesty's coterminous possessions." The battalion was a federal unit, but its soldiers were mostly derived from the local Minnesota settler population. Hatch had traveled extensively in Dakota Territory, worked as a trader among the Ho-Chunk and Ojibwe, and served as an Indian agent to the Blackfeet in the 1850s. The command marched north through harrowing winter weather and arrived at Pembina on November 13.[9]

Pembina was settled by Red Lake Ojibwe as they moved west after 1790. It became a central Ojibwe stronghold in the borderland of the Red River Valley and a fur trade hub. There was a distinct band of Pembina Ojibwe, but the Turtle Mountain, Red Lake, Pillager, and Lake of the Woods bands visited the settlement frequently. Pembina was also considered by many Métis as their original home. Some still lived in the woods along the rivers, but most had moved north when the international boundary was negotiated and Hudson's Bay Company business could only be conducted (officially) north of the border. The Métis crossed the border—barely noting that fact if they did at all—twice a year and allied with the Ojibwe for the annual buffalo hunt. A U.S. expedition marked the border with a post at the Red River in 1823. But a local immediately rotated it, showing the absurdity of colonial efforts to mark the line. A U.S. officer reported in 1849 that "the post marking the line is thought not to be accurately on the Forty-ninth parallel, but some two or three hundred yards within our territory." In 1860, a journalist accompanied a party across the border and wrote, "Three cheers as we passed the international boundary post. Its inscription, whatever it may have been, had been quite effaced by the hatchets and arrows of Indians." He continued: "Later observations have proved that it is 370 yards south of the parallel of 49°, the true boundary line." This was a borderland, with trade companies, especially the HBC, ignoring the border for their benefit, and Native Americans firmly in power mocking any attempts to mark an imaginary line through their lands. But things were beginning to change quickly in 1863. Just two months before Hatch's arrival, Ojibwe from Pembina and Red Lake signed a treaty with the U.S. government ceding their lands along the Red River. The treaty was yet to be ratified, but its signing and the arrival of U.S. troops signaled the U.S. settler state's intention to remove Native people from the area.[10]

The arrival of U.S. troops at Pembina further motivated Dakhóta people to seek refuge at the Red River Settlement. When reports reached Hatch that Šákpedan's band was moving through St. Joseph, a Métis settlement thirty-five miles west of Pembina, the U.S. commander pursued. Although U.S. and Dakhóta soldiers engaged in a skirmish, the majority of the Dakhóta had already moved to "the other side of the British line," reaching the Red River Settlement on December 11, 1863. The HBC governor, Alexander Grant Dallas, estimated their numbers at 445, rising to 600 a week later, the majority of them women and children. Dallas stated that the Dakhóta were "being hard pressed, have fallen back upon us, as their chiefs plainly told me, to live or die with us, in preference to perishing amidst the snow drifts of the prairies." The HBC government decided to supply the Dakhóta with food and ammunition with the promise that it would only be used to hunt game. Still, the governor knew the dangerous diplomatic implications, writing, "The American Government may probably hear exaggerated reports of our having supplied the Sioux with ammunition, and make a complaint against us." He also acknowledged that the Dakhóta had violated the Ojibwe's border, writing, "The Chippeways and Saulteaux are much alarmed at this invasion of their territory, and will not long tolerate it quietly." The governor worried that if violence began, he would have to ask the U.S. military at Pembina for assistance.[11]

Back across the border, Red River settlers had communicated with Hatch, telling him they were "very tired of [the Dakhóta] and are devising means to get rid of them." U.S. Army officers began crossing the border and visiting the settlement to procure supplies and communicate with the inhabitants. The porous nature of the border and isolation of the region from imperial centers allowed U.S. soldiers to visit the Red River Settlement, but Hatch knew he could not cross with his entire command. Since Šákpedan and Wakȟáŋ Ožaŋžáŋ's band was out of reach, Hatch focused his efforts on more reports of Dakhóta at St. Joseph. He sent a detachment there hoping his men would "get some scalps." On December 16, 1863, U.S. soldiers surrounded a camp of Dakhóta at St. Joseph who were reportedly members of Šákpedan's band. At dusk, they attacked and killed six Dakhóta people, scalped them, then burned their lodges. In official reports, Hatch described the affair as a battle, but a field reporter described it as more of a massacre, with a boy and a woman among the dead.[12]

Red River settlers exerted enough pressure on Dallas to remove the Dakhóta that he finally wrote to Hatch. Dallas reported that the Dakhóta were still in the settlement and that Šákpedan was among them. Brigadier General Henry Sibley, commander of the Minnesota District, told Hatch that "no terms will be made with the murdering remnant of the lower bands now at or near Fort Garry," though women and children would be spared. Hatch sent an officer to the Dakhóta camp demanding their unconditional surrender. Many Dakhóta, including Šákpedan and Wakȟáŋ Ožaŋžáŋ, refused, but the U.S. demands caused the band to fracture into two groups—one under Šákpedan and one under The Leaf. Others considered the ultimatum and decided to surrender. The majority who surrendered were women and children, numbering in the hundreds. U.S. Army officers and the British trader Andrew Bannatyne provisioned and escorted several of the groups that surrendered across the border.[13]

Hatch was not satisfied and still wanted to capture the Bdewákhaŋthuŋwaŋ leaders that the government deemed the last holdouts from the U.S.-Dakhóta War. Meanwhile, Sibley forbade Hatch to cross the line and elevated the border issue to state and federal authorities. Minnesota governor Stephen Miller argued that if the British government could not enforce its own neutrality, it needed to "permit the refugee savages to be pursued by our troops wherever they may go." U.S. Secretary of State Seward chastised the HBC government for feeding the Bdewákhaŋthuŋwaŋ and argued that U.S. troops should be allowed to pursue them if the British authorities could not control the situation. Clearly, U.S. officials were angry that their colonial counterparts were not as advanced in the project of settler colonialism. The border was politically important to federal officials but not to Hatch and his men. Determined to extend his reach, Hatch formed a plot with civilians on the other side of the border to capture as many Bdewákhaŋthuŋwaŋ as possible, especially their leaders. The evidence indicates that Lieutenant Cochrane of Hatch's command crossed the border and spoke with John McKenzie at his home outside of Fort Garry. Cochrane "employed [McKenzie] to use his best endeavors to secure the surrender of the Sioux murderers." McKenzie agreed and assembled a group to aid in his work. McKenzie "and his true and devoted friend," an interpreter named Onisime Giguere, led the operation.[14]

McKenzie and Giguere visited Šákpedan's band and attempted to convince them all to surrender with a letter from Hatch. Šákpedan reportedly said, "All the Sioux that wanted to shake hands with the Yankees, the Yankees now have; we will never make peace with them. They are all liars and this letter . . . you now have was written by one of them. Do you think I will believe it?" Upon this refusal, Giguere threatened that the rations from the HBC would be stopped. As a result of that threat, the leaders went to McKenzie's house to discuss matters. There, "Mr. McKenzie went to work with whisky, laudanum and chloroform, and succeeded in getting them drunk and asleep." With the aid of Giguere, Andrew Bannatyne, an Indian agent named Lane, another individual named Kingsley, and accomplices who were never identified, McKenzie had them tied to sleds. McKenzie, Giguere, and Kingsley abducted the leaders and brought them across the border to Pembina during the night of January 17–18, 1864. Hatch had the two men placed in chains and imprisoned in the guardhouse.[15]

Hatch believed that the abduction had been legal since no U.S. soldiers had taken part in the actual act, and Dallas was of the same opinion. Others, especially British Canadians from farther east, did not agree. The *Canadian News* stated that giving up the Dakhóta was contrary to "British practice" because they had "sought refuge under the British Flag." The newspaper called the abduction a "gross violation of International Law . . . committed by persons acting under the authority of the United States Government." American newspapers shot back stating that the Dakhóta should be given over to U.S. authorities under the Webster-Ashburton Treaty. Yet no formal extradition request appears to have ever been made, and it is unclear if the treaty covered such a case, since the sovereignty of Native people was interpreted in various ways at the time.[16]

Throughout the rest of the winter, the Dakhóta survived and adapted to their situation. It seems the band divided into smaller groups as the pressure mounted to turn over Bdewákhaŋthuŋwaŋ, whom the U.S. government had condemned as "guilty." Relations between the Dakhóta and Ojibwe varied, with some instances of violence and some of peace. The Bdewákhaŋthuŋwaŋ moved northwest to White Horse Plains, Long Lake, and Lake Manitoba. Those on the lakes began "catching immense quantities of jack-fish," a common late-winter harvest for the Native Americans of the region. The HBC administration, still under attack by U.S. newspapers for harboring the Dakhóta, continued to defend its actions. The *Nor'wester,* published at the Red River Settlement, argued that the Dakhóta were "refugees"—"the bulk of them women and children"—and that a "christian country" could not allow them to starve. The situation continued to escalate. The settlers of the White Horse Plains met in council at Fort Garry and developed a plan to transport the remaining Dakhóta across the border into the custody of the U.S. military using their own means. Since Hatch had again been told not to cross, and the settlers wished the Dakhóta gone, they felt this was the best way to enforce their sovereignty. Yet they were motivated by another fact: U.S. authorities threatened to prevent the settlers and the Métis "from crossing the boundary line in the usual annual pursuit of buffalo" if they drove "the Sioux into the open country instead of into their power." With the U.S. Army threatening to end the fluidity of the borderland, the settlers made common cause with the U.S. military. Some Métis Red River settlers defied easy categorization within a colonizer-colonized dichotomy, and in a transborder alliance, enlisted in Hatch's battalion for service at Pembina.[17]

By early March, Hatch was becoming desperate to capture or kill the remaining Dakhóta north of the line, fearing they would move out onto the vast expanse of the western plains. He wrote Dallas about his desire to "secure" the Dakhóta. In the letter, delivered across the border by a U.S. officer, Hatch appeared to obey his superiors but perhaps hinted to Dallas he could make decisions on the ground: "I cannot however, take any steps which may by any chance place soldiers under my command in such a position that they may appear as trespassers upon British soil. Therefore, the locality of the 49th parallel never having been officially determined, I do not feel justified in moving in pursuit of these murderers towards the point where they are now encamped, without the consent of your excellency."

In his reply, Dallas stated that, though the Dakhóta were unwelcome, they were "refugees." However, he wanted to disabuse them of the idea that they could commit violence "in one territory and take refuge in the other." Dallas, pushed by the more aggressive U.S. colonial agents, and expressing his desire to control the Dakhóta, gave Hatch permission to cross the border. Here, Dallas turned his back on old fur trade alliances with the Dakhóta that had been pivotal during imperial struggles with the United States. He realized that the era of competing with the United States was over and the time for coexistence and cooperation in enforcing settler sovereignty had come.[18]

As news of Dallas's capitulation spread, those closer to British metropoles expressed disbelief. A Montreal newspaper exclaimed, "It is hardly possible to conceive that the Governor of Red River would have assumed so great a responsibility, without instructions from the Imperial Government." The governor had essentially hauled "down the British flag" and abandoned the "sacred right of asylum." Yet, whether U.S. troops would have crossed the border in pursuit of the Dakhóta is unclear, for Hatch and his men were ordered south to Fort Abercrombie, another U.S. post on the Red River. All of the Dakhóta prisoners except Šákpedan and Wakȟáŋ Ožaŋžáŋ were marched south to Fort Snelling by another U.S. Army unit.[19]

Hatch's battalion reached Fort Abercrombie in early May with their prized prisoners. The major initially made arrangements to have soldiers from another unit march the Dakhóta leaders to Fort Snelling. Expressing their need to exact retribution for what had been done to settlers in Minnesota in 1862, Hatch's men threatened to kill Šákpedan and Wakȟáŋ Ožaŋžáŋ rather than let someone else take them to St. Paul. Hatch gave in to their threats, ordering a detachment of thirty men from the battalion to escort the prisoners to Fort Snelling. Hatch eventually decided to go south with them. The march began on May 18, and on May 27, under cover of darkness, the Dakhóta leaders were brought through St. Paul and turned over to District Command at Fort Snelling.[20]

Šákpedan and Wakȟáŋ Ožaŋžáŋ were imprisoned at Fort Snelling for six months before they were tried by a U.S. military tribunal. The two men were tried separately for murder and general participation in the war. In both trials, only hearsay testimony was heard against them. Both men were convicted and sentenced to death. The Bdewákhaŋthuŋwaŋ leaders made mention of their time north of the forty-ninth parallel in their defense. Šákpedan requested that he be given time to obtain legal counsel. The commission refused. At the end of his trial, he lamented, "I went up in the British Territory. I always remained on English ground and intended to remain there and would have remained there forever, but I was taken away from there." Wakȟáŋ Ožaŋžáŋ secured legal counsel, and his lawyers argued that the court had no jurisdiction in the case because their client had been captured on British territory. The lawyers cited the Trent Affair as legal precedent: "Neutral ground protects an enemy under all circumstances. No government can acquire rights by its own wrong or by the wrong of any of its citizens. No state can reach over into the domain of a foreign and neutral power and drag from its protection any criminal by force." This argument rested on the idea that a formal extradition process should have been followed because Wakȟáŋ Ožaŋžáŋ was a citizen and soldier of a sovereign Native American nation, recognized in colonial law.[21]

The commission, regarding the two men as being "under the protection of the United States," was not swayed by these arguments. When the verdicts were sent to Washington, D.C., for approval, Sibley wrote that they were abducted by residents of the British settlements, not by U.S. citizens, and therefore their imprisonment and execution were legal. The Judge Advocate General in Washington agreed. For nearly another year, the Dakhóta leaders were held at Fort Snelling. On November 11, 1865, the U.S. government executed them outside the walls of the fort. By that time, the questions surrounding their capture had mostly faded. Two years later, in 1867, the Minnesota state government further legitimized the borderland abduction by paying McKenzie and Giguere "for moneys expended and services rendered by them in the capture of the Indian chiefs Little Six and Grey Iron."[22]

The Bdewákhaŋthuŋwaŋ Dakhóta of Šákpedan and Wakȟáŋ Ožaŋžáŋ's band continued to live on in the northern plains. From the abduction of their leaders in January of 1864 through 1866, the band flits in and out of the historical record. Struggles over leadership, confrontations and peace efforts with the Ojibwe, and some conflicts with settlers occurred during that time. Some of the band moved west and joined other groups of refugee Dakhóta, while others returned to the Red River Settlement in subsequent winters. In the years following the events of 1863–65, the northern plains borderland continued its shift from a borderland to a bordered land as colonial governments asserted their sovereignty. The Treaty of Old Crossing was ratified on April 12, 1864, and Canada confederated in 1867. The HBC gave up its land in 1870, ending its two-hundred-year-long presence in the region. The U.S. Army, determined to secure the area, established a post at Pembina that same year. Settler colonists quickly flooded the territory once colonial borders were firmly established. The forty-ninth parallel was surveyed in a joint U.S.-British effort from 1872 to 1874. The surveyors met at a place shaped by the multicultural borderland: Pembina. Though vast and porous, the surveyed border was patrolled by the U.S. Army to the south, and the Royal Canadian Mounted Police began patrolling it to the north in 1873.[23]

The story of Šákpedan, Wakȟáŋ Ožaŋžáŋ, and their people reveals a borderland in transition and a border as a site of colonial struggle. The forty-ninth parallel—a colonial political construct—was at times real and at other times imagined or ignored. Imperial governments and settler polities used the border to enforce their sovereignties, but local colonial agents also flouted the border and colluded to enforce their own sovereignty and control of indigenous populations. The Bdewákhaŋthuŋwaŋ used the region to resist U.S. settler colonialism, seek refuge, and play colonial states off of one another. But their strategy was based on an era of imperial contest between Britain and the United States, one in which alliances with Native Americans and the existence of borderlands were valued. This era was being replaced by one of intercolonial alliances cemented by the settler colonial need to suppress Native peoples and solidify borders. In crossing the border, and especially in Wakȟáŋ Ožaŋžáŋ's trial, the Bdewákhaŋthuŋwaŋ deployed colonial law as a form of resistance. But this strategy was also unsuccessful in the face of the U.S. settler state's need to quell Dakhóta defiance in the wake of the U.S.-Dakhóta War. All of these overlying and intermingling interpretations of sovereignty brought about by the events of 1863–65 accelerated the transformation of the Red River borderland into a bordered land. This dramatic shift in the North Country identifies it as a unique historic and geographic site—a pivot point. The fur trade society of the previous two hundred years, with its nexus in the Northwoods and Great Lakes, began to end, and the era of open warfare between Native Americans and colonial governments on the Great Plains to the west began.

NOTES

1. This chapter uses the Lakota/Dakota orthography developed by the Lakota Language Consortium. The orthography is taught at Sitting Bull College, the University of Minnesota, other universities, and several community organizations.

2. For a discussion of Minnesota's unique borderland society, see Wingerd, *North Country*.

3. Pond, *The Dakota or Sioux in Minnesota*, 12–13, 78; Anderson, *Little Crow*, 119, 133, 138.

4. For an account of Dakhóta crossings into British Canada prior to Šákpedan and Wakȟáŋ Ožaŋžáŋ's arrival, see McCrady, *Living with Strangers*, 17–30. Also see Anderson, *Little Crow*, 171–76; Beck, *Columns of Vengeance*, 80, 154–68.

5. Beck, *Columns of Vengeance*, 169; "A Sioux Retreat," *Winnipeg Nor'Wester*, October 28, 1863.

6. Eastman, *Indian Boyhood*, 13.

7. Peers, *Ojibwa of Western Canada*, 154–56. Historians have defined the region this history takes place in as the "Northern Plains." See Evans, *Borderlands of the American and Canadian Wests*, xvi–xvii.

8. Peers, *Ojibwa of Western Canada*, 156–59; "The Selkirk Treaty and Map, July 18, 1817." For a discussion of the "medicine line," see LaDow, *The Medicine Line*, 3; Evans, *Borderlands of the American and Canadian Wests*, 131.

9. Tiling, "Hatch's Battalion of Cavalry at Pembina, Dakota Territory," 3–7; Hill, "People of Note: Edwin Aaron Clark Hatch," 134; *Expedition Against the Sioux Indians—1864: Report of Brig. Genl. Henry H. Sibley, Commanding District of Minnesota*, Headquarters, District of Minnesota, Department of the Northwest, St. Paul, Minn., October 10, 1864, in Board of Commissioners, *Minnesota in the Civil and Indian Wars, 1861–1865* (St. Paul, MN: Pioneer Press, 1893), 2:523.

10. Treuer, *Warrior Nation*, 30–31, 34; *Pembina Settlement, Letter from the Secretary of War: Transmitting Report of Major Wood, Relative to His Expeditions to Pembina Settlement and Condition of Affairs on the North-Western Frontier of the Territory of Minnesota, March 19, 1850*, U.S. House of Representatives, 31st Cong., 1st Sess., Committee on Military Affairs, Document No. 51, 8, 19; LaDow, *The Medicine Line*, 7; Manton Marble, "To Red River and Beyond [Second Paper]," *Harper's New Monthly Magazine*, October 1860, 583–84.

11. Major Edwin Hatch to his wife, November 22, 1863; Hatch to his wife, November 25, 1863; Hatch to his wife, January 11, 1864, Edwin Hatch and Family Papers, Minnesota Historical Society, St. Paul; Alexander Grant Dallas to Thomas Fraser Esq., December 11 and 18, 1865, Papers Relating to the Sioux Indians, Printed by the House of Commons, June 17, 1864, Minnesota Historical Society; Oliver, *The Canadian North-West*, 1:530; Ens, "The Border, the Buffalo, and the Métis of Montana," 141.

12. Hatch to Brig. Genl. H. H. Sibley, December 21, 1863, in Board of Commissioners, *Minnesota in the Civil and Indian Wars*, 2:545; Major C. W. Nash, "Narrative of Hatch's Independent Battalion of Cavalry," in Board of Commissioners, *Minnesota in the Civil and Indian Wars*, 1:599; Major Edwin Hatch to his wife, December 17, 1863, Edwin Hatch and Family Papers; "From Pembina," *St. Paul Daily Press*, January 6, 1864.

13. Dallas to Fraser, January 15, 1864, Papers Relating to the Sioux Indians; Hatch to his wife, January 11, 1864; Nash, "Narrative of Hatch's Independent Battalion," 599; Sibley to Hatch, January 5, 1864, and Sibley to Major General John Pope, February 5, 1864, in Board of Commissioners, *Minnesota in the Civil and Indian Wars*, 2:547; "The Sioux," *Winnipeg Nor'Wester*, January 18, 1864; "The Sioux," *Winnipeg Nor'Wester*,

February 5, 1864; "The Sioux," extracts from a Montreal newspaper, Sioux Correspondence, a manuscript collection of published correspondence and newspaper extracts held at the Minnesota Historical Society.

14. "The Good News from Pembina," *St. Paul Daily Press,* February 3, 1864; Gluek, "The Sioux Uprising," 322–23.

15. "The Good News from Pembina," *St. Paul Daily Press,* February 3, 1864; "Two Very Bad Indians," *St. Paul and Minneapolis Pioneer Press,* May 23, 1886; Folwell, *A History of Minnesota,* 2:443–44.

16. "Kidnapping Two Indian Chiefs," *Canadian News,* March 3, 1864; "Neutrality," *St. Paul Daily Press,* January 20, 1864; Dallas to Lord Lyons, February 25, 1864, Sioux Correspondence. See Article X of *A Treaty to Settle and Define the Boundaries between the Territories of the United States and the Possessions of Her Britannic Majesty in North America,* US-GB, August 9, 1842, T.S., 576, https://avalon.law.yale.edu/19th_century/br-1842.asp.

17. Dallas to Sibley, February 25, 1864, Sioux Correspondence; Peers, *Ojibwa of Western Canada,* 160; "The Sioux," *Winnipeg Nor'Wester,* January 18, 1864; "The Sioux," *Winnipeg Nor'Wester,* February 5, 1864; "Neutrality," and "Public Meeting—The Sioux," *Winnipeg Nor'Wester,* February 18, 1864; "Wayside Jottings: On the Road to Georgetown," *Winnipeg Nor'Wester,* July 2, 1864; "Roster of Company D," in Board of Commissioners, *Minnesota in the Civil and Indian Wars,* 1:607.

18. Hatch to Dallas, March 4, 1864, and Dallas to Hatch, March 7, 1864, Sioux Correspondence.

19. Sibley to Pope, March 21, 1864, and Assistant Adjutant General R. C. Olin to Hatch, April 15, 1864, in Board of Commissioners, *Minnesota in the Civil and Indian Wars,* 2:549, 551; "It will be seen . . . ," *Montreal Evening Telegraph and Daily Commercial Advertiser,* April 13, 1864; Veracini, *Settler Colonialism,* 57.

20. Nash, "Narrative of Hatch's Independent Battalion," in Board of Commissioners, *Minnesota in the Civil and Indian Wars,* 1:601; "Wayside Jottings," *Winnipeg Nor'Wester,* July 13, 1864.

21. Isch, *Guilty as Charged*; Folwell, *History of Minnesota,* 2:445–50.

22. Sibley to Judge Advocate General Holt, December 14, 1864, and Holt to the President, Bureau Military Justice, March 25, 1865, Alan R. Woolworth Papers, 143.E.1.1.B, Box 24, Manuscript Collection, Minnesota Historical Society; "The Execution," *St. Paul Pioneer,* November 12, 1865; Auditor, Executive Council Files, Records related to payment of McKenzie, Minnesota State Archives Record, 111B.11.3, Minnesota Historical Society; Minnesota State Legislature, "An Act for the Relief of John H. McKenzie and Onesime Giguere," March 7, 1867, *Special Laws, Chapter CLIV,* 390. The firsthand account of the abduction, written by McKenzie, was published by the Minnesota legislature in 1867. The single copy in existence was held by the Minnesota Historical Society but is now lost. Wakȟáŋ Ožaŋžáŋ is frequently identified as "Grey Iron" in colonial sources.

23. For Sitting Bull's involvement in the Punitive Expeditions, see Beck, *Columns of Vengeance,* 123–24, 222–23, 242, 253; Treuer, *Warrior Nation,* 66; LaDow, *The Medicine Line,* 9–11, 54; Meyer, "The Canadian Sioux," 15; Ens, "The Border, the Buffalo, and the

Métis," 143; "The Sioux," *Winnipeg Nor'Wester,* March 31, 1864; "Fighting between the
Sioux and Chippewas," *Winnipeg Nor'Wester,* May 10, 1864; "Sioux Outrages," *Winnipeg Nor'Wester,* September 16, 1864; "Arrival of the Sioux," *Winnipeg Nor'Wester,*
December 3, 1864; "The Sioux," *Winnipeg Nor'Wester,* August 1, 1865; "Sioux at Portage
La Prairie," *Winnipeg Nor'Wester,* October 2, 1865.

BIBLIOGRAPHY

Primary Sources

Board of Commissioners, eds. *Minnesota in the Civil and Indian Wars, 1861–1865.* 2 vols.
St. Paul, MN: Pioneer Press Company, 1890.
Eastman, Charles A. *Indian Boyhood.* New York, NY: Dover, 1971.
Hatch, Edwin, and Family. Papers, 1805–1939. Manuscript Collection, Minnesota Historical Society, St. Paul, MN.
Isch, John. *Guilty as Charged: The 1862–1864 Military Commission Trials of the Dakota:
Including the Trial Transcripts and Commentary.* [MN?]: The author, 2010.
Miller, Stephen. *Annual Message of Governor Miller, to the Legislature of Minnesota,
Delivered January 4, 1865.* St. Paul, MN: Frederick Driscoll, State Printer, 1865.
Oliver, Edmund Henry. *The Canadian North-west: Its Early Development and Legislative
Records,* vol. 1. Ottawa, ON: Government Printing Bureau, 1914.
Papers Relating to the Sioux Indians, Printed by the House of Commons, June 17, 1864.
Manuscript Collection, Minnesota Historical Society, St. Paul, MN.
"The Selkirk Treaty and Map, July 18, 1817." Hudson's Bay Company Archives, Archives
of Manitoba, Winnipeg, CA. https://www.gov.mb.ca/chc/archives/hbca/spotlight
/selkirk_treaty.html.
Woolworth, Alan R. Papers, 1774–2008. Manuscript Collection, Minnesota Historical
Society, St. Paul, MN.

Secondary Sources

Anderson, Gary Clayton. *Little Crow: Spokesman for the Sioux.* St. Paul: Minnesota
Historical Society Press, 1986.
Anderson, Gary Clayton, and Alan R. Woolworth, eds. *Through Dakota Eyes: Narrative Accounts of the Minnesota Indian War of 1862.* St. Paul: Minnesota Historical
Society Press, 1988.
Beck, Paul N. *Columns of Vengeance: Soldiers, Sioux, and the Punitive Expeditions,
1863–1864.* Norman: University of Oklahoma Press, 2013.
Ens, Gerhard J. "The Border, the Buffalo, and the Métis of Montana." In Evans, *Borderlands of the American and Canadian Wests,* 139–54.
Evans, Sterling, ed. *The Borderlands of the American and Canadian Wests: Essays on
Regional History of the Forty-ninth Parallel.* Lincoln: University of Nebraska Press,
2006.
Folwell, William Watts. *A History of Minnesota,* vol. 2. St. Paul: Minnesota Historical
Society, 1961.

Gluek, Alvin C. Jr. "The Sioux Uprising: A Problem in International Relations." *Minnesota History* 34, no. 8 (Winter 1955): 317–24.

Hill, Patrick. "People of Note: Edwin Aaron Clarke Hatch." *Minnesota's Heritage*, no. 7 (January 2013): 134–37.

LaDow, Beth. *The Medicine Line: Life and Death on a North American Borderland*. New York, NY: Routledge, 2002.

Lakota Language Consortium. *New Lakota Dictionary: Lakȟótiyapi-English, English-Lakȟótiyapi & Incorporating the Dakota Dialects of Yankton-Yanktonai & Santee-Sisseton*. 2nd ed. Compiled by Jan F. Ullrich. Bloomington, IN: Lakota Language Consortium, 2008.

McCrady, David G. *Living with Strangers: The Nineteenth-Century Sioux and the Canadian-American Borderlands*. Toronto, ON: University of Toronto Press, 2010.

Meyer, Roy Willard. "The Canadian Sioux: Refugees from Minnesota." *Minnesota History* 41, no. 1 (Spring 1968): 13–28.

Peers, Laura. *The Ojibwa of Western Canada: 1780 to 1870*. St. Paul: Minnesota Historical Society Press, 1994.

Pond, Samuel W. *The Dakota or Sioux in Minnesota as They Were in 1834*. St. Paul: Minnesota Historical Society Press, 1986.

Tiling, Robert. "Hatch's Battalion of Cavalry at Pembina, Dakota Territory, 1863–1864." Paper prepared for the 14th Annual Dakota History Conference, 1982. https://mnpals-mhs.primo.exlibrisgroup.com/permalink/01MNPALS_MHS/ge68jo/alma990016120250104294.

Treuer, Anton. *Warrior Nation: A History of the Red Lake Ojibwe*. St. Paul: Minnesota Historical Society Press, 2015.

Veracini, Lorenzo. *Settler Colonialism: A Theoretical Overview*. New York, NY: Palgrave Macmillan, 2010.

Westerman, Gwen, and Bruce White. *Mni Sota Makoce: The Land of the Dakota*. St. Paul: Minnesota Historical Society Press, 2012.

Wingerd, Mary Lethert. *North Country: The Making of Minnesota*. Minneapolis: University of Minnesota Press, 2010.

3

WHERE THE MEN ARE MEN AND THE WOMEN ARE, TOO

Finnish Gender Stereotypes in
the Upper Midwest

At an October 2006 concert in Stoughton, Wisconsin, the musical comedy group Da Yoopers, from Michigan's Upper Peninsula (UP), asked of the audience, "Are there any transplanted Yoopers here tonight?"[1] The question elicited wide response from the audience, and soon band leader Jim "Hoolie" DeCaire asked what towns were represented. When a woman to my left and I shouted "Hancock!" and "Toivola!" respectively, Hoolie looked toward us and replied, "Oh, these girls are from the Copper Country. This is a special place . . . where the men are men and the women are, too!" And with this quip, DeCaire introduced an age-old stereotype surrounding the gendered nature of the Northwoods culture that exists in the Upper Peninsula itself as well as in northern Wisconsin and Minnesota and just across Lake Superior in southwestern Ontario.

While the rural Northwoods can be understood to have a culture in which women are stereotyped as tougher than their more southerly, urbanized counterparts, why should an association with a cultural stereotype of tough, even masculine, women thrive in Upper Midwestern areas such as the Copper Country? Culturally, the Northwoods region of the Upper Midwest is unique in the diversity of European immigrant groups that settled there, starting in the 1840s and ending, for the most part, around 1920. Around Lake Superior, in addition to Native Ojibwe, Odawa, Potawatomi, and Menomini peoples, one finds the descendants of Italians, Cornish, Swedes, Croatians, French and French-Canadians, Germans, and, most notably in the Copper Country and other pockets across the western Lake Superior region, Finns.[2]

This four-county area located on and adjacent to the Keweenaw Peninsula in the western UP has a storied, rough-and-tumble history that perfectly complements the stereotypes of the local ethnic groups and their interethnic shared culture. These stereotypes developed across the region but were intensified in population pockets, including the Copper Country, Minnesota's Iron Range, and the Thunder Bay, Ontario, area. As interethnic contact took place in worksites, neighborhoods, public schools, and other parts of the social commons, regional identities grew, and Finnish ethnicity often made a strong imprint on these.

The Finns flocked to the region beginning in the 1860s, first for jobs in Michigan copper mines and then spreading out to Minnesota, Wisconsin, and Ontario. Their wives, daughters, and sisters soon joined them, becoming by 1910 the local ethnic majority in areas like the Copper Country. By that time, Finns were also considered to be culturally significant across the Upper Peninsula and the western Lake Superior region in general, and folk ideas about their supposed generic traits and characters were similarly invoked and developed across the region.[3] Of the interethnic regional situation, the historian A. William Hoglund says that by 1920, "Because of their strong presence in Michigan and Minnesota, Finns gained cultural leadership among their compatriots."[4]

This situation led to Finns having a strong influence over the development of regional interethnic cultures. The linguist Kathryn A. Remlinger has documented the influence the Finnish language had on the regional dialect of the Upper Peninsula, pointing out the fact that though the dialect is the result of English as negotiated by a number of first-language Indigenous and immigrant language speakers, "often the perception of UP English is that it sounds 'Finnish.'"[5]

Other non-Finnish cultural artifacts incorporated into the cultural commons of the Upper Midwest, such as the Cornish pasty, a meat pie popularized in area mining districts, are now believed by many to be a cultural contribution of the Finns. In fact, this belief is even held by many ethnic nonimmigrant Finns in the region.[6] It is important to note that while conflating one group's meat pies with similar dishes brought over by one's own ancestors is minor, relegating the contributions of other ethnic groups in the region to generalized images of Upper Midwesterners erases the unique traits others have contributed to the group. In this chapter, my intent is to reveal what the Finns are considered to have contributed to gendered stereotypes and how they negotiate them through cultural performance. The stories of other ethnic groups within this dynamic exist in different forms and are equally deserving of attention.

The geography of the region and the settlement patterns of people exert their own influence over the perception of local culture. The largely rural region is dotted with villages boasting a few hundred citizens, with communities such as Marquette, Michigan, population 25,000, considered to be a destination for commerce and culture, and cities such as Duluth, Minnesota, and Thunder Bay, Ontario, each closer to 100,000 citizens, seen as downright urban. The heavily forested landscape is dotted with hundreds of small lakes. Lake Superior moderates temperatures and dumps legendary lake-effect snows, especially on the south shore.[7] The region also has immense mineral deposits of copper and iron, which provided much of the original stimulus for white settlement in the region.[8]

Most important to an understanding of the significance of the geography, for the purpose of this chapter, is the fact that the topography is very reminiscent of Finland with its rocky coasts and numerous inland lakes; dark forests and white birches; icy, turbulent seas; and hardscrabble agricultural lands. It is, though, a coincidence that Finns should settle here: the earliest immigrants were recruited from the mines of Norway's Finnmark to come to such a place, which later facilitated Finns moving from industrial to agricultural work in the region.[9]

The perceived cultural uniqueness of Finns is best elaborated in stereotype by the folklorist Richard Dorson in his 1952 book, *Bloodstoppers and Bearwalkers,* comparing stereotypes of Finns to those of Native Americans when he said that they both "derive from a shadowy Mongolian stock [. . . ;] live intimately with the fields and woods [. . . ;] possess supernatural stamina, strength, and tenacity [. . . ;] drink feverishly and fight barbarously [. . . ;] practice shamanistic magic and ritual"; and "are secretive, clannish, inscrutable, and steadfast in their own peculiar social code."[10]

Konrad Berkovici, writing of Finns in the farming community of Embarrass, Minnesota, in 1925, also describes stereotypes he learned while visiting the area. Berkovici was told about "black Finns" who would, once a week, visit a small building on their farmstead as a family, dressed in sheets, where they would practice "witchcraft." Berkovici discovers that what was described was, in fact, sauna bathing.[11] Claims that Finns were "wild-eyed radicals who wanted to turn the Government topsy-turvy" were discounted by Berkovici as a particularly distrustful interpretation of Finnish participation in consumer and producer cooperativism. At several points in his visit, Berkovici reveals an apparent relationship between the treatment Finns receive due to stereotypes and their response to the prying eyes of outsiders as a result. His commentary, for the most part, acknowledges this situation and serves to characterize the Finns as perhaps foreign but still perfectly normal humans.[12]

Where his stereotypes remain, however, is in his description of Finnish farm wives. Of Finnish gender difference, and of Finnish women in particular, he states: "The Finns owe a great deal of their success to their women. Huge, blue-eyed, and golden-haired, they are as a rule taller than the men and as broad-shouldered." He goes on to state that Finnish men are poor farmers, but that their wives excel at it and that, due to their expertise, discussion about local farming was an area in which women prominently engaged.[13]

The sociologists Eleanor Palo Stoller and Chris Susag, both conducting research across the United States in the 1990s, revealed stereotypical traits among primarily third-generation ethnic Finns. Positive stereotypes included a tendency toward hard work, cleanliness, honesty, and persistence in completing tasks and goals often tied to the Finnish concept of *sisu*.[14] Negative stereotypes included a tendency toward alcoholism, detrimental self-effacement, and depression.[15] While not commonly articulated, folk ideas about the upper classes as well as social research reflect an egalitarian attitude that is seen in ideas about gender and class in Finland and the United States.[16] These observations, drawn from ethnic Finns primarily in the Upper Midwest, illustrate general stereotypes the group holds about themselves. While many were not framed as gendered norms or roles, several can be correlated with gendered stereotypes. One informant related to Stoller the idea that cleanliness was evidenced by "the popularity of Finnish maids or 'cleaning ladies,'" a phenomenon to be discussed later that is widely recognized within the Finnish ethnic community, and especially among elders who remember when this was still common in the mid-twentieth century.[17] Generally speaking, alcoholism can be associated with males, as other stereotypes attest.

The Finns have thus been particularly notable for their cultural differences with their neighbors, and these traits, real and imagined, are recognized, elaborated, and exploited by Finns and those with whom they interact.[18] They have been alternately admired and ridiculed through folk images created by outsiders, and it is through imagery created and perpetuated by the region's Finns themselves that we find a discourse that both counters and embraces outsiders' ideas. Most important to this discourse, perhaps, is the masculinity with which Finns are portrayed. Representations of men and women consistently rely on images as described by Dorson and Berkovici above, continuing with Hoolie DeCaire's description of Copper Country women, more likely to be of Finnish heritage than not, as being essentially masculine, or tough in a way that contradicts mainstream ideals of femininity. Next I identify and analyze key characters and character types found in folk images of Upper Midwestern Finns and describe how folk discourse handles women within the community who attempt to break the mold.

RELEVANT FINNISH FOLK CHARACTERS AND CHARACTER TYPES

No discussion of folk characters in Finnish North America could begin without discussion of the characters and types that were brought with the immigrants from Finland. These folk images not only served to categorize people in the homeland, but they also provided people with fodder for the creation of North American types. The most famous and obvious source of material is the *Kalevala*, the national epic of Finland, and a symbol around which Finns worldwide rally as important to their culture.

In the *Kalevala*, five main masculine figures all feature widely different personalities, but all have distinct problems with women. Väinämöinen, the world's oldest and wisest man, is too old to attract a bride despite other numerous attributes. Ilmarinen, the smith, is so shy around women that he second-guesses his chances to woo a bride for whom he built a magical object. Joukahainen, brazen and boastful, must trade his sister Aino to Väinämöinen in exchange for his life after a brutal singing duel. Kullervo, embittered by a cruel life and thoughts of revenge, murders his farm mistress and then unintentionally commits incest with a long-lost sister, leading to the ultimate demise of his entire family. Lemminkäinen, the ardent lover, just cannot stay away from women, *any* of them, leaving his mother and wife to suffer the consequences of his actions and of his double standards for them.[19]

The adult women of the *Kalevala*, too, are strong and superhuman just like the men, but they are portrayed as being heroic through sacrificing their power and sometimes their lives or personal dignity due to the rash actions of men, or as being villains for standing up for themselves and their families' interests. The two farm wives, Louhi and Lemminkäinen's mother, hold a lot of power in their own homes, although their relationships with their children are problematic. Lemminkäinen's mother dotes on and solves problems for a son she knows to be wild, even resurrecting him from death. Louhi, though married until her husband dies in a duel, is very much the leader of her people, negotiating a heavy brideprice for the hand of her daughter and even carrying her people to battle transformed as an eagle in one poem of the epic. However, for these very traits, she is reviled.

Young women, meek and powerless, are largely pawns for strategic marriages, and they must remain virgins until the appointed time. Aino, Joukahainen's sister, commits suicide rather than marry Väinämöinen. Lemminkäinen, after courting all the maidens of the village, pursues Kyllikki, who is saving herself for a better match. Rather than respect Kyllikki, he kidnaps her, forcing her to agree to a marriage with him to save face. The Maid of Pohjola is largely a silent pawn before marriage, but after, she abuses the young serf Kullervo until he kills her. The final young woman in the poem, Marjatta, is expelled from her family home when she reveals that she is pregnant despite being a virgin, and she is forced to deliver her baby alone in a stable and face the ridicule and judgment of Väinämöinen when she brings her baby to be baptized.

Recurrent themes and figures in modern Finnish American folk culture can be seen to have direct connections to the human characteristics of *Kalevala* characters. Väinämöinen, an old bachelor wizard, can be found in images of modern-day Finnish American elderly bachelors, who often live alone in the backwaters or with a sibling or parent. Ilmarinen can be found in recurrent images of painfully shy Finnish men. Joukahainen and Lemminkäinen are the forebears of youthful, rebellious Finns who challenge elders and make public celebrations a place of danger.

Young women are compared to the virginal Aino, and as they age, to the strong and resourceful Lemminkäinen's mother. Although Louhi could also be seen in a positive light as worthy of emulation, she is portrayed as an enemy of the people of Kaleva (i.e., the Finns), and so those features that are so respected in a Finnish woman are considered negative for her. Her daughter is not able to escape her outsider status, despite marrying into the Kaleva people: she is eventually murdered for the cruel traits she exhibits.

As the folklorist Patricia E. Sawin highlights, the *Kalevala* was compiled when Finland was in the process of nation-building, and the development of a national epic by the folklorist Elias Lönnrot was an important part of this process. In so doing, however, Lönnrot, piecing together diverse poems from a vast geographic, temporal, and purposed base of oral poetry, created a set of masculine heroic characters that fit the national project—and a complementary set of female characters who were only represented in a positive light when their acts served to support the often violent acts of the male heroes, to the detriment of themselves or other women.[20]

While these character images came over with immigrant Finns to some extent, some of whom may have read the literary epic, it is important to highlight that many of the early Finnish immigrants fled from famine, land shortages, and military conscription.[21] Even back in Finland, they would have been too busy—and too lowly—to participate in the fit of nationalism sweeping the largely Swedish-speaking elite at the time. And so while it is highly likely that immigrants knew of the epic and sometimes even the source poetry behind it, it appears that the later recognition of the epic among subsequent generations may have strengthened its importance in the Upper Midwest, deepening internalization of Kalevalaic traits among the region's Finns today.[22]

A well-known masculine character type that came over with the immigrants is that of the "knife-fighting Finn." The folklore surrounding knife fights comes from two primary genres: songs still performed to some extent today and jokes or anecdotes about individual Finns remembered for their expertise with the weapon, known in Finnish as a *puukko*. The ballad "Isontalon Antti ja Rannanjärvi" is the best known of these songs, although "Anssin Jukka ja Härmän Häät" and "Ketolan Jukka" were performed at least through the first half of the twentieth century.[23] Kenneth Porter, in 1955, discusses his experiences with a cycle of knife-fighting ballads surrounding the character "Hansi Joki," mentioning that the lines he still remembered were, "And many a time with my guts in my lap / I sprawled upon the dancing floor."[24]

Many of these songs centered on drunken young men who, like Lemminkäinen, broke into violence at festive events in small villages in the Finnish region of Pohjanmaa or Ostrobothnia, from whence most Finnish immigrants came. "Isontalon Antti ja Rannanjärvi" is based on true events, and the characters in the song were real men who served time for their deeds.[25] Dorson recounts a tale about Finnish American knife-fighting in *Bloodstoppers and Bearwalkers,* detailing a preferred method for holding the knife that results in shallow scratches across the skin that would draw a lot of blood but not result in death. In this story, the victim of the fight was found by a church congregation one Sunday "lying like dead with his chest all crisscrossed and bloody with knife cuts." When a physician came to attend to the man, "too weak to move," he poured turpentine on the wounds, resulting in the victim screaming "Saatana!" (Satan) and getting up.[26]

Another image of men that crossed the ocean is that of the *noita,* a Finnish wizard who derives from Finnish and Sámi pre-Christian traditions. In *Bloodstoppers and Bearwalkers,* Dorson encounters multiple tales of the *noita,* all of which present "a religious magician, a wizard, or a healer" who uses his supernatural powers, among other things, to avenge wrongs committed by landowners against the peasants.[27]

Finnish men or women might be practicing *loihtijat,* singers of charms. A charm is a formulaic verse concerning the origin and harnessing or banishment of something a person wants control over, including physical ailments, dangerous animals, and even the process of brewing ale. A characteristic teaching of the *Kalevala* is that anyone could control a formidable situation if they knew, and could describe, the most about the given circumstances.[28] This is demonstrated in the singing duel between Väinämöinen and Joukahainen, in which Joukahainen claims to know of the world's origins, but Väinämöinen's knowledge of this supersedes Joukahainen's: Väinämöinen was there when it happened, and his understanding of these things allows him to vanquish his young challenger.[29]

Richard Dorson and Marjorie Edgar describe charms, or *loitsuja,* used to guarantee a certain outcome, such as protecting one's cows from predatory animals, stopping blood flow from an open wound, or healing an injury like frostbite or a bruise.[30] Men were often more associated with blood-stopping charms and women with healing and protective charms. These surviving items of folklife, carried across the sea with immigrants and used in everyday life, contributed to the reputation of Finnish people as being supernaturally mysterious.

Finnish men and women were also recognized for traditional medical techniques, including massage, cupping blood, and sauna usage, in which many ritualized curative practices took place.[31] Cupping and sauna-based healing traditions continued in Finnish ethnic communities across North America. In the Copper Country, Eelu Kiviranta of the farming community of Nisula was a well-known cupper, masseur, and topical couplet writer, about whom colorful tales continue to circulate.[32]

The connections between Kalevalaic imagery, considered to be purely folkloric and even mythical in nature, and generic characters such as healers, wizards, and knife fighters, all of whom straddle the line between folk fantasy and historical characters, are made in folk characters, named and unnamed, found in Upper Midwestern Finnish communities. Examination of the male and female characters reveals a latent concern for community maintenance in certain aspects as well as a continued privileging of traits considered to be "strong" and "masculine" in nature. Even women who may succeed at this, however, remain in the background as compared to their husbands in the folklore record.

MASCULINE CHARACTERS IN FINNISH ETHNIC FOLKLORE

Saint Urho

Arguably the most famous folk character in Finnish North America, Saint Urho was invented in 1956 in Minnesota's Iron Range. The identity of his originator is disputed, with Richard Mattson of Virginia, Minnesota, and Sulo Havumäki of Bemidji, Minnesota, holding equal claims.[33] Saint Urho was created to counter the Irish Saint Patrick, whose festival day was a cause for great celebration in the Iron Range. Urho's "feast day" has come to be celebrated on March 16, the day before Saint Patrick's Day, thus overshadowing local Irish festivities.[34]

The story of the saint, created haphazardly in 1956, states that an invasive plague of pests (grasshoppers most commonly, but in some traditions frogs) invaded Finland approximately 12,000 years ago. The pests attacked allegedly plentiful and bounteous grapevines in Finland, thereby threatening the year's wine production. This prospect terrified the Finns, who feared complete ruin until one man, the brave Urho, singlehandedly chased the plague from Finland with a pitchfork. In the dominant variant, he chanted, "Heinäsirkka, heinäsirkka, menee täältä hiiteen!" (Grasshopper, grasshopper, go from here to hell!).[35]

The story of Saint Urho is now celebrated across North America, with his biggest festivals being thrown in his home territory of northern Minnesota.[36] Urho is associated with the colors green and purple, which celebrants wear, and with grape juice and wine, the products of that which he saved. Revelers often recite an ode to the saint, written in 1956 by Mattson's coworker Gene McCavic, which tells the legend of the saint in the dialect known as Finglish. As Urho's popularity has grown, others, Finnish and not, have been free to add their own details to the story of the saint. Urho is associated with a specific burial place, and two major statues have been constructed in his honor in the towns of Menahga and Finland, Minnesota.[37] Additionally, Urho has a wife, who will be discussed later.

The meaning behind Saint Urho becomes apparent when we consider the dominant discourse surrounding Finnish history. As one of the last Christianized areas of Western Europe with a pre-Christian worldview utilizing shamanic elements, Finnish Christianity acknowledges a strong affinity with nature carried down from earlier beliefs and practices.[38] With no written language of its own before ca. 1550, Finland exists in the written record through the words of outsiders, beginning with Tacitus in 98 CE. Furthering the dominance of outsiders in shaping images of Finland and Finns is the fact that Sweden colonized Finland beginning with the first crusade of Henrik of Uppsala between 1155 and 1156 and ending with the ceding of Finland to the Russian Empire in 1809.[39]

The creation and use of Saint Urho, in this context, serves as a counterstatement to the idea that Finland's history and religion begin only in the twelfth century. Saint Urho thus initiates a fantasy of a history older even than that of the biblical record.[40] Additionally, by using the term "saint," a connection is made with Christianity, 10,000 years before its founding. Using Saint Urho in this light, then, negates images of Finland as having given the nation no history and no god, but rather says in a tongue-in-cheek manner that Finland is perhaps the oldest and godliest of all nations.

Heikki Lunta

Created as a character in a 1970 radio jingle for a snowmobile race that featured a Finnish name and was performed in a strong regional accent, Heikki Lunta is known as the "Finnish Snow God."[41] Heikki Lunta's creator, David Riutta, of Calumet, Michigan, wrote a song in which Lunta does a dance to make snow fall on behalf of the Range Snowmobile Club of nearby Atlantic Mine. The club worried that snow would not fall in time for an annual race; apparently, however, Heikki Lunta's magic worked. The song was so popular on the radio station WMPL that many claim that the races were cancelled after repeated play and a subsequent blizzard. The "Heikki Lunta Snow Dance Song" and a B-side tune, "Heikki Lunta, Go Away," were pressed as a 45-rpm record, and copies made their way to various locations across the country. The winter continued to be harsh for the rest of the season, and thus Heikki Lunta became canonized as a part of the local lore and was further imprinted upon local consciousness.

Riutta's friends and coworkers imagined the snow god as a stereotypical Finnish bachelor who lived alone in the woods using his innate understanding of nature and his ability to build useful contraptions from nothing. These attributes, as well as his ability to conjure snow through a dance, make Heikki Lunta into a modern parallel of Väinämöinen. By the late 1990s, however, Heikki's story had developed to the point that it is alleged that "he married his childhood sweetheart, Aino Mäkinen, or some other Copper Country Finnish girl."[42] She is not, however, commonly discussed.

Heikki Lunta appeared at regional winter events in which local and tourism-related interests comingled. The imagery of the "snow god" played with Finnish American and Upper Midwestern stereotypes, fostering a place for discussion and reflection of these ideas within the community. After their arrival in North America, Finns had developed a reputation that differentiated them from their neighbors and put them up to scrutiny, sometimes resulting in discrimination. Differences included the previously cited stereotypes of Finns provided by Richard Dorson, Finns' reputation for being politically radical in the workplace, and even nineteenth- and early twentieth-century racial theories categorizing Finns as Asian and not white.[43] At the same time, however, ethnic Finns foster a strong sense of group identity through social organizations, festivals, churches, and similar means.

FEMININE CHARACTERS IN FINNISH ETHNIC FOLKLORE

Both Heikki Lunta and St. Urho are loosely associated with female companions over time, but these associations are tenuous and these women do not appear in costumed events celebrating the figures. A poem by Priscilla J. Harvala on the website *Saint Urho: Legendary Patron Saint of Finland* tells the story of Urho's wife, Sinikka, whose unseen supporting role gives Urho his power in the first place, even claiming that "it was said by many that maybe Sinikka was the sainted hero."[44] She performs the duties of both man and wife to compensate for Urho while he is out saving the grapevines.

More notorious than the feminist Sinikka is the decidedly camp "Queen Helmi." A fixture at the annual St. Urho's Day celebration in Finland, Minnesota, the Queen Helmi Drag Contest is an event in which male competitors vie to provide "the beloved saint a wife."[45] Photographs and internet videos of this event show contenders with long, curly wigs in evening gowns and negligees, faces covered with copious makeup contrasting with blackened-out teeth and unshaven facial hair. The commentary on the nature of women in the community is apparent: the proper mate for such a manly, heroic Finn can only be found in a masculine character.[46] While drag performances have become increasingly common in the Northwoods, this is the only one in which performers maintain clear signals of masculinity and dressing down. That such a performance is only found in this Finnish American festival also signals folk ideas about the Finns.

Heikki Lunta's wife, mentioned previously, is Aino Mäkinen, a Finnish immigrant everywoman. This character was invented for a series of plays performed at Finlandia University in Hancock, Michigan, during the late 1990s. Another wife to the snow god, Aili, is mentioned in a song by the Marquette, Michigan, Finnish American reggae band Conga Se Menne. The song, "Guess Who's Coming" reveals only that Heikki and Aili enjoy the sauna, eating traditional Finnish American foods and listening to regional bands, including the Oulu Hotshots and Da Yoopers.[47] Whatever the particulars, she, just like Sinikka, is invisible, and both are only seen when their work and activities coincide with or compensate for those of their husbands, much like the women of *Kalevala*.

EXTRAORDINARY ORDINARINESS

The essential elements of everyday stereotypes of Finnish American women center around strong women working on farms, raising armies of children, wringing dollars out of dimes, and placidly fighting off family disasters and crises as though there was no other way to live. While I am not arguing here that this situation would have been different for the other working- and poverty-class immigrant and Indigenous Northwoods women, it is a stereotype that is replayed time and again in oral histories, family memorates, and even ethnic fiction about Finnish Americans. Combined with the imagery of Finnish women in the immigration era engaging in stereotypically masculine activities out of necessity, this idea lays the basis for the future that young Finnish American women could expect.

This image of traditional Finnish American womanhood was updated and presented by the comedy troupe Nyt Naura/Laugh Now, who performed during the first decade of the 2000s. Three sisters from Michigan's Copper Country, the women of Nyt Naura presented images of coffee time at home in an era recently bygone but residually still present. Wearing white head scarves still known as *huivit,* as well as long blue and white striped denim aprons, the "Suomalainen Sisters" provide an image of gendered traditionality that deepens the discourse.

Seated around a table set for coffee with a traditional Finnish cardamom bread, *nisu,* the sisters portrayed recurrent moments between close women: reminiscing about the past, laughing over their father's interactions with prospective suitors, remembering family tragedies, and praising the *sisu,* or Finnish inner strength, that continued to bind them together. Using the Finnish American dialect in deep voices, the sisters sang Bobby Aro's "Highway Number Seven," a song performed from the perspective of a man.

While their actions thus far mostly portrayed a strength developed through tough times and hard work, it is through their discussion of past loves that Nyt Naura described gendered toughness. In a 2006 performance, the sisters discussed the mishaps created by a boyfriend's first visit to the home, situated on a dirt road in the deep woods. The young man, likely from Lower Michigan, is upset by the thick mud that clings to his new, shiny leather shoes as he gets out of his car. The darkness of the backwoods and the quiet ways of the family he visits are unnerving. It is finally too much for the young man when he is invited to join the father for a sauna bath. In a recorded performance found on the Nyt Naura website, two sisters listen, rapt, while the third recounts this event: "You mean to tell me, Mr. Kyrö . . . you and I just met . . . but you want me to go to that isolated building back there, take off all our clothes, sit on the highest part of the sauna, throwing water on hot rocks and hitting each other with sticks? And then jump in the snowbank? I'm sorry, sir, but I don't even think so!" (Nyt Naura, 2006).[48]

The storyteller Jenny "Jingo" Vachon (1918–2009) of Toivola, Michigan, wrote many of her best-known vignettes about Finnish Northwoods life in three published volumes in the 1970s. In "The Pest," she describes a male suitor, "a refined gentleman," who has come to visit her sister in terms similar to those offered by Nyt Naura, though the actions took place a half century earlier. He comes in a "well-tailored suit and shiny shoes" and his spotless new car, and though the action centers on the pesky younger sister, Jingo, the difference between outside men and farm-raised Finnish young women is made clear.[49]

The fact that these young men contrast so sharply with the people they visit and fail so miserably at the tests given to them highlights the idea that they are not tough enough to survive the rigors of daily life that these girls are expected to face. It makes these women tougher than these men, and by extension, more masculine. Traditional Finnish girls growing up in the north must ignore the mud that fills the yard for a significant portion of the year; keep the stove full of wood for the long, cold winters; and be able to withstand the searing heat of a good sauna followed by the deep cold of jumping in the snow. They must display a toughness and fortitude not expected of their contemporaries from suburbia, male or female.

Because of these deeply held visions of Finnish women, as well as the necessary toughness that all women who live in this environment and culture must develop, a generalized conception of women from the Northwoods persists. Just like men, they wear flannel shirts year-round and drink the least expensive beer. They chop wood and prepare endlessly for the ever-coming winter. To break this mold, however, results in further marginalization in the popular imagination. Both require that women leave their home community and reinvent themselves into something seemingly at odds with what they are made to be in their "native" context.

Jingo Vachon also mentions young Finnish women from her community taking jobs as domestic servants in the homes of the well-to-do both near and far, including the urban community of Detroit. According to Vachon, "In those days, the only passport needed for a maid's job in a high class home was a Finnish name, a Finnish accent, and a strapping peasant build. When you stated your home address as some place in the Copper Country of the Upper Peninsula, that cinched it!"[50] The social historians Carl Ross and Varpu Lindström highlight the important role that domestic employment played among Finns for the first few generations living in North America.[51] While at first able to find work in rural mining communities in boarding houses and mining bosses' homes, many Finnish women were also able to gain employment in affluent homes.

Women in this setting were expected to be meek and pliant, contrary to the image of the strong Finnish farm wife. This exchange of control of the household, however, was traded for freedom in the wider community; no elders were there to disapprove. For the immigrant woman who would eventually marry an American or a Canadian, working in the home of wealthy employers was an opportunity not only to learn English but also to learn "household skills, cooking, and keeping house American style."[52]

Other benefits of leaving rural home villages for urban areas included learning upper-class culture and having enough money for stylish clothes, modern appliances, and other items. This change in lifestyle became a source of pride for the woman in question, but it also caused a gulf with the folks at home. One folkloric reaction to such a woman, thought to have become "high-tone," is found in the creation of the character, Hilda Hitooni.

The folklorist James P. Leary once attended a community performance in Oulu, Wisconsin, in which the Hilda Hitooni character served as a counterstatement to the "traditional" local couple, Sulo and Rauha Kantapää. Sulo and Rauha have large, fake noses and wear old clothes. Hilda, from Lake Worth, Florida, is the cousin who has escaped the Northwoods, moving to an upper-class "Finn town" in the South. She is very feminine and flaunts her newfound social status. She gets to be feminine because she escaped, but she is also derided for making this choice.

Jingo Vachon writes about a few such women. Anni, in "The Throne That Pinched," is a Toivola native who, after two years as a servant in a home in Detroit, has married a factory foreman, who has secured her a comfortable, suburban lifestyle. When, years later, she returns to Toivola for the community's annual midsummer festival, she presents a stark contrast to the folk she left behind:

> Anni was resplendent in a sky blue satin dress that matched her eyes, very, very Frenchy looking delicate shoes with four-inch heels, and mink hides, at least three, draped around her shoulders! Her flaxen hair was now a beautiful reddish-gold and sculptured and scalloped to perfection. All eyes were on her and she so dominated the scene hardly anyone gave her husband and boy a glance as they quietly faded into the group. Her four inch heels sank down into the sandy sod and she almost lost her balance. Swiftly regaining her composure, she daintily lifted her feet and minced toward one of the picnic tables, eyeing the whole scene with a supercilious air.[53]

Anni's transition from a farm girl with a peasant build "like the rest of us" to a haughty, pampered housewife who has returned home to brag about her "house, her furniture, her high class friends, her social life, and everything else she could think of" does not sit well with the community.[54] Her concern that the wooden picnic tables would cause runs in her silk stockings and her discomfort at the mosquitoes and other aspects of rural life increase the ire of her audience until she draws attention to the fact that she must use the outhouse, a task she now detests due to her assumed exclusive use of indoor plumbing in Detroit. When she faces an embarrassing situation in the outhouse requiring public assistance due in no small part to her "softening" over the years, she becomes the laughing stock of the community and leaves in embarrassment. Her espousal of conspicuous consumption and modernity have alienated her from her community.

In the folkloric record, those women who are not masculine and tough are those who either place themselves in the home of another or who leave the community for one vastly different. It is in these new environments that their mainstream femininity can be cultivated and celebrated, but because of this choice, they may distance themselves emotionally from their families.

I have found no characters reflecting the modern "softening" of men in the Finnish ethnic community. Part of this may stem from the fact that in many of the northern areas with high concentrations of Finns, the men noticeably out-number the women.[55] It is not important to censure the men for leaving, while, in the interest of maintaining balance in the community, it may be considered so with women. In any case, though, women are considered to be masculine, strong, and marginal within the community and meek, "high-tone," and still marginal when they leave.

In recent decades, the increasingly clear presence of local community members who are LGBTQ+ has had long-term positive effects on the region as a whole, though the pain felt by those experiencing homophobia from would-be friends and family has doubtlessly been intense.[56] Everyone in the Northwoods who comes out continues to reshape the ways in which gender and sexuality are conceived locally, and this, too, is an area of study that deserves more attention in a number of fields. They, too, contribute to folklore that intersects gender and ethnicity.

It will be interesting to see how character types will continue to develop as the gendered dynamics of the ethnic community and their traditional settle-ment regions continue to change. As individual ethnic Finns age and create their own folkloric commemorations of their culture, we may someday find females whose exploits—like those of Saint Urho and Heikki Lunta—are as memorable as those of the *Kalevala* heroines. We may find LGBTQ+ reflections in the folkloric mirror. In the meantime, further research on folk representa-tions of gender among Finns and others in the Upper Midwest will illuminate how individuals define their roles in different situations, and eventually, how these images contribute to their senses of self.

NOTES

1. The term "Yooper" refers to a resident of Michigan's Upper Peninsula, based on the common abbreviation of the Upper Peninsula: "UP." See Arnold R. Alanen, "Yoopers," in *The American Midwest: An Interpretive Encyclopedia,* eds. Andrew R. L. Cayton, Richard Sisson, and Chris Zacher (Bloomington: Indiana University Press, 2006), 106.

2. See, for instance, Larry D. Lankton, "American Themes/Keweenaw Stories," in *New Perspectives on Michigan's Copper Country,* eds. Alison K. Hoagland, Eric C. Nord-berg, and Terry S. Reynolds (Hancock, MI: Quincy Mine Hoist Association, 2007), 15–16.

3. Bureau of the Census, *Thirteenth Census of the United States Taken in the Year 1910: Statistics for Michigan* (Washington, D.C.: Government Printing Office, 1913), 606; Matti E. Kaups, "The Finns in the Copper and Iron Ore Mines of the Western Great Lakes Region, 1864–1905: Some Preliminary Observations," in *The Finnish Experience in the Western Great Lakes: New Perspectives,* eds. Michael G. Karni, Matti E. Kaups, and Douglas J. Ollila Jr. (Turku, Finland: Institute for Migration, 1975), 55–56.

4. A. William Hoglund, "Finns," in *The American Midwest*, 241.

5. Kathryn A. Remlinger, *Yooper Talk: Dialect as Identity in Michigan's Upper Peninsula* (Madison, University of Wisconsin Press, 2017), 45.

6. See William G. Lockwood and Yvonne R. Lockwood, "The Cornish Pasty in Northern Michigan," in *Michigan Folklife Reader*, eds. C. Kurt Dewhurst and Yvonne R. Lockwood (East Lansing: Michigan State University Press, 1988), 362–64. This is also commonly expressed in the Finnish American internet community, for instance, in Facebook groups such as American Finnish People, where members commonly discuss pasties.

7. For the effect annual snowfall has on regional folklife, see Marsha Penti, "Copper Country: Snow Country," in *1987 Festival of Michigan Folklife* (East Lansing: Michigan State University Museum, 1987), 53–56.

8. Larry Lankton, *Cradle to Grave: Life, Work, and Death at the Lake Superior Copper Mines* (New York and Oxford: Oxford University Press, 1991).

9. Armas K. E. Holmio, *Michiganin Suomalaisten Historia* (Hancock, MI: Book Concern, 1967), 125–26; see also 161–62.

10. Richard M. Dorson, *Bloodstoppers and Bearwalkers: Folk Traditions of Michigan's Upper Peninsula*, 3rd ed., ed. James P. Leary (Madison: University of Wisconsin Press, 2008), 123.

11. Konrad Berkovici, *On New Shores* (New York: Century, 1925), 101–2; 113.

12. Berkovici, *On New Shores*, 109, 112, 113.

13. Berkovici, *On New Shores*, 115.

14. Eleanor Palo Stoller, "Sauna, Sisu, and Sibelius: Ethnic Identity among Finnish Americans," *The Sociological Quarterly* 37, no. 1 (Winter 1996): 154; Chris Susag, "Ethnic Symbols: Their Role in Maintaining and Constructing Finnish American Culture," *Siirtolaisuus/Migration*, no. 4 (Winter 1998): 4–5. "*Sisu*" can be simply translated as grit, or more elaborately as persistence beyond normal expectations.

15. Stoller, "Sauna, Sisu, and Sibelius," 155; Susag, "Ethnic Symbols," 5–6.

16. Klaus Helkama and Anneli Portman, "Protestant Roots of Honesty and Other Finnish Values," in *On the Legacy of Lutheranism in Finland: Societal Perspectives*, eds. Kaius Sinnemäki, Anneli Portman, Jouni Tilli, and Robert H. Nelson (Helsinki: SKS, 2019), 81–86.

17. Stoller, "Sauna, Sisu, and Sibelius," 154.

18. Finland has been a cultural crossroads between Lutheran Sweden and Orthodox Russia and, since the twentieth century, Western democracy and the Soviet Union/the Russian Federation. Before independence, Finland was part of Sweden (1200s to 1808) and then Russia (1809 to 1917), giving it a liminal status between the two countries. Finally, the Finnish language belongs to the broader Uralic language family, while both Swedish and Russian belong to the broader Indo-European family. The area has long been marginalized by its two neighbors and noted for significant cultural differences. See Henrik Meinander, *A History of Finland* (New York: Columbia University Press, 2011).

19. For concise details on the characters, plot, and history of the *Kalevala*, see Irma-Riitta Järvinen, *Kalevala Guide* (Helsinki: Finnish Literature Society, 2010).

20. See Patricia E. Sawin, "Lönnrot's Brainchildren: The Representation of Women in Finland's 'Kalevala,'" *Journal of Folklore Research* 25, no. 3 (September 1988): 187–217.

21. See Timo Orta, "Finnish Emigration Prior to 1893: Economic, Demographic and Social Backgrounds," in *The Finnish Experience in the Western Great Lakes Region: New Perspectives*, eds. Michael G. Karni, Matti E. Kaups, and Douglas J. Ollila (Turku, Finland: Institute for Migration, 1975), 30–33; see also Meinander, *A History of Finland*, 109, 119.

22. Marianne Wargelin-Brown, "The Kalevala as Western Culture in Finland and America," in *The Best of Finnish Americana*, ed. Michael G. Karni (Iowa City, IA: Penfield Books, 1994), 189. Stoller also discusses this briefly in "Sauna, Sisu, Sibelius," 157, 164. Although *Kalevala* was not widely read among early immigrants, a fraternal order called the Knights of Kaleva was founded in 1898 by the Finnish immigrant John Stone. This organization takes its inspiration from the epic, which has inspired the creation of materials central to the group's social functions, including rituals enacting characters from the epic and reading groups for study of the epic. While the published history of the order claims that *Kalevala* was commonly known across Finland, the source poetry that forms the basis of the epic was primarily a living tradition in the Russian borderlands of Karelia by the early 1800s. See Alfons Ukkonen, *A History of the Kaleva Knighthood and the Knights of Kaleva* (Beaverton, ONT: Aspasia Books, 2002), 10–11, 20–21, 326–28.

23. Marjorie Edgar, "Ballads of the Knife-Men," *Western Folklore* 8, no. 1 (January 1949): 53–57. See also Joyce E. Hakala, *The Rowan Tree: The Lifework of Marjorie Edgar, Girl Scout Pioneer and Folklorist: With Her Finnish Folk Song Collection "Songs from Metsola"* (St. Paul, MN: Pikebone Press, 2007), 124–27, 129.

24. Kenneth Porter, "Notes and Queries: Hansi Joki, the Terrible Finnish Knife-Man," *Western Folklore* 14, no. 2 (April 1955): 134.

25. Matti Kuusi, ed., *Suomen Kirjallisuus I: Kirjoittamaton Kirjallisuus* (Helsinki: Finnish Literature Society, 1963), 437.

26. Dorson, *Bloodstoppers and Bearwalkers*, 124. The folklorist James P. Leary also mentions the stereotype of Finnish men as having an affinity for fighting as illustrated in jokes. See Leary, ed., *So Ole Says to Lena: Folk Humor of the Upper Midwest*, 2nd ed. (Madison: University of Wisconsin Press, 2001): 86.

27. Dorson, *Bloodstoppers and Bearwalkers*, 131–34.

28. Järvinen, *Kalevala Guide*, 57.

29. Elias Lönnrot, *The Kalevala*, trans. Keith Bosley (Oxford: Oxford University Press, 1989), 28–29.

30. Marjorie Edgar, "Finnish Charms from Minnesota," *Journal of American Folklore* 47, no. 186 (October–December 1934): 381–83; Dorson, *Bloodstoppers and Bearwalkers*, 162–63.

31. See Ilmar Talve, *Finnish Folk Culture* (Helsinki: Finnish Literature Society, 1997), 231–32.

32. See Eelu Kiviranta, *A Rascal's Craft: Musings of a Finnish-American Immigrant* (Troy, MI: Momentum Books, 2010).

33. Hilary-Joy Virtanen, "Forging a Leader for a New Heritage: Finnish Americans and St. Urho," in *Pyhä Urho: Fakeloresta Folkloreksi/ St. Urho: From Fakelore to Folklore*,

eds. Anne Heimo, Tuomas Hovi, and Maria Vasenkari (Turku, Finland: University of Turku, 2012), 63–65.

34. Virtanen, "Forging a Leader," 64.

35. Joanne Asala, ed., *Finnish-American Folklore: The Legend of St. Urho* (Iowa City, IA: Penfield Books, 2001), 8.

36. See Matti Kaups, "A Commentary Concerning the Legend of St. Urho in Minnesota," in *The Best of Finnish Americana*, ed. Michael G. Karni (Iowa City, IA: Penfield Books), 175–76; Asala, *The Legend of St. Urho*; Virtanen, "Forging a Leader."

37. Virtanen, "Forging a Leader."

38. Meinander, *A History of Finland*, 7; Matti T. Salo, "The Pre-Christian Religion of the Finns," in *The Faith of the Finns: Historical Perspectives on the Finnish Lutheran Church in America*, ed. Ralph J. Jalkanen (East Lansing: Michigan State University Press, 1972), 1–18.

39. Meinander, *A History of Finland*, 8–10, 71–73.

40. Asala, *The Legend of St. Urho*, 9.

41. The name "Heikki Lunta" translates literally into Finnish as "Henry Some-Snow." The name was inspired by the then popular country musician Hank Snow. The word for snow is in its partitive form because as Finnish language receded from regular use, the most commonly used forms of Finnish words were remembered, incorrectly or not. Because snow is an uncountable substance, it is most frequently discussed using the partitive word form. See Hilary-Joy Virtanen, "Take the Power Back: Cultural Memory, Resurgence, and Heikki Lunta," *Journal of Finnish Studies* 11, no. 1 (August 2007): 60.

42. Finnish Genealogical Society, quoted in Virtanen, *Not Just Talking about the Weather: Tradition, Social Change, and Heikki Lunta* (Madison: University of Wisconsin Center for the Study of Upper Midwestern Cultures, 2006), https://heikkilunta.csumc.wisc.edu/.

43. Much has been written on Finns in the labor and socialist movements, but works detailing many aspects of Finnish leftist movements in the United States are found in Michael G. Karni's and Douglas J. Ollila's edited volume *For the Common Good: Finnish Immigrants and the Radical Response to Industrial America* (Superior, WI: Työmies Society, 1977). For more on racial theories and their application to Finns, see Peter Kivisto and Johanna Leinonen, "Ambiguous Identity: Finnish Americans and the Race Question," in *Finns in the United States: A History of Settlement, Dissent and Integration*, ed. Auvo Kostiainen (East Lansing: Michigan State University Press), 75–88.

44. Priscilla J. Harvala, "Sinikka, St. Utho's [*sic*] Wife, the Real Hero?," *Saint Urho: Legendary Patron Saint of Finland*, www.sainturho.com/urhowife.htm, 2001.

45. Asala, *The Legend of St. Urho*, 46.

46. Early photographs are found in Asala, *The Legend of St. Urho*, while recent photographs can be found on the Facebook page "St. Urho's Celebration in Finland, MN," https://www.facebook.com/sturho/.

47. Conga Se Menne, "Guess Who's Coming," *Finnish Reggae . . . and Other Sauna Beats* [audio recording] (Negaunee, MI: Conga Records, 1994).

48. The Nyt Naura website was hosted by Michigan Technological University, which employed Sherry Saarinen, one of the sisters in the ensemble. After her retirement in 2014, the page was taken down, so this quoted material from their performance is no longer accessible. This text was transcribed by the author before this material was removed.

49. Jingo Viitala Vachon, *Sagas from Sisula: Sketches and Stories* (L'Anse, MI: L'Anse Sentinel, 1975), 55–56.

50. Vachon, *Sagas from Sisula*, 127.

51. Carl Ross, "Servant Girls: Community Leaders," in *Women Who Dared: The History of Finnish American Women*, eds. Carl Ross and K. Marianne Wargelin Brown (St. Paul: University of Minnesota Immigration History Research Center, 1986), 41–54; Varpu Lindström, *Defiant Sisters: A Social History of Finnish Immigrant Women in Canada* (Toronto: Multicultural History Society of Ontario, 1988).

52. Ross, "Servant Girls: Community Leaders," 46.

53. Jingo Viitala Vachon, *Tall Timber Tales* (L'Anse, MI: L'Anse Sentinel, 1973), 70–71.

54. Vachon, *Tall Timber Tales*, 71.

55. This observation is supported by census data: of the four counties commonly considered to be part of the Copper Country region (Baraga, Houghton, Keweenaw, and Ontonagon), three show consistent patterns of higher male populations in the age groups between fifteen and fifty-four years of age. The 2020 American Community Survey, reporting age groups in five-year increments (i.e., 15–19, 20–24, etc.) shows gender imbalances skewing heavily toward men. In Baraga County, for instance, there are an estimated 301 men between the ages of thirty-five and thirty-nine, with only 135 women of the same age. While this disparity reduces among older age groups (possibly due to shorter male life expectancies and the phenomenon of retired couples settling in the region later in life), the consistency across the age groups associated with marriageable age and family growth provides statistical support for the stereotype of the Copper Country as being "where the men are men and the women are, too." U.S. Census Bureau, *American Community Survey*, 2020 ACS Five-Year Estimates; Table S0101: Age and Sex. Data compiled by the author March 22, 2022, for Baraga, Houghton, Keweenaw, and Ontonagon Counties. Data for St. Louis County, Minnesota (Duluth and the Iron Range), and Marquette County, Michigan (Marquette and surrounding iron mining region), also compiled for comparison, reveal more typical gender parity in population.

56. As a close family member, friend, and colleague of many LGBTQ+ people of Finnish and other ethnicities in the Upper Midwest, I have seen the homophobia that my loved ones face, and I stand with them as often as I can to help secure the dignity, personal safety, and public and private resources they need to live in comfort and grace. I know people who have been shot at, fired, physically assaulted, and kicked out of their family homes as minors—all for living as their authentic selves, or even giving any glimmer that their selves and the gender identities expected of them might not match up. Homophobia is a scourge that has not yet been driven from this community, and indeed, many others.

GREGORY S. ROSE

4

THE NORTHERN BORDERLAND AS AN ENVIRONMENTALLY, AGRICULTURALLY, AND CULTURALLY DISTINCTIVE SUBREGION OF THE MIDWEST IN THE LATE 1800s

Cultural geographers and others have employed unusual data sources to understand what regional terms people apply to parts of the United States based on their knowledge or perceptions of the characteristics that describe and categorize the region surrounding them. Some maps generated from this research show large stretches of sharply defined territory carrying major regional names, while others more finely depict areas within which distinguishing regional characteristics are most recognizable and transitional zones or edges where they are less obvious. The northern edge of the Midwest is best understood through the latter example. Absent is the stereotypical Midwestern landscape of fields of corn and soybeans stretching to the horizon, but despite its differences, this northern area typically is included within the Midwest, forming a distinctive Northern Borderland subregion that includes most of Michigan, Wisconsin, and Minnesota. The subregion's defining characteristics were present even in 1880, before the regional term "Midwest" began to solidify in the early 1900s and before the inhabitants thought of themselves as Midwesterners, let alone as residents of the northern edge of the Midwest.[1]

Multiple studies in the latter half of the 1900s examined perceptions of the Midwest's geographic extent and where its margins might fall. An analysis by Joseph Brownell, published in 1960, surveyed about five hundred postmasters in communities along major arteries radiating outward from Chicago, asking whether they thought their community fell inside or outside the Midwest.[2] From those data, Brownell mapped a "core" Midwest and a "peripheral Midwest."[3] Wilbur Zelinsky in 1980 used the names of businesses to demarcate vernacular or popular regions of North America.[4] One map, among seven others showing various regions within North America, displayed the combined pattern of the terms "Middle West," "Midwest," and "Mid-American," dividing their distribution into a zone where these three represent the dominant identifiers and another zone of secondary or peripheral occurrence.[5] And research by James Shortridge in 1985 examined "popular literature written at the state level" to see whether "local experts" perceived their state to be within or outside the Midwest, discovering a core area of "strongest regional feeling" for being Midwestern surrounded by two zones of successively lesser regional identification.[6] Results in line with these older studies appear when comparing recent maps drawn from internet and social media responses to the perennial question "Where is the Midwest?"[7]

While the specific placement of the northern edge of the area most strongly perceived as Midwestern varies, similarities among the maps are sufficient to suggest that the perceptual Midwest does not fully encompass Michigan, Wisconsin, and Minnesota. The northern edge of the Midwest may exclude Michigan altogether and end in northernmost Indiana or extend no farther north than a line crossing the Lower Peninsula from Detroit to Muskegon or eliminate the Thumb and the Lower Peninsula's northeastern third (map 1). Most to all of the Upper Peninsula is typically left out. The entirety of Wisconsin sometimes may be included in the Midwest, but in other examples, the state is divided in half along an east-west line, placing the south in the dominant zone perceived as being the Midwest but the north in the periphery, or only encompassing a small part of south-central Wisconsin as being the most Midwestern. Similarly, all of Minnesota sometimes falls within the Midwest, while in other instances only Minnesota's south or southwestern third is fully within the Midwest. The "left out" area north of the predominantly Midwestern region, generally including the northern half of Michigan's Lower Peninsula, the entire Upper Peninsula, and the northern two-thirds of both Wisconsin and Minnesota, formed

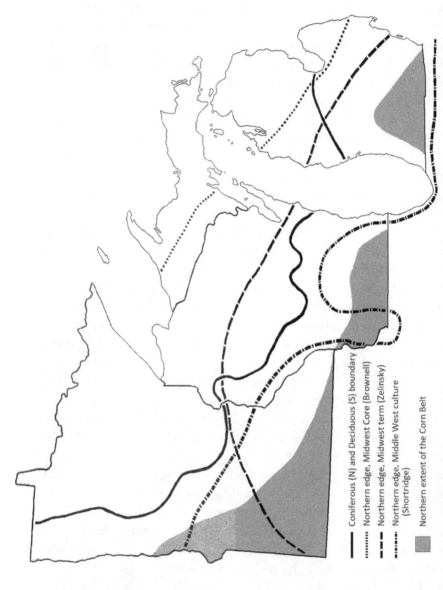

Map 1. The boundary between predominantly coniferous and predominantly deciduous forests; the northern edge of the Corn Belt; and the northern edge of Midwestern regions, according to three cultural geographers.

Coniferous (N) and Deciduous (S) boundary

Northern edge, Midwest Core (Brownell)

Northern edge, Midwest term (Zelinsky)

Northern edge, Middle West culture (Shortridge)

Northern extent of the Corn Belt

a secondary zone less commonly perceived as or weakly associated with the Midwest. Zelinsky took another approach to ascertaining where the Midwest ended by identifying a zone where the term "Northern" was most used in business names. This zone again included territory north of the area commonly viewed as the Midwest: the northern two-thirds of Michigan's Lower Peninsula and the entire Upper Peninsula, the northern/northeastern half of Wisconsin, and Minnesota's northeastern third.[8] South-southwest of the dominant area for "Northern" appeared a narrow band where it was used secondarily.

Beyond the more recent perceptual mapping, a long history exists of evidence for less typical but distinctive Midwestern characteristics in much of Michigan, Wisconsin, and Minnesota that can form the basis for identifying a Northern Borderland subregion. These factors were apparent at least by 1880, a marker date reflecting when population density in the Northern Borderland generally reached at least two to six persons per square mile and indicating a degree of settlement intensity by individuals engaged in economic activity using local physical and agricultural resources.[9]

The environmental elements of temperature and precipitation as recorded in the 1880 Census represent a set of historical data in support of a defined Northern Borderland subregion within the Midwest. These climate factors impacted the agricultural potential of the subregion, further differentiating it from the rest of the Midwest. That year's census contains maps of mean annual, July average, and January average temperatures, permitting contemporary climate conditions to be associated with contemporary vegetative cover and agricultural production.[10] On these maps, the isotherm marking the mean annual temperature of 45 degrees Fahrenheit extended about two-thirds of the way north across the Lower Peninsula of Michigan and a third of the way north in Wisconsin. Cooler mean annual temperatures occurred in the rest of Michigan and Wisconsin and nearly all of Minnesota. The isotherm for a July mean temperature of 70 degrees Fahrenheit cut east-west through the centers of Michigan's Lower Peninsula and Wisconsin and across Minnesota to its northwestern corner, with cooler temperatures northward. Nearly all of the Lower Peninsula and a narrow zone along the Lake Michigan shoreline in Wisconsin experienced 20-to-25-degree Fahrenheit mean temperatures for January. Elsewhere, January's average temperatures did not exceed 20 degrees.[11]

The 1880 Census also provided maps of mean annual precipitation and rainfall during spring/summer, "the six growing months."[12] Annual precipitation amounts generally were highest in Michigan, with a small area in the southwestern part of the state receiving 40 to 45 inches annually. Precipitation totaling between 30 and 40 inches yearly occurred in most of the remainder of the Lower and Upper Peninsulas and in Wisconsin, but westward into Minnesota the amounts declined to 20 inches. Spring and summer rainfall of 20 to 25 inches was measured in Michigan's southwestern Lower Peninsula, Wisconsin's southern half, and the southeasternmost tip of Minnesota. Most of the remainder of the region received 15 to 20 inches during that season except for as little as 10 inches in the eastern and western Upper Peninsula of Michigan and northern Minnesota. Overall, warm-season precipitation was considered sufficient for growing row crops.

The 1880 Census of Agriculture contained a large section describing the nation's "cereal" grain production, including a segment focused on "Indian corn," or maize. Corn occupied nearly 53 percent of all land sown to grain in the United States in 1879.[13] Although corn was "more generally distributed" across the country than any other grain, "the place of its greatest production is on the fertile prairies and river bottoms of the West, and north of the thirty-sixth parallel of latitude," with over half the crop raised between the thirty-ninth and forty-second parallels.[14] Only the southernmost range of Michigan counties fell south of the forty-second parallel, leaving nearly all that state and the entirety of Wisconsin and Minnesota above that latitude. Reflecting their location north of the prime growing latitudes, these three states combined accounted for only 4.7 percent of corn grown in 1879. Immediately to the south, however, Iowa, Illinois, Indiana, and Ohio together produced nearly half of all bushels, with Illinois and Iowa together yielding over one-third.[15]

The 1880 Agricultural Census also examined the relationship between production of major types of grains and mean annual, July, and January temperatures.[16] Over three-quarters of the total corn grown in 1879 was raised where mean annual temperatures were between 45 and 55 degrees Fahrenheit; only the southern two-thirds of Michigan's Lower Peninsula and the southern third of Wisconsin fit within that temperature category.[17] Ninety percent of corn was produced where mean July temperatures reached between 70 and 80 degrees Fahrenheit.[18] The cooler half of this maximum production zone (70 to 75 degrees) included the southern Lower Peninsula of Michigan, southern Wisconsin, and southwestern Minnesota, but the majority of the nation's corn grew farther south in the 75-to-80-degree temperature range. Additionally, according to the census, "the ideal climate for corn" required a frost-free period of at least four and a half months, a standard not met in the more northerly parts of Michigan, Wisconsin, and Minnesota.[19]

Relationships between precipitation and grain production were considered in less detail in the census analysis. However, over 97 percent of grain grew where 15 to 30 inches of spring/summer precipitation was received, and well over 80 percent of corn was raised in areas with spring/summer rainfall totaling 15 to 25 inches.[20] While most of Michigan, Wisconsin, and Minnesota fell within this rainfall range, the more significant limitation for corn production was temperature.

By 1880, many decades before maps of a perceptual Midwest appeared, an area of far less corn production already was discernable north of the greatest concentration of corn growing (see map 1).[21] Although an emerging "Corn Belt" appears on maps of crop production as early as 1840, the notion of such a defined agricultural region first arose about 1880, clearly outlined on maps from that year's census that displayed, county by county, various measures of bushels of corn raised per acre.[22] The incipient Corn Belt expanded from Ohio's Scioto and Miami River valleys, its early nineteenth-century footprint in the Midwest, to generally encompass the western half of Ohio; most of Indiana except the southern quarter; a small section of the south-central Lower Peninsula of Michigan; essentially all of Illinois and Iowa; a piece of south-central or southwestern Wisconsin; and slices of northern Missouri, eastern Nebraska, southeastern Dakota Territory, and southwestern Minnesota, a familiar outline nearly a century and a half later.[23] In contrast, most of Michigan Wisconsin, and Minnesota, where temperature restrictions resulted in different types of or limited agricultural activity and productivity in the late 1800s, lay beyond the northern edge of the Corn Belt.[24]

In the late eighteenth century, many Northern Borderland residents practiced hardscrabble, subsistence agriculture, which included raising corn but not at the levels seen farther south. Statistics for "Indian corn" production for 1879 reveal the contrast between Corn Belt and northern areas within each state.[25] Michigan's Corn Belt counties of Lenawee and Kalamazoo generated, respectively, 1.8 and 1.5 million bushels of maize in 1879, but Crawford and Cheboygan Counties in the northern Lower Peninsula grew fewer than 3,100 bushels each; more moderate temperatures in Leelanau County supported a yield of nearly 55,000 bushels. In the Upper Peninsula, Schoolcraft County grew 184 bushels, whereas none were listed for Marquette County. In Wisconsin, the Corn Belt counties of Grant and Dane each generated between 3.4 and 3.0 million bushels;

Marathon and Oconto Counties in the north accounted for fewer than 25,000 bushels apiece, and Ashland produced none. Overall yields in Minnesota were lower. Faribault and Fillmore Counties in the Corn Belt grew between 750,000 and 1 million bushels each, but many northern counties produced few (Carleton, 2,281 bushels; Pine, 1,150) or none.

Much of the northern Midwest overlapped with what came to be identified as the Dairy Belt, an agricultural zone of pasturage and milch cows from New England through New York, Pennsylvania, and northeastern Ohio.[26] It continued farther westward to include the transition zone between the Corn Belt portions of Michigan, Wisconsin, and Minnesota and the more heavily forested and colder areas farther north. Here, dairying using pastures on rolling topography in cooler areas less suited for commercial-level corn growing (although corn for silage was raised) became a common agricultural activity. Mapping milk production data in the 1880 agricultural census reveals this Dairy Belt, especially when cheese and butter tonnage is measured; fluid milk production data are less revelatory, as perishability concentrated it closer to the urban centers of Detroit, Chicago, Milwaukee, and Minneapolis.[27]

Another distinguishing characteristic of the Northern Borderland in 1880 and today is its forests. Because vegetative cover was considered a marker of soil quality by initial purchasers of federal lands, one responsibility of the surveyors as they began work in Michigan in 1816, continued through Wisconsin, and finished in Minnesota in 1907 was to record plant types encountered along their survey transects.[28] Researchers using these data have captured detailed characteristics of the "pre-settlement" vegetation, identifying a large variety of individual tree types, consolidating them into more general groupings, and yielding maps of forest associations. Their work revealed a vegetational transition within the Northern Borderland loosely separating predominantly coniferous forests northward from deciduous forests southward. The transition sliced westward across Michigan from Saginaw Bay to Ludington (a mixed zone of pines and hardwoods extended about a third of the way south toward Indiana); divided Wisconsin northwestward from south of Green Bay to Minnesota (a triangle of pines and hardwoods continued south to Milwaukee); and cut across Minnesota, starting around Duluth, before turning sharply northward to the state's western border, although an isolated zone of mixed pines and hardwoods appeared southward (see map 1).[29] Also to the south, grasslands were found in southwestern and western Minnesota and in the Prairie Peninsula east of the

Mississippi River that included "outliers . . . as far north as southern Wisconsin and southern Michigan."[30]

Details from surveyors' data indicate that beech and maple trees occurred throughout Michigan, with oaks and hickories as secondary species in the southern half of the Lower Peninsula and hemlocks in the north. White, red, and jack pines; cedars; spruce; and fir trees were more common in the northern half of the Lower Peninsula and the Upper Peninsula, and small prairie remnants appeared in southern Michigan.[31] Wisconsin's northern/northeastern half was a mix of conifers, predominantly pines (white, jack, red), hardwoods (beech and maple primarily), and other deciduous species such as aspen and birch, with a narrow band of boreal forest found in the far northwest.[32] Southern and southwestern Wisconsin hosted a blend of hardwoods (sugar maples, white oaks, basswoods), oak savannas (scattered trees mixed with grasslands), and prairies.[33] The northeastern third of Minnesota was covered by an assortment of northern coniferous trees, including white and jack pines and northern deciduous hardwoods.[34] A narrow transition zone of eastern deciduous forest, largely oaks, hickories, maples, basswoods, and aspens to the north, extended from the state's southeastern to northwestern corners.[35] Upland and wet prairies dominated Minnesota's southwest and western margins, with a mix of forest and prairie in the southeastern corner.

By 1880, clearing of land for farming and extensive lumbering had changed the look and coverage of forests in many places but not its basic distribution.[36] In 1884, the Census Bureau produced an in-depth *Report on the Forests of North America*, including numerous maps displaying the general locations of coniferous and deciduous forests and of certain species, as well as separate maps for Michigan's Lower and Upper Peninsulas, Wisconsin, and Minnesota, showing the tree types currently or previously present in somewhat or largely cut-over lands.[37] Information on these maps conformed in large part to data from the original surveys, defining a similar boundary between northern coniferous forests and southern deciduous forests that trended west and then northwest across central Michigan, Wisconsin, and Minnesota.

Forest resources on the northern margin of the Dairy Belt continued all the way to the Great Lakes and supported development of a Timber Belt.[38] Here, before but most intensively after the Civil War, widespread lumbering of white pine, other conifers, and the hardwoods interspersed with them supplied the nation's seemingly insatiable demand for wood.[39] Rivers, supplemented by narrow gauge railroads built to move logs, sent timber to sawmills at waterpower sites around the region.[40] Forest resources attracted settlers but at significantly lower concentrations than in agricultural regions farther south and, as a frontier with different characteristics from those found on the edge of agricultural expansion, lumbering generated its own extensive folklore.[41] Great Lakes timber provided building materials for construction in the region's cities and on the relatively treeless western prairies and supported industries such as furniture making in Grand Rapids, Michigan.[42]

Underneath the natural vegetation and developed on base material—for the Northern Borderland, primarily glacial till from the Wisconsinan era—distinctive soils evolved with varying potentials for agriculture.[43] The division between the two major soil types in Michigan, Wisconsin, and Minnesota aligned with the deciduous/coniferous forest boundary. North of this boundary, Spodosols (typically featuring low natural fertility) represented the dominant soil.[44] Southward, on the more rolling topography supporting deciduous forests in southern Michigan and Wisconsin and a slice of southwestern and western Minnesota, Udalf soils were typical.[45] On the very southernmost edge of the Northern Borderland, where prairies pushed into a small part of Michigan, a somewhat larger area of southern Wisconsin, and much of southwestern and western Minnesota, fertile Mollisols developed on the grasslands.[46] Only these limited parts of southern Michigan, Wisconsin, and Minnesota where soils were significantly better fell within the incipient Corn Belt on maps accompanying the 1880 Census or on later maps of agricultural regions.[47]

Beyond the Northern Borderland's distinctive climate, types of agriculture, natural vegetation, and soils, the area also differed from the core of the Midwest in the timing and sequence of non-Indigenous settlement. By 1870, a population density of at least eighteen persons per square mile—the minimum required for successful agricultural settlement according to the 1880 Census—extended no farther north than the boundary between deciduous and coniferous forests in Michigan's Lower Peninsula and Wisconsin.[48] By the late 1800s, the area with that density had expanded somewhat to include more of Michigan's Lower Peninsula, except its northeastern quarter, the southern two-thirds of Wisconsin, and most of southern Minnesota. But even with some expansion by 1900, settlement was insufficiently dense to be considered agriculturally successful in a zone from the shores of Lakes Huron, Michigan, and Superior to the northeastern Lower and the entire Upper Peninsula of Michigan, northern Wisconsin, and northern Minnesota. And not just the settlement density for agriculture was insufficient:

environmental limitations kept the area from generating the high production of maize as grain that characterized agriculture in the Midwest's Corn Belt core.[49]

The Northern Borderland was further differentiated by its distinctive mix of non-Indigenous population origins, as indicated by census birthplace information from 1850 and 1880, and by an extensive, detailed literature recounting the lives and experiences of mostly Euro-American immigrants in the three states.[50] Compared to the Northern Borderland, the Corn Belt core of Ohio, Indiana, Illinois, and Iowa contained proportionally more U.S.-born immigrants than foreign born, although rural and urban clusters of foreigners existed, and Southern states provided more of the domestic immigrants (table 1). In contrast, Michigan, Wisconsin, and Minnesota were populated by more and a greater variety of foreign immigrants and attracted more settlers from northern or other Midwestern states. In 1850, no Northern Borderland state counted a southern state among its top-ten immigrant sources, while Kentuckians, Virginians, Tennesseans, and Marylanders heavily occupied the southern Midwest, and Indiana featured a unique concentration of North Carolinians.[51] Immigrants from Pennsylvania and New York settled throughout the Midwest, with Pennsylvanians more common in the southern-tier states while New Yorkers and New Englanders (primarily from Vermont or Massachusetts) mostly settled the north. Across the entire Midwest in 1850, foreigners—commonly Germans, Irish, and English—averaged 25.5 percent of immigrants, but in the northern Midwest, foreign-born settlers accounted for 36.1 percent of the immigrant proportion, over twice that in the southern Midwest states alone. Canadians, plus Norwegians in Wisconsin, were among the top-ten sources of immigrants only in northern-tier states.

While over half of Midwestern immigrants in 1880 had U.S. birthplaces, the foreign proportion (44.3 percent) was notably greater than in 1850, partially reflecting the significant increase of post–Civil War arrivals and partially reflecting the age and mortality of the original domestic pioneers. New Yorkers represented 51.1 percent of Michigan's immigrants in 1850 but 27.5 percent in 1880; 28.3 percent of Wisconsin's immigrants in 1850 but 13.9 percent in 1880; 10.3 percent in Minnesota in 1850 but slightly less (9.8 percent) in 1880. Yet New York remained the top state of origin for the northern Midwest, with Ohio and Pennsylvania next in order. Ohio, Pennsylvania, and New York also were among the top immigrant sources for the southern Midwest, but New York was not first. In 1880, as in 1850, no southern state appeared on the top-ten list of immigrant sources for the northern-tier states of Michigan, Wisconsin, and

Table 1. Top Ten Sources, by Percent of Total, of Domestic and Foreign-Born
Immigrants to Midwestern States, 1850 and 1880

1850	Percent	1880	Percent
Illinois			
New York	16.8	Germany	17.2
Ohio	16.2	Ohio	10.0
Kentucky	12.6	New York	8.8
Germany	9.6	Ireland	8.6
Pennsylvania	9.5	Indiana	6.7
Tennessee	8.4	Pennsylvania	8.2
Indiana	8.1	Kentucky	5.7
Ireland	6.9	England	5.2
Virginia	6.3	Sweden	3.9
England	4.6	Missouri	2.9
Indiana			
Ohio	27.3	Ohio	29.9
Kentucky	15.1	Germany	12.9
Pennsylvania	10.1	Kentucky	11.9
Virginia	9.3	Pennsylvania	8.2
North Carolina	7.0	Illinois	4.4
Germany	6.5	Virginia*	4.3
New York	5.5	New York	4.2
Ireland	2.9	Ireland	4.1
Tennessee	2.8	North Carolina	3.3
Maryland	2.3	England	1.8
Iowa			
Ohio	21.7	Ohio	13.6
Indiana	14.0	Illinois	11.6
Pennsylvania	10.4	Germany	9.9
Kentucky	6.3	New York	9.3
New York	5.7	Pennsylvania	8.7
Virginia	5.5	Indiana	6.7
Illinois	5.1	Ireland	5.0
Germany	5.1	Wisconsin	4.6
Ireland	3.4	England	2.5
Tennessee	3.0	Norway	2.4
Michigan			
New York	51.9	New York	27.5
Ohio	5.7	Canada	17.9
Canada	5.4	Germany	10.7
Ireland	5.1	Ohio	9.2
Vermont	4.4	Ireland	5.2
England	4.1	England	5.2

1850	Percent	1880	Percent
Germany	3.9	Pennsylvania	4.3
Pennsylvania	3.7	Indiana	2.2
Massachusetts	3.2	Holland	2.1
Connecticut	2.6	Vermont	1.5
Minnesota			
Canada	29.9	Germany	13.9
New York	10.3	Norway	13.1
Maine	7.7	New York	9.8
Wisconsin	6.3	Wisconsin	9.2
Ireland	5.7	Sweden	8.2
Ohio	5.1	Canada	6.2
Pennsylvania	4.8	Ireland	5.3
Illinois	3.5	Illinois	3.4
Germany	3.1	Ohio	3.3
New Jersey	2.4	Pennsylvania	3.1
Ohio			
Pennsylvania	13.9	Germany	23.0
Germany	8.0	Pennsylvania	16.5
Virginia	6.0	Ireland	9.4
New York	6.0	New York	7.7
Ireland	3.6	Virginia*	7.6
Maryland	2.6	England	5.0
England	1.9	Kentucky	3.9
New Jersey	1.7	Indiana	3.3
Connecticut	1.6	Maryland	2.4
Massachusetts	1.3	Wales	2.2
Wisconsin			
New York	28.3	Germany	29.6
Germany	15.6	New York	13.9
Ireland	8.7	Norway	7.9
England	7.8	Ireland	6.7
Ohio	5.0	Canada	4.7
Vermont	4.2	England	4.0
Pennsylvania	3.9	Ohio	3.3
Canada	3.5	Pennsylvania	3.1
Norway	3.1	Illinois	2.6
Massachusetts	2.6	Bohemia	2.2

*Virginia in 1880 included both Virginia and West Virginia.

Sources: Bureau of the Census, *The Seventh Census of the United States: 1850* (Washington, D.C.: Robert Armstrong, Public Printer, 1853), xxxvi–xxxviii; Department of the Interior, Census Office, *Compendium of the Tenth Census, 1880* (Washington, D.C.: Government Printing Office, 1885), 464–69, 482–87.

Minnesota, whereas each southern-tier state except Iowa had three southern states among the top ten.

By 1880, the foreign proportion of immigrants had increased throughout the Midwest, but at 55.9 percent, their presence in the northern Midwest was notably higher than the 35.5 percent in the southern Midwest. Foreign natives represented 65.0 percent of immigrants in Wisconsin, 56.0 percent in Minnesota, and 46.6 percent in Michigan. Germany provided the largest percentage of the entire Midwest's foreign born in 1880, and their presence increased considerably after 1850. Ohio's Germans in 1850 represented 8 percent of immigrants but by 1880 they accounted for 23 percent; in Wisconsin they rose from 15.6 percent of immigrants in 1850 to 29.6 in 1880. On average across the three Northern Borderland states in 1880, Germany provided the largest proportion of immigrants, followed by Norway and Canada, although Canada was first in Michigan. Some foreign countries on the northern Midwest's list in 1850 contributed significantly more immigrants in 1880. For Wisconsin, 3.1 percent of immigrants in 1850 were Norwegians and 7.9 percent in 1880; Norwegians, not in Minnesota's top ten in 1850, represented 13.1 percent of its immigrants in 1880; Canadians formed 5.4 percent of Michigan's immigrants in 1850 and 17.9 percent in 1880. New European countries—Norway in Iowa, Sweden in Illinois, Wales in Ohio—appeared among the top-ten sources in 1880 for the southern Midwest but never exceeded 4 percent of immigrants. New countries also appeared among the northern Midwest's leading immigrant sources in 1880, including Sweden (8.2%) for Minnesota, Bohemia (2.2%) for Wisconsin, and Holland (2.1%) for Michigan.

The 1880 Census included county-by-county tables of the twenty leading birthplace states and foreign countries, permitting immigrant concentrations to be mapped within Michigan, Wisconsin, and Minnesota.[52] For some sparsely populated northern counties, however, the notion of "concentration" should be viewed in the context of overall low density. The average percentage of a state's immigrants born in another state or country formed the standard measure, with a county containing a concentration if its immigrant percentage exceeded the statewide average.

Settlers from New York and Vermont (the leading New England source) heavily occupied the Dairy Belt region. New Yorkers accounted for over one-quarter of Michigan's immigrants and 10 percent, plus or minus, of Wisconsin and Minnesota's. In all three states, Vermont natives accounted for 1.5 to 2 percent of immigrants. Counties with concentrations of New Yorkers and

Vermonters overlapped heavily in the southern part of lower Michigan, south-central Wisconsin, and southern Minnesota (map 2). Ohio and Pennsylvania also provided many northern Midwest settlers, particularly in the western half of Michigan's Lower Peninsula, the western half of Wisconsin, and sprinkled throughout Minnesota.

Foreign immigrants concentrated in Michigan's eastern and northern Lower Peninsula and throughout the Upper Peninsula; mostly in the eastern half of Wisconsin, especially near Lake Michigan; and from southeastern to north-western Minnesota (map 3). In Wisconsin, the most German of the Northern Borderland states in 1880, they concentrated very heavily in counties along and near the eastern shoreline north and somewhat west from Milwaukee (map 4). Germans in Minnesota commonly settled in the south-central portions of the state, while in Michigan, the least German of the three states in 1880, they appeared near Detroit and Saginaw Bay.

Natives of Norway and Sweden together represented Minnesota's largest foreign immigrant group in 1880, accounting for 21.3 percent of immigrants.[53] In Wisconsin, they formed 9.2 percent of immigrants but only 1.5 percent in Michigan. Among Norwegians and Swedes, those born in the former country accounted for two-thirds of the Northern Borderland's settlers. At 83.4 percent, Norwegians dominated in Wisconsin and represented 61.5 percent of the total in Minnesota, but Swedes formed three-quarters of the two groups in Michigan. Because census tables of nativity by county placed Norwegians and Swedes into a single category, they cannot be separated at that level. Together, Norwegians and Swedes concentrated in western Minnesota and along both sides of the Mississippi River; in Michigan, they located primarily in the northwestern Lower Peninsula and the Upper Peninsula (see map 4). Danes in Minnesota lived among the Norwegians and Swedes, but in Wisconsin they settled apart in the center and northeast.

Although immigrants from Finland were not directly identified in the state-wide tables for 1880, natives of Russia—which annexed Finland—were listed for Michigan, Wisconsin, and Minnesota, although they were too few to appear in the county tables.[54] The number of Finns among the 1,560 Russian immigrants in Michigan, 2,272 in Minnesota, and 812 in Wisconsin in 1880 is unclear. Other Slavs, including nearly 13,000 natives of Poland, lived in the three states.[55] How-ever, many sources identify Finns as a distinctive population in the northern Midwest: one claimed that 1,135 of the 3,400 Finnish natives residing in the United States in 1880 lived in Michigan.[56]

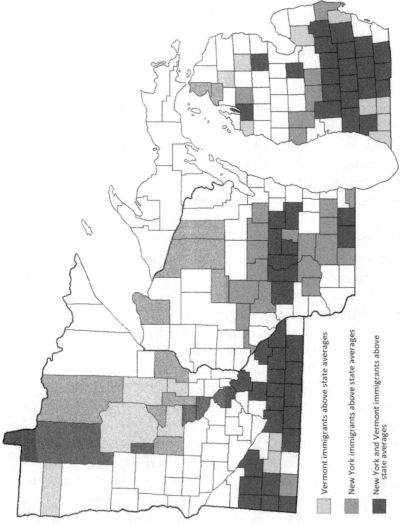

Map 2. Counties with immigrants from Vermont, New York, or both states that exceeded each state's average immigrant percentage in 1880. Natives of Vermont represented 1.6 percent of all immigrants in Minnesota, 2.0 percent in Wisconsin, and 1.5 percent in Michigan. Natives of New York represented 9.8 percent of all immigrants in Minnesota, 13.9 percent in Wisconsin, and 27.5 percent in Michigan.

Vermont immigrants above state averages

New York immigrants above state averages

New York and Vermont immigrants above state averages

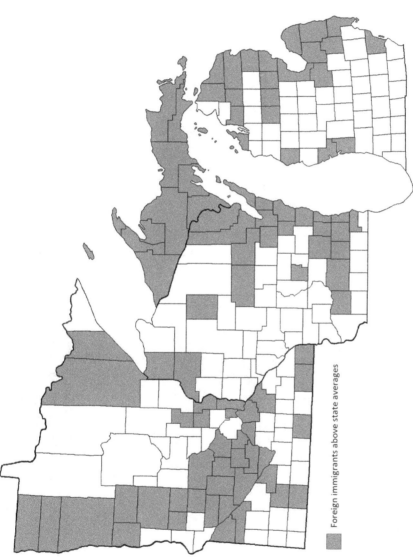

Foreign immigrants above state averages

Map 3. Counties with foreign immigrants exceeding each state's average percentage in 1880. Foreign immigrants represented 56.0 percent of all immigrants in Minnesota, 65.0 percent in Wisconsin, and 46.6 percent in Michigan.

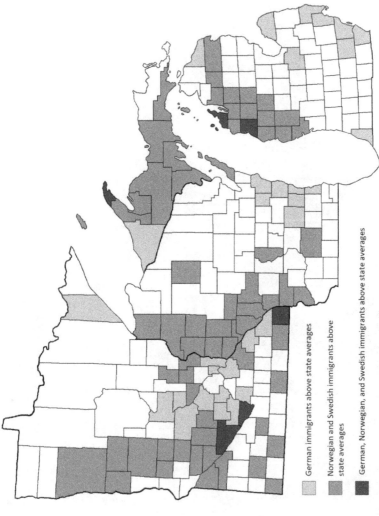

Map 4. Counties with immigrants from Germany, Norway and Sweden combined, or both sources that exceeded each state's average immigrant percentage in 1880. Natives of Germany represented 13.9 percent of all immigrants in Minnesota, 29.6 percent in Wisconsin, and 10.7 percent in Michigan. Natives of Norway and Sweden combined represented 21.3 percent of all immigrants in Minnesota, 9.2 percent in Wisconsin, and 1.5 percent in Michigan.

German immigrants above state averages

Norwegian and Swedish immigrants above state averages

German, Norwegian, and Swedish immigrants above state averages

Canadian immigrants mostly concentrated in the northernmost parts of the Northern Borderland, almost perfectly overlapping counties in the coniferous forest zone, but they were rare farther south. In Michigan, Canadians accounted for 17.9 percent of immigrants (the largest foreign source), concentrating in the Thumb and northern Lower Peninsula and throughout nearly the entire Upper Peninsula. They were also common in northern Wisconsin and Minnesota. Counties with greater proportions of Irish natives were found in southeastern Michigan, its Upper Peninsula, and southeastern Minnesota. Natives of England and Wales formed a single category in the county nativity tables.[57] They scattered throughout Minnesota but were strongly represented in southwestern Wisconsin, southeastern Michigan, and the western Upper Peninsula. Had English and Welsh natives been separately listed, it might have been possible to differentiate between the Cornish and Welsh laborers who worked the Michigan and Wisconsin copper, iron, and lead mines.[58]

What was the cultural impact of these Northern Borderland settlers? Folklore has generated the notion that for some immigrants, notably Scandinavians, the similar environment and rigorous climate of their old and new homes drew them to the Borderland and, as hardy denizens of a distinctive North, they and their neighbors became a defining characteristic of the region.[59] The "Doctrine of First Effective Settlement" extends this concept to the full group of Euro-American settlers in the Northern Borderland. It posits that the "later social and cultural geography" of a region was created by those people filling unoccupied areas, or, in this case, displacing an existing Indigenous population, to "establish a viable, self-perpetuating society."[60] Compared to the rest of the Midwest in 1880, the Northern Borderland's distinctive mix of population and ethnicities, as revealed by censuses from the last half of the nineteenth century, included higher proportions of settlers born in New York, New England, and foreign lands, notably Canada, Scandinavia, and Germany. And the area contained Native American reservation lands, something not found in other parts of the eastern Midwest.[61] History chronicled in secondary sources, plus surnames, traditions, and cultural events still found in the Northern Borderland, indicate that this ethnic imprint endures. Another piece of evidence comes from a recent study examining the "genetic (identity-by-descent, IBD) connections among 770,000 genotyped individuals of U.S. origin," which included a map showing the "Distribution of ancestral birth locations in North America associated with IBD clusters."[62] According to their genetics, distinctive groupings of New Englanders and New Yorkers appear in Michigan's southern Lower Peninsula, Finns gather in the

Upper Peninsula and northeastern Minnesota, and Scandinavians are found in southwestern Wisconsin and southeastern and western Minnesota. No other place in the Midwest displays a similar collection of those ethnic groups.

The distinctive environmental, agricultural, ethnic, and settlement history characteristics of the Northern Borderland, already identifiable in the late 1800s, provide the basis for defining that area as a subunit within the Midwest. Further, perceptual maps of the vernacular Midwest from the late twentieth century through today place much of Michigan, Wisconsin, and Minnesota north of the area predominantly considered Midwestern. Is the divergence from the Midwest's most common defining elements great enough that the Northern Borderland should not even be considered part of the Midwest? If so, then the same question could be posed for other edges of the Midwest—east, south, and west—where appear variant sets of environmental, agricultural, and settlement histories common to those areas but different from those found in the center of the Midwest. Yet, as is the case for other Midwestern edges, the northern areas of Michigan, Wisconsin, and Minnesota are connected to the rest of their states. And as often as not, regional boundaries are drawn in alignment with state boundaries. Another way to seek an answer to the question employs the model of core, domain, and sphere conceived by the geographer D. W. Meinig. The core is "a centralized zone of concentration" that best represents "the particular features characteristic of the culture under study," the domain "refers to those areas in which the particular culture under study is *dominant*" but less so than in the core, and the sphere is "the zone of outer influence" where the "culture is represented only by certain of its elements."[63] By these descriptors, the Corn Belt from western Ohio through Iowa forms the core of the Midwest; the domain on the north side is represented by the Dairy Belt through central Michigan, Wisconsin, and Minnesota; and the sphere incorporates the forested zone northward from the deciduous-coniferous transition line to the shores of the Great Lakes. The distinguishing elements that characterize the environment, agriculture, ethnicity, and settlement of the Northern Borderland places it then, and arguably now, within the Midwest's domain and sphere but not within its Corn Belt core—still Midwestern but a distinctive subregion on its northern margins.

NOTES

1. James R. Shortridge, "The Emergence of 'Middle West' as an American Regional Label," *Annals of the Association of American Geographers* 74, no. 2 (1984): 209–20;

James R. Shortridge, *The Middle West: Its Meaning in American Culture* (Lawrence: University Press of Kansas, 1989), 13–26.

2. Joseph W. Brownell, "The Cultural Midwest," *Journal of Geography* 59, no. 2 (1960): 81.

3. Brownell, "The Cultural Midwest," 83.

4. Wilbur Zelinsky, "North America's Vernacular Regions," *Annals of the Association of American Geographers* 70, no. 1 (1980): 1–16.

5. Zelinsky, "North America's Vernacular Regions," 8.

6. Shortridge, *The Middle West*, 97.

7. David Montgomery, "We Mapped 'the Midwest' for You, so Stop Arguing," *City-Lab, Bloomberg*, August 29, 2019, https://www.citylab.com/life/2019/08/where-is-the -midwest-map-geography-great-lakes-rust-belt/597082/, accessed January 23, 2020; Spencer Quain, "As a Geography Undergrad, I Just Had to Have a Go at It," Twitter, January 29, 2020, https://mobile.twitter.com/SpencerQuain/status/1222658437084930050, accessed January 29, 2020.

8. Zelinsky, "North America's Vernacular Regions," 10.

9. Department of the Interior, Census Office, *Statistics of the Population of the United States at the Tenth Census, 1880* (Washington, D.C.: Government Printing Office, 1883), map between pages xx and xxi.

10. Department of the Interior, *Statistics of the Population*, Maps 19, 20, 21.

11. Department of the Interior, Census Office, *Report of the Productions of Agriculture as Returned at the Tenth Census, 1880* (Washington, D.C.: Government Printing Office, 1883), 15/395.

12. Department of the Interior, *Statistics of Population*, Maps 24, 25; Department of the Interior, *Report of the Productions of Agriculture, 1880*, 15/395.

13. Department of the Interior, *Productions of Agriculture*, 90/470.

14. Department of the Interior, *Productions of Agriculture*, 90/470, 92/472.

15. Department of the Interior, *Productions of Agriculture*, 90/470.

16. Department of the Interior, *Productions of Agriculture*, 11/391–93/473.

17. Department of the Interior, *Productions of Agriculture*, 14/394, 92/472.

18. Department of the Interior, *Productions of Agriculture*, 14/394, 92/472.

19. Department of the Interior, *Productions of Agriculture*, 92/472; Henry D. Foth and John W. Schafer, *Soil Geography and Land Use* (New York: John Wiley, 1980), 148; Christopher R. Laingen, "The Agrarian Midwest: A Geographic Analysis," in *Finding a New Midwestern History*, eds. Jon K. Lauck, Gleaves Whitney, and Joseph Hogan (Lincoln: University of Nebraska Press, 2018), 147.

20. Department of the Interior, *Report of the Productions of Agriculture*, 15/395, 16/396.

21. Oliver E. Baker, "Agricultural Regions of North America: Part IV—The Corn Belt," *Economic Geography* 3, no. 4 (1927): 447–65; Laingen, "The Agrarian Midwest," 146; U.S. Department of Agriculture, "Generalized Types of Farming in the United States," *Agriculture Information Bulletin No. 3* (Washington, D.C.: U.S. Department of Agriculture, 1950), https://naldc.nal.usda.gov/download/CAT87210699/PDF, accessed January 20, 2020; U.S. Department of Agriculture, "Generalized Types of Farming in

the United States," http://usda.mannlib.cornell.edu/usda/AgCensusImages/1959/05/06/971/Table-26.pdf, accessed January 20, 2020; "Corn for Grain 2021: Production by County for Selected States," (U.S. Department of Agriculture, 2021), https://www.nass.usda.gov/Charts_and_Maps/Crops_County/cr-pr.php, accessed January 20, 2020.

22. John C. Hudson, *Making the Corn Belt: A Geographical History of Middle-Western Agriculture* (Bloomington: Indiana University Press, 1994), 1–14; Laingen, "The Agrarian Midwest," 145–48; William Warntz, "An Historical Consideration of the Terms 'Corn' and 'Corn Belt' in the United States," *Agricultural History* 31, no. 1 (1957): 40–45; Department of the Interior, *Report of the Productions of Agriculture*, Maps 6 and 7.

23. Hudson, *Making the Corn Belt*, 8–9, 88–109; John C. Hudson and Christopher R. Laingen, *American Farms, American Food: A Geography of Agriculture and Food Production in the United States* (Lanham, MD: Lexington Books, 2016), 25–27, 30–32; Laingen, "The Agrarian Midwest," 145–48.

24. Ralph E. Neild and James E. Newman, "Growing Season Characteristics and Requirements in the Corn Belt," in *National Corn Handbook-40: Climate and Weather* (West Lafayette, IN: Purdue University Cooperative Extension Service, 1990), https://www.extension.purdue.edu/extmedia/NCH/NCH-40.html, downloaded August 28, 2019.

25. Department of the Interior, *Report of the Productions of Agriculture*, 193, 194, 211.

26. Oliver E. Baker, "Agricultural Regions of North America: Part V—The Hay and Dairying Belt," *Economic Geography* 4, no. 1 (1928): 44–73; Baker, "Agricultural Regions of North America: Part IV—The Corn Belt," 448, 451; Hudson and Laingen, *American Farms, American Food*, 54; U.S. Department of Agriculture, "Generalized Types of Farming in the United States."

27. Gregory S. Rose, "The Dairy Belt of Southern Michigan, Wisconsin, and Minnesota, 1850–1880: Midwest or New England Extended?" (paper presented at Midwestern History Conference, Grand Rapids, MI, May 30, 2019).

28. Dennis A. Albert, Patrick J. Comer, and Helen Enander, *Atlas of Early Michigan's Forests, Grasslands, and Wetlands* (East Lansing: Michigan State University Press, 2008), ix; John Fraser Hart and Susy S. Ziegler, *Landscapes of Minnesota: A Geography* (St. Paul: Minnesota Historical Society, 2008), 47.

29. E. Lucy Braun, *Deciduous Forests of Eastern North America* (New York: Free Press, 1950), map of forest regions and sections.

30. Braun, 185, map; Edgar Nelson Transeau, "The Prairie Peninsula," *Ecology* 16, no. 3 (1935): 423–37.

31. Albert, Comer, and Enander, *Atlas of Early Michigan's Forests*, viii–xxviii; Lawrence M. Sommers, ed., *Atlas of Michigan* (East Lansing: Michigan State University Press, 1977), 18–19, 45; Braun, *Deciduous Forests*, 185–91; Transeau, "The Prairie Peninsula."

32. John T. Curtis, *The Vegetation of Wisconsin: An Ordination of Plant Communities* (Madison: University of Wisconsin Press, 1959), frontispiece, 204–08, 533–34, 536, 548; Robert C. Ostergren and Thomas R. Vale, eds., *Wisconsin Land and Life* (Madison: University of Wisconsin Press, 1997), 99–102.

33. Curtis, *The Vegetation of Wisconsin*, frontispiece, 104–5, 133, 519, 522, 552, 566; Ostergren and Vale, *Wisconsin Land and Life*, 99–102.

34. Braun, *Deciduous Forests*, 383; Hart and Ziegler, *Landscapes of Minnesota*, 44, 47.

35. Braun, *Deciduous Forests*, 180–85.

36. Michael Williams, "Clearing the United States Forests: Pivotal Years 1810–1860," *Journal of Historical Geography* 8, no. 1 (1982): 12–28.

37. Department of the Interior, Census Office, *Report on the Forests of North America* (Washington, D.C.: Government Printing Office, 1884), 551, 554, 558, Portfolio Maps 1, 2, 6, 8.

38. Hart and Ziegler, *Landscapes of Minnesota*, 89–103; Theodore J. Karamanski, *Deep Woods Frontier: A History of Logging in Northern Michigan* (Detroit: Wayne State University Press, 1989); Rolland H. Maybee, *Michigan's White Pine Era, 1840–1900* (Lansing: Michigan Historical Commission, 1960); Mark Wyman, *The Wisconsin Frontier* (Bloomington: Indiana University Press, 1998), 246–78.

39. Thomas R. Cox, *The Lumberman's Frontier: Three Centuries of Land Use, Society, and Change in America's Forests* (Corvallis: Oregon State University Press, 2010), 163; Hart and Ziegler, *Landscapes of Minnesota*, 89–98; Maybee, *Michigan's White Pine Era*; Ostergren and Vale, *Wisconsin Land and Life*, 82; Gregory S. Rose, "On the Path toward National Eminence: Economic Development in the Old Northwest, 1850–1860," in *The Making of the Midwest: Essays on the Formation of Midwestern Identity, 1787–1900*, ed. Jon K. Lauck (Hastings, NE: Hastings College Press, 2020), 157–81; Sommers, *Atlas of Michigan*, 12.

40. Cox, *The Lumberman's Frontier*, 127, 161.

41. David C. Smith, "The Logging Frontier," *Journal of Forest History* 18, no. 4 (1974): 96–106.

42. Scott Richard St. Louis, "A 'Self-Made Town': Semi-Annual Furniture Expositions and the Development of Civic Identity in Grand Rapids, 1878–1965," *Michigan Historical Review* 44, no. 2 (2018): 37–65.

43. Braun, *Deciduous Forests*, 24–26; Foth and Schafer, *Soil Geography and Land Use*, 38–41; John Fraser Hart, "The Middle West," *Annals of the Association of American Geographers* 62, no. 2 (1972): 259.

44. Foth and Schafer, *Soil Geography and Land Use*, 203, 205, 144, 148.

45. Foth and Schafer, 149–53.

46. Foth and Schafer, 116.

47. Department of the Interior, *Report of the Productions of Agriculture*, Maps 6–9; Hudson and Laingen, *American Farms, American Food*, 23, 30; Laingen, "The Agrarian Midwest," 146.

48. Hart, "The Middle West," 260–61; Hart and Ziegler, *Landscapes of Minnesota*, 111; Ostergren and Vale, *Wisconsin Land and Life*, 138; Sommers, *Atlas of Michigan*, 70; Wyman, *The Wisconsin Frontier*, 295.

49. Hart, "The Middle West," 263.

50. Bureau of the Census, *The Seventh Census of the United States: 1850* (Washington, D.C.: Robert Armstrong, Public Printer, 1853), xxxvi–xxxviii; Department of the Interior, Census Office, *Compendium of the Tenth Census, 1880* (Washington, D.C.: Government Printing Office, 1885), 464–69, 482–87; Gregory S. Rose, "American and European

Immigrant Groups in the Midwest by the Mid-Nineteenth Century," in *Finding a New Midwestern History*, eds. Jon K. Lauck, Gleaves Whitney, and Joseph Hogan (Lincoln: University of Nebraska Press, 2018), 73–95. Examples of detailed literature include: Regina Donlon, *German and Irish Immigrants in the Midwestern United States, 1850–1900* (London: Palgrave Macmillan, 2018); Jon Gjerde and Carleton C. Qualey, *Norwegians in Minnesota* (St. Paul: Minnesota Historical Society, 2002); Jean Lamarre, *The French Canadians of Michigan: Their Contribution to the Development of the Saginaw Valley and the Keweenaw Peninsula, 1840–1914*, Great Lakes Books series (Detroit: Wayne State University Press, 2003); Jeffrey W. Hancks, *Scandinavians in Michigan* (East Lansing: Michigan State University Press, 2006); Hart and Ziegler, *Landscapes of Minnesota*, 105–19; June Drenning Holmquist, ed., *They Chose Minnesota: A Survey of the State's Ethnic Groups* (St. Paul: Minnesota Historical Society, 1981); John C. Hudson, "North American Origins of Middlewestern Frontier Populations," *Annals of the Association of American Geographers* 78, no. 3 (1988): 395–413; Jeremy W. Kilar, *Germans in Michigan* (East Lansing: Michigan State University Press, 2002); Russell M. Magnaghi, *Cornish in Michigan* (East Lansing: Michigan State University Press, 2007); D. Aiden McQuillan, "French-Canadian Communities in the Upper Midwest during the Nineteenth Century," in *French America: Mobility, Identity, and Minority Experience across the Continent*, eds. Dean R. Louder and Eric Waddell (Baton Rouge: Louisiana State University Press, 1993), 117–42; Susan Gibson Mikoś, *Poles in Wisconsin* (Madison: Wisconsin Historical Society Press, 2012); Ostergren and Vale, *Wisconsin Land and Life*, 137–330; Sommers, *Atlas of Michigan*, 74–78; Robert P. Swierenga, "The Settlement of the Old Northwest: Ethnic Pluralism in a Featureless Plain," *Journal of the Early Republic* 9, no. 1 (1989): 73–105; Robert P. Swierenga, ed., *The Dutch in America: Immigration, Settlement, and Cultural Change* (New Brunswick, NJ: Rutgers University Press, 1985); Richard K. Vedder and Lowell E. Gallaway, "Settlement Patterns of Canadian Emigrants to the United States, 1850–1960," *The Canadian Journal of Economics/Revue canadienne d'economique* 3, no. 3 (1970): 476–86; William E. Van Vugt, *Britain to America: Mid-Nineteenth-Century Immigrants to the United States* (Urbana: University of Illinois Press, 1999); Brian C. Wilson, *Yankees in Michigan* (East Lansing: Michigan State University Press, 2012); Wyman, *The Wisconsin Frontier*, 185–214; Richard H. Zeitlin, *Germans in Wisconsin* (Madison: Wisconsin Historical Society, 2013).

51. Gregory S. Rose, "Quakers, North Carolinians and Blacks in Indiana's Settlement Pattern," *Journal of Cultural Geography* 7, no. 1 (1986): 35–48.

52. Department of the Interior, *Statistics of Population*, 513–16, 534–35.

53. Department of the Interior, *Compendium of the Tenth Census*, 464–69, 482–87.

54. Auvo Kostiainen, ed., *Finns in the United States: A History of Settlement, Dissent, and Integration* (East Lansing: Michigan State University Press, 2014), 56–57, 110.

55. Department of the Interior, *Compendium of Tenth Census*, 482–87.

56. Kostiainen, *Finns in the United States*, 60–62.

57. Department of the Interior, *Statistics of Population*, 513–16, 534–35.

58. Magnaghi, *Cornish in Michigan*.

59. See Hilary-Joy Virtanen, "Where the Men Are Men and the Women Are, Too: Finnish Gender Stereotypes in the Upper Midwest" in this volume; Hancks, *Scandinavians in Michigan* pp. 46–65.

60. Wilbur Zelinsky, *The Cultural Geography of the United States* (Englewood Cliffs, NJ: Prentice-Hall, 1973), 13. One could easily argue that because the area's Indigenous population established the truly first effective settlement, the Euro-Americans might better be termed the "most recent effective settlers."

61. Barry M. Pritzker, *A Native American Encyclopedia: History, Culture, and Peoples* (New York: Oxford University Press, 2000), 398–481.

62. Eunjung Han, Peter Carbonetto, Ross E. Curtis, et al., "Clustering of 770,000 Genomes Reveals Post-colonial Population Structure of North America," *Nature Communications* 8, no. 14238 (2017), https://www.nature.com/articles/ncomms14238?proof =true, 1, 6, downloaded June 3, 2019.

63. D. W. Meinig, "The Mormon Culture Region: Strategies and Patterns in the Geography of the American West, 1847–1964," *Annals of the Association of American Geographers* 55, no. 2 (1965): 213–16.

5

THE UPPER PENINSULA AND THE REPORTER

John Bartlow Martin's *Call It North Country*

In the summer of 1940, a former *Indianapolis Times* reporter who now made his living as a freelance writer in Chicago for sensationalistic true-crime magazines pondered where he and his new wife, Fran, could travel for their honeymoon. Since his boyhood in Indiana, John Bartlow Martin had sought relaxation through outdoor pursuits, continuing to do so as his writing career blossomed by retreating to rented cottages in northern Wisconsin on fishing expeditions with his editors from *Official Detective Stories* (known in the trade as *OD*) and *Actual Detective Stories of Women in Crime* (*AD*). Convinced that Wisconsin had become "too civilized, too crowded with tourists, too organized," he sought a more remote spot for time alone with his new bride. The couple decided to try Michigan's Upper Peninsula, a region that Martin later described as "a wild and comparative Scandinavian tract—20,000 square miles of howling wilderness on the shores of Lake Superior." The couple picked out "an isolated town on the map with a name we liked, Michigamme," Martin recalled. They rented a camp—as cottages and cabins were called in the region, a holdover term from the days when lumberjacks lived all winter in logging camps—without electricity or running water at the town of Three Lakes, named for the nearby Ruth, George, and Beaufort Lakes. "Some honeymoon!" Martin recalled, "But it was on the shore of a beautiful lake and it shared the shore with only a few other camps, and the fishing was excellent, and we met people who remained our friends until they died."[1]

When the Martins first visited, Three Lakes consisted of just one country store, Numi's Service Station, operated by Earl Numinen, the son of a Finnish immigrant. As the social center for the tiny community, the store offered local residents and tourists such supplies as gasoline from its two pumps (only one actually worked), fresh fruits and vegetables (once a week), beans, cigarettes, socks, Finnish boot grease, slabs of bacon, and a mosquito repellent known as Wood's Lollacapop. On Friday evenings, Numinen's father fired up the sauna, or Finnish steam bath, and those who braved its overwhelming heat included miners attempting to sweat the hematite out of their pores and a few poor souls looking for relief from their hangovers. "A day lived at the store is like a year lived elsewhere," Martin said. The Martins' honeymoon marked the first of many summer trips to the Upper Peninsula in the years to come. The couple purchased a camp of their own on Three Lakes, and Martin discovered that those who lived in the region did not bend over backward to welcome outsiders. "You will have to do nearly everything for yourself," he warned would-be tourists. "The region is not geared to make your visit painless." The lack of modern conveniences and the clannishness of the locals could be maddening, he said, but if an outsider adjusted his thinking and fit into the region's ways, he could find "no better vacation spot."[2]

Although a newcome to the region, Martin, from the first, believed that he could write something about this wild country and its "magnificent waterfalls, great forests, high rough hills, long stretches of uninhabited country, abundant fish and game." With the aid of a Chicago bookstore owner and a New York publisher, Martin, who had begun to break out of the true-crime field with "serious nonfiction" contributions to prestigious national magazines, saw his wish come to fruition with the publication on May 15, 1944, of *Call It North Country: The Story of Upper Michigan*. The book won favorable reviews from the *New York Times* and such established Midwestern periodicals as *Minnesota History* and the *Wisconsin Magazine of History*. Although the book went out of print for a time, in October 1986 (the sesquicentennial of Michigan's statehood),

Wayne State University Press republished *Call It North Country* as part of its Great Lakes Books series. Martin had been able to capture in his first book not only the region's wild beauty but the character of those who lived there—people "among the finest and friendliest on earth," who, he said, "when they know you and like you, there is absolutely nothing they will not do for you. But this takes time, you must not push, they have to find out about you."[3]

Since leaving his job at the *Times* for the uncertain life of a freelance writer in Chicago, Martin had become a mainstay for both the *OD* and *AD* and their often imperious editor Harry Keller, who liked his employees to call him "Papa," perhaps imitating the famed writer of the period, Ernest Hemingway. In his work for the true-crime trade, Martin learned the uses of such techniques as "description, dialogue, characterization, and perhaps above all narrative pull—that mysterious invisible force that pulls the reader forward." The stories he wrote for the pulp journals served as perfect training for his later career writing serious fact pieces for *Harper's* and the *Saturday Evening Post,* as they taught him how to conduct research and how to interview people. "I worked as hard at this writing as at any I ever did and, given the constrictions of the genre, made it as good as I could," he recalled. At his peak, Martin produced on his manual typewriter a million words a year, at first selling about a third of them, and later half, at two cents a word. "Toward the end Keller was taking just about every-thing I could write. . . . None of this seemed extraordinary to me," said Martin. "I had set out to be a freelance writer and I was one."[4]

Martin's desire to capture the Upper Peninsula's unique character and history came at a time when he had begun to grow tired of the true-crime market, which he once referred to as writing about "monsters and ogres and fiends in human form." Francis S. Nipp, Martin's high school classmate, an English teacher earning his doctorate at the University of Chicago, and a person Martin described as a "a natural editor," convinced his friend to become a regular reader of *The New Yorker.* He also encouraged him to start submitting his writing to *Harper's.* Although it had a small circulation (109,787 in 1940) and offered its contributors paltry fees (usually $250 per article) in comparison to other magazines, *Harper's* reached a vital audience, what one of its editors described as "the intelligent minority" of opinion makers in the United States, "the thinking, cultured reader who seeks both entertainment and an enlarged and broadened point of view." Martin submitted pieces to the magazine and soon found himself under the tutelage of Frederick Lewis Allen, who had, since taking over as the periodical's editor in October 1941, striven to print within its pages "the exciting, the creative, the lustily energetic, the freshly amusing, the newly beautiful, the illuminating, the profound." Martin also received assistance from Allen's associate editors, especially George Leighton, who usually handled his submissions. Martin discovered that East Coast editors felt out of touch with the rest of the country, and because he lived in the Chicago suburbs, they often asked him what people cared and thought about in the Midwest. "Just as farm boys yearn to go to New York, so do New York editors yearn to know what's on the farm boy's mind," said Martin. "Sometimes they sounded almost anxious." Although later in his career he received invitations to leave the Midwest for positions on the staff of East Coast magazines, including *Life* and the *Post,* Martin always declined the offers, "feeling that, first, I wanted to stay freelance and, second, that this Midwest was where things were happening and there were no writers, while New York was where not much happened and there were a million writers."[5]

Seeking to learn more about being a writer, Martin became a familiar figure at the Argus Book Shop at 333 South Dearborn Street, the place where the literary action happened in Chicago. The bookstore was owned and operated by Ben Abramson, whom Martin remembered as a "red-haired gnome-like little man with a mottled complexion who not only sold books but also read them—and loved them. He liked to encourage young writers." Abramson's daughter, Deborah, recalled that when her father liked an author's work, "he went all out for him or her. He not only pushed their books, when money was a problem . . . he sent them checks and found them jobs when he could." Abramson also maintained close relationships with his customers. Even when they had not been in his store for some time, Abramson, blessed with a phenomenal memory, could greet them "as if they had left just a few minutes ago, continuing a conversation about writing or [book] collecting which he had begun perhaps six months ago," his daughter noted. Abramson advised Martin to read Henry Watson Fowler's timeless 1926 stylebook, *A Dictionary of Modern English Usage,* telling him to pay attention to the section on rhythm. "I had never read anything about writing so exciting," Martin said. "I was beginning to take writing seriously." He also absorbed new works by John Steinbeck and Ernest Hemingway, and old books by E. M. Forster and Aldous Huxley, studying them to try and adapt their fictional devices to his own fact writing. Years later, Martin remembered how he took the streetcar to the Criminal Courts Building and Cook County Jail on Chicago's southwest side. While the streetcar clattered its way to its destination, passing along the way the city's Jewish and Italian neighborhoods and Greek coffee shops, Martin sat, engrossed, reading a copy of Marcel Proust's *Remembrance of Things Past.*[6]

Impressed by Martin's commitment to his craft, Abramson corresponded with one of the most influential figures in American publishing—Alfred A. Knopf Sr., a man referred to by H. L. Mencken as "a perfect publisher," and someone Martin had considered an idol since his high school days. Founding his own publishing firm in 1915, Knopf over the years had brought to print the works of such notable writers and thinkers as Thomas Mann, Sigmund Freud, Willa Cather, W. Somerset Maugham, Kahlil Gibran, and Langston Hughes. "Never had I dreamed I might write for him," Martin said of Knopf, "might even meet him." Abramson's February 22, 1943, letter to Knopf introduced him to Martin, whom the bookseller described as "a magazine writer who has been successful in that field, has for many years traveled in, and studied, and read about the Lake Superior country. That is, the Michigan Peninsula and Minnesota. He would like to do a book on either the Peninsula or the State of Michigan as a whole." Abramson thought Martin's idea might fit into the series of regional books Knopf had been publishing, and if Knopf had not yet assigned that particular region to a writer, Abramson suggested that he "might perhaps be interested in communicating with him [Martin]."[7]

Knopf expressed interest in Martin to Abramson, and in March, Martin wrote to the publisher outlining how he planned to approach the project, noting that he had become well acquainted with the Upper Peninsula and for a long time had believed there "is a good book in the country—its history, flavor, folklore, people, mines, wilderness." Martin noted that he had recently read Richard G. Lillard's *Desert Challenge: An Interpretation of Nevada* (1942, published by Knopf), and he thought a book about the north country could "well fit into a similar pattern." Martin continued:

> The book might be written about the entire Lake Superior Country, embracing parts of Wisconsin, Michigan, Minnesota and Ontario. But there is such a great wealth of material about the Upper Peninsula alone that I think it might be best to confine the book to the Upper Peninsula. There are other considerations, too. The U.P. is, really, the essence of the whole Lake Superior Country. I think it is better to do a really solid book about a small area than a more superficial book about a larger one.[8]

To bolster his proposal, Martin explained to Knopf that he had already consulted such standard works as A. P. Swineford's *History and Review of the Copper, Iron, Silver, Slate, and Other Material Interests of the South Shore of Lake Superior* (1876); the early annual reports of the Michigan Commissioner of

Mineral Resources; and more recent books on specific aspects of the region's history, including Walter Havighurst's *Long Ships Passing: The Story of the Great Lakes* (1942) and Angus Murdoch's *Boom Copper: The Story of the First U.S. Mining Boom* (1943). "I have noticed that the more recent writers have relied for historical material on the standard published works and have not gone very deeply into original sources," Martin told Knopf. "This is not to say that a good book cannot now be written about the *whole* story of the Upper Peninsula from these secondary sources. For it can; the entire subject has not been covered adequately in one volume, to my knowledge."[9]

For his book, Martin suggested a different approach. He told Knopf that he wanted to attempt to obtain old correspondence and unpublished diaries "kept by early settlers of the country, to study the early newspapers, to recount certain stories I have picked up in personal conversations about the early days." After establishing the region's historical background, Martin said he would like to write the latter portion of his book based on his personal observations, including "several sketches of characteristic Upper Peninsula men and women, either living or recently dead, together with personal experiences, anecdotes, etc." By doing so, Martin, a reporter, not a historian, believed he could capture "the flavor and the way of life of the Upper Peninsula in a way that has not yet been touched. Above all, I would like to put the emphasis of the entire book on people, with the politics, geology, geography, etc., covered thoroughly but handled as background." Knopf was quick to respond to Martin's plans, writing him on March 23 thanking him for his "long and interesting" letter. The publisher said it was his firm's belief that Martin should confine his work to the Upper Peninsula. "I am sure we would be definitely interested in publishing such a book," wrote Knopf, who later gave Martin a $1,000 advance for the project.[10]

During the summer of 1943, Martin, assisted by Fran, drove to the Upper Peninsula to conduct research, visiting the Marquette County Historical Society, consulting newspaper clipping files, reading books, and interviewing a number of people in the region's logging and mining communities—lumberjacks, miners, trappers, newspapermen, saloonkeepers, local historians, police officers, shop owners, retired prostitutes, game wardens, and plain citizens, "some of them," Martin noted, "old-timers with long memories." He realized that his work on the Upper Peninsula could be what came to later be known as social history, as it portrayed "how the American people talked, worked, and behaved." The stories he garnered from the people he interviewed were important because nearly everybody whose recollections of the old days were "entombed" in the book were themselves entombed not long afterward. "It wasn't a bad idea to get them down on paper for our children," Martin said. There were, however, times in the book when he resorted to what those in television called a "docu-drama" technique. A few of the scenes in the book were not based on written documents or eyewitness accounts but were occurrences "that simply *ought to* have happened or *must* have happened." (Martin, who eventually produced sixteen books, never again wrote one in this manner.)[11]

In his research, Martin concentrated on the Marquette Iron Range, the Copper Range, and the wilderness in between. Two people were especially helpful: John D. Voelker, a liberal Democrat and Marquette County district attorney, who was also a budding author and remained a close friend for the rest of Martin's life, and Cal Olson, born eight years after President Abraham Lincoln's assassination and the caretaker at the camp where the Martins stayed at Three Lakes. "It was he," Martin said of Olson, "who took me around and introduced me to the people who had in their heads and in their characters the essence of the Upper Peninsula." Also helpful were L. A. Chase, head of the social science department at the Northern Michigan College of Education and corresponding secretary for the Marquette Historical Society, and William H. Newett, editor of the *Ishpeming Iron Ore* newspaper. Newett had been encouraging Martin to write a book about the Upper Peninsula for the past three years and gave the author access to his extensive private library. In addition to furnishing him "a great amount of information and guidance," Chase and Newett read Martin's manuscript prior to its publication, enabling him to "avoid numerous errors."[12]

In August, Martin wrote Keller telling him that he had "driven a couple thousand miles, covering the whole UP [Upper Peninsula]. . . . I've got a cardboard box completely filled with notes, another box of art, and something like 50 books (in addition to probably another 100 books etc. I've consulted in historical societies). So there isn't any question of having enough material; it's a question of what to throw away." Martin estimated that he had gathered enough information to produce three or four books—"one on logging, one on copper mining, one on iron mining on each of the three iron ranges"—so the problem that presented itself "is going to be compression and organization." In his travels, Martin had managed to finagle his way onboard an ore boat taking on cargo in Marquette, Michigan, as well as obtaining permission from a company to go underground in one of its iron mines. "My first trip down; and it's quite an experience," he told Keller. "When I came up after being under about four hours, the superintendent said, 'Well, do you want the job?' I told him I guessed not. Writing isn't so bad after all."[13]

Organizing his research material and turning it into a cohesive narrative structure plagued Martin for a time. He shared his early struggles with his friend Nipp, who expressed his sympathy and offered some guidance. He advised against dividing the book by subject or sections, preferring a "straight chronological division with related threads, I think that would be best, but that's dangerous with some subjects especially, and it's difficult in the sense that there needs to be a real, not just an arbitrary assimilation. The fact that it's bothering you is promising at that; better than wondering: What the hell am I going to do with this?" When finished with his manuscript, Martin sent it off to Knopf. The publisher, he remembered, responded promptly and succinctly, telling him his work "was satisfactory and he was putting it into production." The writer expressed some disappointment at Knopf's measured response to what he had produced, saying to Nipp he had hoped his publisher might be "enthusiastic" about the book, which Knopf had decided should be titled *Call it North Country* and released in early 1944. Nipp reminded Martin about Knopf: "He's published books before." Martin did receive a piece of advice from an editor at Knopf's firm about writing that he never forgot: "Remember, one beaver trapper is like a hundred."[14]

Both Martin and Fran spent hours reviewing proofs sent to them by Knopf. "Proofreading," Martin wrote Keller, "is a job unfit for human consumption. I had no idea it was as big a job as it is." Although he was getting "pretty sick of Michigan," Martin was surprised to find only a few places where his writing had failed to deliver as promised, and he believed the book stood "up pretty well." He and Fran were also responsible for preparing the book's index. "God! Publishers certainly get their thousand dollars' worth," Martin joked. In spite of all the hard work, he mused that an author seeing his first book in type "probably is a kick never repeated. You sign a contract then go out and do a lot of legwork then type page after page of copy and send it in—and then nothing happens, and you begin to wonder if maybe you weren't just sort of making it up. Then along come the proofs and bang—it's really going to be a book after all." *Call It North Country* also marked the first time Martin used his full name, John Bartlow Martin, for his byline, as there were other authors who wrote under the name John Martin. He later had second thoughts about his decision, believing the name was too long to print or pronounce, "like a pompous Christian divine's, but once I did it I was stuck with it."[15]

Fascinating, often larger-than-life characters populate *Call It North Country*, from trappers and surveyors to ore miners, lumberjacks, and prostitutes, all in a wild wilderness region isolated from state government in Lansing, Michigan, and which, by all logic, should have been part of Wisconsin. One memorable event Martin included was the grand funeral of the celebrated Silver Street prostitute Lottie Morgan from Ironwood, Michigan's bawdy sister city, Hurley, Wisconsin, whose murder remains unsolved. "She was, an admirer recalls, strictly a high-class girl," Martin reported. "Like most of her sisters, she worked out of a saloon. Her clients were men of means, for she accumulated a certain amount of expensive jewelry, which subsequently became the subject of much speculation." A large crowd packed the Hurley Opera House to pay their respects at her funeral. Martin also included famous names, such as William Austin Burt, who painstakingly surveyed the region and discovered the first iron deposits, as well as Detroit automotive magnate Henry Ford, who at one time owned a million acres in the Upper Peninsula. The discovery of iron and copper set a pattern for the region, which Martin described as "boom-and-bust country, mineral land, timberland. Yet it always had remained wilderness country." Martin also captured the charm and anguish of one of the wilderness's distinguishing attributes—its solitude. He wrote:

> There is the solitude of winter, when nothing moves in the woods but the wind through the tall timber. There is the dark solitude of a lake on a moonless night, when the only sound is the cry of a loon, long and high and weird, like the laughter of a woman gone mad. There is the solitude of the deep woods, and the solitude of the wild Big Lake, Superior, and the special solitude of the deep black holes that men have thrust thousands of feet down into the copper and iron ranges.[16]

Martin's friend Olson, to whom the author dedicated *Call it North Country*, served as the book's backbone, as his life touched on the region's essential toughness—a place where natives described its climate as "ten months of winter and two months of poor sledding." For most of his life, except for a brief time as a gold miner, Olson's father worked underground in the iron mines near Ishpeming, finally dying of "miner's consumption," most likely silicosis, a lung disease caused by inhaling crystalline silica dust. Too sick to work underground, Olson's father tried to work on the surface, but missed his old life and returned to the job he knew. "He was a miner, not a laborer; a miner he had lived and a miner he died," Martin wrote. The year after Olson was born, Ishpeming's

1,500 residents battled and contained a major fire that threatened to consume the community, and he remembered the tension between him and his Swedish comrades and the tough Irish kids they often fought in territorial battles. Olson had an eclectic career, working as a printer's devil, a teamster, a bartender, and a diamond driller. For a short time, he tried working in an iron mine, but could not take, as Martin wrote, "the weird dark world underground," quitting after working just two shifts. Olson knew many of the spirited men who attempted to tame the wilderness—Pete Moore, Neil Steffens, Dan Spencer—and shared "their independence and their feel for this hard lonely country, this Upper Michigan," Martin noted. "He belonged to it, and it to him."[17]

Call it North Country, which had a second printing by Knopf in July 1944, sold well for a regional book, approximately ten thousand copies, Martin estimated, and received solid reviews from major newspapers in New York and Chicago. James Gray, a *New York Times* reviewer, described the book as offering a "detailed, vigorous, and understanding interpretation" of the people who lived in the Upper Peninsula, and praised Martin as a "young and hearty observer." A reviewer in the *Chicago Sun* indicated that the book's writer possessed an eye for "telling details," and because Martin told his story in a succinct manner, his account of Upper Michigan and its people proved to be "entertaining, informative reading, revealing in a corner of our great country how Americans got that way."[18]

Periodicals published by Midwestern historical societies were also, for the most part, kind to Martin's book. Havighurst, the author of *Long Ships Passing,* reviewed *Call It North Country* for the *Wisconsin Magazine of History* and said that though the writing seemed "a bit gaudy in places," Martin's work had nevertheless been "generally discriminating in its appraisals and honest in its affection for a hard country and a primitive way of life." The reviewer placed the book within a social and economic history that had developed in regional writing in those times. "A professional historian may grow impatient with its impressionism, its lack of historical sequence, and its subjective coloring," Havighurst wrote, "but these very qualities win for it a wider audience than formal history can command." Martin had been wholly successful, he added, in "his blending of past and present, of geography and economics, of broad historical movements and a writer's feeling about them."[19]

Although the reviewer for the *Minnesota History* magazine, L. A. Rossman, wrote that *Call It North Country* was a book that "all who care for the North Country and local history should read and possess," and in some ways Martin's work had "elements of greatness," it did fall short of excellence in other ways. In particular, the reviewer hit the author hard for his depiction of the lumberjack in the Upper Peninsula "as a besotten and dissolute man," which, Rossman said, had never been true. In his book, Martin had written with gusto about what happened after fallen timber had been successfully driven down the Menominee and Manistique Rivers to towns such as Manistique, Escanaba, and Menominee. "Like the logs they drove down-river," Martin wrote of the lumberjacks, "they jammed the broad straight streets from sidewalk to sidewalk, a surging flood of bearded men, fighting, drinking, swearing, whoring. . . . Here the girls were waiting, and twenty-four hours a day the drab buildings bulged with ribald song and brawling." Rossman disputed Martin's view, noting that he had been "misled by traditional stories about the lumberjack as well as about the North Country in general. There may have been dissolute people in the timber and copper country, but they also were to be found near meat-packing plants and in large cities. The pioneers of the North were great men and the world ought not to live with distorted memories of them."[20]

Writing for the *Pacific Northwest Quarterly*, Milo Milton Quaife, a Michigan and Great Lakes historian and secretary of the Burton Historical Collection at the Detroit Public Library, had a clear understanding of the book's defects and strengths, noting that Martin was a journalist by training, not a historian, and his expertise was in being a "keen observer and first-rate reporter." Quaife called *Call It North Country* "invaluable" to anyone seeking to become better acquainted with the Upper Peninsula and wrote that the book stood as an "excellent contribution to the regional history of the United States." The reviewer also noted that the book's "lively style and choice of contents will prove shocking to the dry-as-dust university type of historical specialist. Needless to add it will be read and enjoyed by scores for every single reader the output of the Ph.D. specialist commands."[21]

Martin was most pleased, however, by the book's acceptance by the people it described and by its longevity. Voelker wrote his friend in June 1944 offering his opinion on *Call It North Country*, and said he felt "envious as hell" because it was the book he should have written if he were not "so goddamn lazy. Your handling of a mass of information, which could be awfully dull, is blown full of life and interest. Implicit in the writing is your love for this wild broken land and its people." Voelker said Martin was in the perfect position to handle the subject, as nobody who lived in the Upper Peninsula "could bring to the story the perspective you have. Yours is not the love of a mother for a besotted son, but of a son for a roaring, aging and pathetic old man. Your book is simply grand and you should feel proud as hell. Your flashes of wry humor were beautiful." On his many trips to the Upper Peninsula, Martin often came across old copies of *Call It North Country* in other people's houses or on bookshelves in camps. These were copies that had been "almost read literally to pieces, their spines cracked, pages loose, pages pencil-marked and with coffee spilled on them, books that have really been read. That is the readership an author appreciates."[22]

For the 1986 republication of *Call It North Country,* Martin provided a new foreword for his book and noted that those born and raised in the Upper Peninsula "never really leave it." The same could be said of him. In a career that included working as a speechwriter for every Democratic presidential candidate from Adlai Stevenson in 1952 to George McGovern in 1972, serving as U.S. ambassador to the Dominican Republic in John F. Kennedy's administration, and writing the definitive biography of Stevenson, Martin, when facing trouble and heartache (particularly following the assassinations of John and Robert Kennedy), found refuge by retreating to the wild north country. After vacationing at Three Lakes for a few years, Martin said the town had begun to be too crowded with tourists, "a trailer camp sprang up, and the lake became polluted with water-skiers." He and Fran began to look for a more remote location for their retreat. "After several years," Martin recalled, "we walked in to Smith Lake, and eating lunch in a grove of majestic hemlocks on a high granite cliff overlooking the lake, we knew this was the place." Starting in 1966 and ending two years later, Martin oversaw the construction by Finnish carpenters of a thirty-foot by thirty-foot log cabin with a large living room, kitchen, bedroom, indoor bathroom, and an enormous fireplace built out of fifty tons of native rock. Initially, Martin and his sons, Fred and Dan, while living in tents, rebuilt the one-room trapper's shack they had discovered on the property. When it was ready, the Finnish carpenters used it as a temporary camp, "living in it while they constructed the big camp up on the cliff, built it slowly, painfully, log by chipped and fitted log, a beauty." Every board and every nail that went into its construction, as well as the equipment for building it, had to be hauled to the site either by Jeep or by hand. "We learned a good deal about carpentry and plumbing, building Smith Lake," said Martin. "Not until 1968 were Fran and I able to use the big camp, and work on its interior and its outbuildings [including a sauna] continued for several years. But we succeeded."[23]

During his retirement in the 1980s after teaching at Northwestern University's Medill School of Journalism, Martin spent much of his time on a project close to his heart—a first-person account about Smith Lake. He called his manuscript "Sometimes in the Summer," borrowing the title from a line out of a book by his writer friend Voelker that Martin said was one of the most exquisite sentences he had ever read in English: "Sometimes in the Summer in the nighttime, when there was a moon there was a mist, so that the fields looked like a lake." (He later retitled the manuscript "Ten Summers," which, as he told Voelker, was "probably not an improvement.") Martin wrote and rewrote the Smith Lake book, changing and rewording each sentence and sometimes altering the manuscript's concept. "Having nearly always avoided writing in the first person, I found doing so extremely difficult, the hardest writing I ever did," he said. Martin loved the book when he finished it, considering it one of the best pieces of writing he had ever done. Unfortunately, publishers failed to share his enthusiasm for its qualities, and the manuscript languished, unpublished. "It was frustrating to him that he could not make clear to others—editors, his agent— what was so special about this place," said Martin's son Fred. "The woods, the clear dry air, the animals and fish, the difficult circumstances of living in the wilderness, the solitude: it all meant so much to him." Ever since he had taken on the Upper Peninsula for *Call it North Country,* Martin had grown used to having difficulty convincing anyone who did not know how special the Upper Peninsula was to read or care about the region he cherished. "In that respect," he noted, "it resembles the old saying about Latin America—the people of the United States will do anything for Latin America except read about it."[24]

Every spring, Martin and Fran packed up their car with the essentials, including manuscripts, books, and a few clothes, and drove to their camp at Smith Lake, staying there for three or four months, enjoying the solitude and wildlife. They could watch a moose swim the length of the lake, observe a fierce mink chasing their family cat, Miss Prettyface, or encounter a bear wandering up to their porch. Martin remembered Fran telling him that if she sat on their porch and stared at the lake and trees long enough, she might see an eagle perched on top of the tallest pine tree near their camp; one day, she did.[25]

Medical problems intruded on Martin's beloved sanctuary. In March 1983, he wrote Voelker that Fran had to drive them to the Upper Peninsula because his vision had become so poor he could no longer be trusted to safely pilot their car. By the next spring, the Martins between them had "too many unresolved medical problems for both of us to go to such a remote place," so, for the first time in forty-four years (except years when they were out of the country), said Martin, he and Fran could not spend their summer in the Upper Peninsula. By

1985, they were well enough to spend a month at Smith Lake, from June 15 to July 15, thanks to their sons, Fred and Dan, who arranged their vacations so they could drive their parents to their camp and stay with them. Diagnosed with throat cancer in 1986, Martin received the grim news stoically. "He described to me in detail what path the cancer would take that was unstoppably killing him and how he would die," Fred remembered, "in the same matter-of-fact tone that he had used with me before when, say, giving driving directions to Upper Michigan." Martin died at Highland Park Hospital on January 3, 1987, at the age of seventy-one; Fran died on February 26, 1994. That spring, the bodies of Fran and John Bartlow Martin were buried side by side at the Herman Cemetery in Herman, Michigan, located just a few miles from their camp at Smith Lake.[26]

NOTES

1. John Bartlow Martin, *It Seems Like Only Yesterday: Memoirs of Writing, Presidential Politics, and the Diplomatic Life* (New York: William Morrow, 1986), 33, 36; John Bartlow Martin, "The Heartland's Backyard Frontier," *Chicago Tribune*, July 31, 1983; John Bartlow Martin, *Call It North Country: The Story of Upper Michigan* (Detroit, MI: Wayne State University Press, 1986), 42; "For Personal and Otherwise" memo, undated, John Bartlow Martin Papers, Manuscripts Division, Library of Congress, Washington, D.C. (hereafter cited as Martin Papers).

2. John Bartlow Martin, "Boy Hunt," *Harper's*, December 1944, 39–40; Martin, *Call It North Country*, viii, 263.

3. Martin, *Call It North Country*, 257, 260; John Bartlow Martin, "Wilderness North of Chicago," *Harper's*, May 1954, 74.

4. Martin, *It Seems Like Only Yesterday*, 28–29, 32; John Bartlow Martin, "For Personal and Otherwise" memo, undated, Martin Papers.

5. Martin, *It Seems Like Only Yesterday*, 37–38, 43–44; Darwin Payne, *The Man of Only Yesterday: Frederick Lewis Allen* (New York: Harper and Row, 1975), 83, 154, 222–23; and John Bartlow Martin, Memo on Memoirs, December 5, 1980, Martin Papers.

6. John Bartlow Martin, Rough Draft of Memoir, Martin Papers; D. B. Covington, *The Argus Book Shop: A Memoir* (West Cornwall, CT: Tarrydiddle Press, 1977), 15, 25, 27; Martin, *It Seems Like Only Yesterday*, 29.

7. Herbert Mitgang, "Alfred A. Knopf, 91, Is Dead; Founder of Publishing House," *New York Times*, August 12, 1984; Martin, *It Seems Like Only Yesterday*, 39; Ben Abramson to Alfred Knopf, February 22, 1943, Martin Papers.

8. John Martin to Alfred Knopf, March 19, 1943, Martin Papers.

9. Martin to Knopf, March 19, 1943.

10. Martin to Knopf, March 19, 1943; Alfred Knopf to John Martin, March 23, 1943, Martin Papers.

11. Martin *Call It North Country*, vii–viii, 273.

12. Martin, *It Seems Like Only Yesterday*, 40; Martin, *Call It North Country*, 275. In 1958, under the pen name Robert Traver, Voelker wrote *Anatomy of a Murder*, a best-selling, fictionalized version of a 1952 case he had been involved with in Big Bay in the Upper Peninsula, defending a man charged with killing the owner of a bar who had allegedly raped his wife. The director Otto Preminger turned the book into a movie starring James Stewart, released on July 1, 1959. See Richard D. Shaul, "Backwoods Barrister," *Michigan History* 85 (November/December 2001): 82–87.

13. John Martin to Harry Keller, August 24, 1943, Martin Papers.

14. Francis Nipp to John Martin, [?], 1943, Martin Papers; Martin, *It Seems Like Only Yesterday*, 41. Martin confided to Keller in a letter that the book's title, *Call It North Country*, "isn't too good nor is it terrible, I think. It was his [Knopf's] idea." John Martin to Harry Keller, January 4, 1944, Martin Papers.

15. John Martin to Harry Keller, January 25, 1944, Martin Papers; Martin, *It Seems Like Only Yesterday*, 41.

16. Martin, *Call It North Country*, 8–9, 180–83; Martin, "Wilderness North of Chicago," 72.

17. Martin, *Call It North* Country, 192, 197–98, 211.

18. Martin, *It Seems Like Only Yesterday*, 41; James Gray, "Michigan Peninsula," *New York Times*, May 21, 1944; August Derleth, "Life in the Upper Michigan Country," *Chicago Sun*, May 28, 1944.

19. Walter Havighurst, review of Martin's *Call It North Country*, in *Wisconsin Magazine of History* 28 (March 1945): 352–53.

20. L. A. Rossman, review of Martin's *Call It North Country*, in *Minnesota History* 25 (September 1944): 276; Martin, *Call It North Country*, 138–39.

21. Milo Milton Quaife, review of Martin's *Call It North Country*, in *Pacific Northwest Quarterly* 13 (December 1, 1944): 444.

22. John D. Voelker to John Martin, June 3, 1944, Martin Papers; Martin, *Call It North Country*, viii.

23. Martin, *Call It North Country*, viii; Martin, "The Heartland's Backyard Frontier"; Martin, *It Seems Like Only Yesterday*, 276–77; Dan Martin, e-mail, March 11, 2014; and Fred Martin, memo to author, October 8, 2013.

24. Martin, *It Seems Like Only Yesterday*, 343–44; John Frederick Martin, "John Bartlow Martin," *American Scholar* 59 (Winter 1990): 98; John Bartlow Martin to John Voelker, April 26, 1977, Voelker Papers, Central Upper Michigan Peninsula and Northern Michigan University Archives, Marquette, MI.

25. John Bartlow Martin to Arthur Schlesinger Jr., January 15, 1978; John Bartlow Martin memorandum on medical history to Doctor Saul A. Mackler, January 1, 1979; and John Bartlow Martin memorandum on recent medical history, March 25, 1979, all in Martin Papers; Martin, *It Seems Like Only Yesterday*, 342–43.

26. John Bartlow Martin to John Voelker, March 6, 1983; June 24, 1984; and May 20, 1985, all in Voelker Papers; Dan Martin, e-mail to author, March 24, 2014; J. F. Martin, "John Bartlow Martin," 97.

JACOB A. BRUGGEMAN

THINGS SEEN AND HEARD

Regional Identity and History in Sigurd F. Olson's
Environmental Ethic

When Sigurd F. Olson and his wife, Elizabeth, moved to Ely, Minnesota, in the winter of 1929, they took up in a cold, dank former coal shed, and set out to make a life for themselves in a town once known for its rough reputation. Elizabeth was pregnant, and Sigurd, having quit his graduate work in Wisconsin's geology program to start earning money, took a job teaching at the Ely high school.[1] One of Olson's students from those years, Helen Denley Barnes, wrote to him decades later in the 1970s to express her gratitude for his teaching. "You perhaps thought you were teaching us biology and I am sure that is what you were paid to do," Barnes wrote, "But for me and many others the textbook knowledge was the least of what you imprinted in our lives." More significant than any such "textbook" learning was Olson's "contagious" "love of life and keen appreciation of the beauty of the world." Olson's outlook, to borrow Barnes's words, oriented students toward "a richer and deeper life."[2]

Olson's life was indeed one of "rich" and "deep" engagement with his community, the country, and the natural world, and many more than Barnes considered Olson a teacher. When the Sigurd F. Olson Environmental Institute in Ashland, Wisconsin, was dedicated in 1981, the ceremony included dozens of activists, students, and even former Wisconsin senator Gaylord Nelson. Commemorating Olson's legacy as a conservation leader *and* teacher, a young man performed a song entitled "They Called Him Bourgeois":

They called him Bourgeois, our teacher he has been
He showed us how to love the living land
how to feel the pulse of life, how to listen to the wind.

As Bill McAllister of the *St. Cloud Times* wrote about this song, the title "Bourgeois" "meant leader to the French-Canadian voyageurs," and Olson had earned the honorific by sustaining the voyageurs' spirit.[3] Here, "bourgeois" did not identify a class, like "bourgeoisie," nor does it describe the economic and cultural attitudes associated with the adjective "bourgeois,"[4] but denoted either a current or future partner in a French Canadian company's fur trade.[5] So when Northland College students brought Olson's canoe into the auditorium at the dedication, they did so dressed in the garb of French Canadian voyageurs.[6]

More than a teacher, however, Olson was a leader in the American conservation movement and a prolific nature writer. So much so that he remains the only individual to have received the highest honors from the four foremost organizations working toward conservation—the Sierra Club, the Izaak Walton League, the Wilderness Society, and the National Wildlife Federation—*and* the highest award given for nature writing, the John Burroughs Medal.[7]

Olson's significance in the countrywide conservation movement cannot be understated. To take just several examples of his involvement, Olson assisted the Wilderness Society president Howard Zahniser in writing the Wilderness Act.[8] He helped the conservationist Leo Drey protect the forests, springs, and caves of Missouri's eastern Ozark area from plans for a mass recreation area.[9] In Alaska, Olson helped conduct a survey that ultimately provided the foundation for Denali National Park's increase in size.[10] In Oregon, Olson helped conserve the Cascades in the late 1950s.[11] Olson lobbied against a Bureau of Reclamation plan to build a dam near Echo Park, part of a park system that stretches along the border between Colorado and Utah.[12] Later in the same decade, Olson assisted in David Brower's and Frank Masland's efforts to protect Utah's Rainbow Bridge

National Monument.[13] Moreover, on the national stage, Olson served as vice president of the Wilderness Society from 1963 to 1967, as its president from 1968 to 1971, and as a member and president of the National Parks Association's board of trustees. This captures only a fraction of those conservation efforts in which Olson was engaged.[14]

Despite his national involvement, however, the lion's share of Olson's conservation efforts focused on Minnesota, and especially the Quetico-Superior region in the state's northern reaches.[15] Olson's conservation efforts were essential to that region's preservation. Indeed, alongside Bud Heinselman and other conservationists, Olson was crucial in the 1964–65 fight to protect the million-acre Boundary Waters Canoe Area. In the late 1970s, he contributed significantly to the citizen-led effort to push new protections for this area through Congress in the form of the 1978 Boundary Waters Canoe Area Wilderness (BWCAW).[16] And throughout the 1960s and early '70s, Olson played a central role in the campaign to establish Voyageurs National Park.[17] Cumulatively, these efforts led many a Minnesotan to cherish Olson. Ernest Oberholtzer, a fellow Minnesotan and one of Olson's colleagues, one of the eight original Wilderness Society founders, and one of the first three members of President Franklin D. Roosevelt's Quetico-Superior Committee, captured a widespread sentiment when he described Olson as "a bright star [of] hope at Ely."[18]

Olson's dedication to Minnesota and the North Country was nowhere more evident than in his writing about the Quetico-Superior wilderness along the U.S.-Canadian borderlands.[19] In his academic work, this area often occupied his research agenda, ranging in subjects from the predatory relationships among wolves and the organization of their packs, to the coniferous forest biome, to the phenomenon of "fish-eating deer."[20] But Olson's contributions to scholarship pale in comparison to his nonfiction oeuvre, which perennially returned to the U.S.-Canadian borderlands and the Quetico-Superior. Olson's literary life was quite productive. His books included *The Singing Wilderness* (1956), *Listening Point* (1958), *The Lonely Land* (1961), *Runes of the North* (1963), *Open Horizons* (1969), *Wilderness Days* (1972), *Reflections from the North Country* (1976), and *Of Time and Place* (1982).[21] (Readers interested in Olson might begin with his autobiography, *Open Horizons, or Reflections from the North Country,* quite possibly his most popular book.)

Olson's writings, observes the historian Mark Harvey, were his "distinctive contribution" to conservation in Minnesota.[22] Therein, to borrow former Wilderness Society and Sierra Club president George Marshall's words, "He made the wilderness and life sing."[23] Those in Olson's orbit, be they students like Barnes or allies in the conservation movement like Marshall, nearly all seemed to agree.

■ ■ ■

Born in Chicago on April 4, 1899, Sigurd was the youngest son of Lawrence, a Swedish Baptist minister, and Ida May, a devout follower of the faith. When the Olson family left Chicago and set sail for Sister's Bay, Wisconsin, in 1906, Sigurd, then at the spry age of seven, was struck by the natural environment he observed in transit. As David Backes writes in his biography, "[Sigurd] excitedly watched flocks of gulls, listened to their cries, and cast his eyes out over the broad, wind-swept waters of Lake Michigan."[24] Though we see here a young Sigurd fascinated by the natural world, it was in Wisconsin where Olson developed his commitment to and reverence for it. Once there, Olson joined the cadre of twentieth-century American literati inspired by Wisconsin's landscapes, including the likes of Frederick Jackson Turner, John Muir, Frank Lloyd Wright, and Georgia O'Keefe.[25] Indeed, remarking on the importance of Wisconsin's wilds, William Cronon wrote that "rarely has so unlikely a landscape evoked such passionate responses from figures of such intellectual importance."[26]

What animated Olson's conservation efforts, as David Backes elegantly argued, was a "wilderness theology." Olson's "theology" offered a "sacramental vision of life and evolution" in which the universe was an "extension of God," and so "all life, human and nonhuman," required care and conservation. Olson's God, if conceived of as a Christian one in childhood, eventually took on a cosmic character, becoming less that of a particular God than that of an unmoved or prime mover whose design and influence was emergent, whose energy was evident in the "logic or reason behind the character of the universe."[27]

Olson observed this divine ordering in nature, which for him was a wellspring of psychological and spiritual renewal. Like Ralph Waldo Emerson and Henry David Thoreau, whose writings emphasized sensory experiences and an individual's awareness of such experiences, Olson "viewed nature-inspired epiphanies as the lodestone of everyday life." These epiphanies could be passing or rapturous, but never failed to "bring joy and wonder and a sense of meaning."[28] It is thus no surprise that scholars read Olson alongside Thoreau, Emerson, Muir, Leopold, and John Burroughs.[29] Indeed, as one reviewer in South Bend, Indiana, wrote of Olson's *Of Time and Place,* it "recalls Thoreau's 'Walden.'"[30]

While Backes's articulation of Olson's intellectual, religious, and philosophical attitudes as a wilderness theology provides critical insight into the moral dimensions of Olson's public activities and private thoughts, I attempt in this chapter to further account for the influence of regional identity and history therein. As such, I aim to emphasize the importance of Minnesotan, North Country, and Midwestern identity and history in Olson's public writing. To this end, I refer to Olson's worldview as an "environmental ethic" rather than a wilderness theology—a terminological shift that attempts to capture the broader influence of regional ecologies and histories on his thought. Indeed, as Olson observed in *Of Time and Place,* his concepts of ecology seemed to emerge from "the land itself and its rich history."[31] Rather than replacing Backes's biographically informed concept of wilderness theology with "environmental ethic," this shift simply acknowledges that Olson's worldview was as complex as the environs he fought to preserve.

I do not offer a complete consideration of Olson's writing in this chapter. Still, I draw from many of his books, Backes's biography, and newspaper clippings to clarify the fundamental relationship between Olson's ethic and regional identity. Focusing on the centrality of the "lost region" in Olson's thought, I attempt to resituate his environmental ethic and public writing in the growing scholarship on the Midwest's history and identity to which this volume will contribute.[32] Though I may be guilty in this chapter of perpetuating a tendency in environmental histories toward "imagined landscapes," it is not without good reason.[33]

Olson's writings, a primary function of which was the construction of "imagined landscapes" for the public to engage with, were bestsellers consumed across the country. Olson's ethic was not merely a series of musings on Minnesota's "imagined landscapes," but a serious and coherent engagement with a cultural inheritance, to use William Sewell's definition, that informed "a concrete and bounded world of beliefs and practices."[34] Furthermore, Olson's ethic entailed an attendant "sociological imagination"[35] that considered the modern individual to be at a crossroads between two ways of life: one ahistorical and anthropocentric, the other biocentric and marked by what Olson referred to as a recognition of, and reverence for, nature's inherent beauty and its particular manifestations in one's region.[36]

Conservation thus became more than stewardship of divine creation strictly understood, but rather the active preservation of the places in which Olson thought individuals could encounter the cosmic truths of "timelessness" and "oneness," and the histories and ecologies particular to any given region. Not unlike the epistemological commitments of other authors and environmental thinkers on the Great Plains, Olson's ethic might be conceived of as a kind of "ecological memory."[37] Olson committed himself to conservation so that generations to come could "breathe the spirit of the past" in *specific* places, places "practically unchanged from the days of discovery." Wilderness areas like Minnesota's Quetico-Superior should be preserved "wherever" possible.[38] Such areas constituted "silent sanctuaries," or respites "of spirit," as Olson described Cumberland Island, in which "we perpetuate the eternal perspectives."[39] Indeed, as Olson wrote in the *Milwaukee Journal,* preservation was "the salvation of the human soul."[40]

Olson's environmental ethic equipped him with a particular ability and self-imposed responsibility for ecological resistance—a "pattern of action"—which enabled him to defend a range of places, from small brooks to a whole region.[41]

Small brooks, falling leaves, and the sound of howling wolves were as precious as the region writ large. Indeed, they were the threads with which the whole was woven. Central to Olson's ethic were these characteristics of the Quetico-Superior and his memories of them. Olson thus attempted, if imperfectly, to integrate the entirety of the nonhuman into his environmental ethic. Riverside flora and fauna, trout, wolves, and even nonorganic elements of the environment, such as rocks or the silence of natural spaces, were all essential components of his ethic. These creatures and features of Minnesota's landscapes, what we might cumulatively describe, in Aldo Leopold's words, as the "biotic community," constituted a dynamic and vibrant wilderness ripe for engagement and exploration.[42]

The storied landscapes of Olson's writing drew primarily from his experiences in Minnesota and the Quetico-Superior wilderness at its borders with Canada. Two categories of regional experience dominate Olson's writing: first, a respect for the French voyageurs of the region's past and the modern men who inherited their legacy, and second, a reverence for the region's unique environmental features and the activities associated with them. In the pages that follow, I trace these two fundamental engagements with regional identity side by side, intertwined, as it were, drawing primarily from Olson's books, and supplemented with other writings where necessary.

■ ■ ■

The fundamental relationship between Olson's environmental ethic and regional identity is no more evident than in his descriptions of the wilderness men and fellow friends of the region whom he admired. In reflecting on his youth, Olson identified one such man as a family friend who took him hunting while he was still too young to hold a gun. This mentor, in Olson's words, was possessed of "a sense of awareness perhaps, that in later years I was quick to recognize in others, a belonging and easy familiarity with woods or mountains, but above all to a boy there was a friendliness and companionship that transcended all other considerations."[43] Men of the wilderness lifestyle made up a constellation of influence and inspiration in Olson's life. They reminded him of the famed deerslayers and foodsmen in the region's histories, and Olson came to "[dream] their dreams and [see] the woods as they did."[44] Olson continued to read about the old voyageurs and their adventures, so much so that, in his own words, "I knew intuitively how they felt, for their frontiers were also mine."[45] Writing of his Scandinavian ancestors who populated the region, Olson observed that as his awareness of the landscape and its history grew, "their legacy of terrain became my own."[46] As a young man, this "terrain" became so enchanted for Olson that he wrote of animals and natural objects as friends: "I felt I must be on a first-name basis with flowers and trees, birds, fish, insects, and mammals, even the rocks and lichens of its hills and valleys, must know this country and so completely identify myself with it there would be no question of my belonging. I wanted to feel as other creatures did instinctively, that this terrain was mine, and that any place I chose to go was where I belonged."[47]

The feeling only intensified as Olson grew older and became a wilderness guide in the Quetico-Superior. And soon enough, "the land and all its creatures were old friends."[48] Indeed, Olson came to know the land as if it were an old neighborhood: "I knew the haunts of moose and deer, nesting places of herons, ospreys and eagles, beaver dams and flowages that connected lakes, the places where mink, otter and muskrat lived. I found the cliffs where Indian pictographs had been painted by ancient tribes, sites of old villages and trading posts, steeped myself with the kind of information I believed my parties would want."[49]

As a guide, Olson drew upon the voyageurs, the wilderness men he admired, and the region's history in an attempt to re-create and inhabit the historical environment they knew and loved for those he guided. Olson's engagement with the voyageurs' legacy took many forms, including a Minnesota Historical Society search for fur trade artifacts in the Basswood Lake country northeast of his home in Ely.[50] Afterward, Olson was interviewed and stated that the region's famed names, like Maligne, Deux Rivieres, Lac la Croix, Grand Marais Lac des Milles Lacs, alongside the physical artifacts themselves, "suggest the sound and smell of the wilderness and the feel of the unknown."[51] On occasion, Olson even put his engagement with the *voyageur* and the region's history into song.

With a French-Canadian friend, Pierre LaRonge, to whom Olson was known as François, old poetry of the voyageurs found new life in Pierre's voice on their expeditions together. "The Voyageur" by Henry Drummond was decidedly Pierre's favorite. As Olson recorded Pierre's rendition of it,

> So dat's de reason I drink tonight
> To de men of de Grand Nor'west
> For hees heart was young, an hees heart was light
> So long as he's leevin dere—
> I'm proud of the sam blood in my vein,
> I'm a son of de Nort' Win' wance again—
> So we'll fill her up til de bottle's drain
> An drink to de Voyageur.[52]

In song and other practices, Olson continuously engaged the past—even by way of cooking. Indeed, he "made pan bread or bannock, even cakes and pies in a reflector oven, steaked and broiled fish, and made various stews and combinations" to re-create the wilderness experience of the voyageurs and wilderness guides from whom there remained "much to learn."[53] Friends like Buck Sletton of the U.S. Marine Corps; Gunder Graves of the lumberjack profession; the Yugoslavian brothers, guides Frankie and Steve Mizera; and Olson's first guide turned friend, Matt Heikkila—these men were the actors in Olson's world. In his own words, "These were the men I wanted to know and work with."[54] In the years Olson spent with these men, he learned skills ranging from how to recognize "an old canoeman [. . .] by the easy way he sits in a canoe" to, thanks to his woodsman friend Johnny Sansted, how to flour a fish in a paper bag, to the utility of a pinch of salt in bringing out the flavor in dried fruit, a trick learned from fellow guide Frank Carney.[55] This active engagement with the region's history repeatedly produced déjà vu for Olson, who observed that when "on the trail," he was possessed by a feeling "that somewhere or sometime I have done a particular thing before." Rather than fleeting moments, these emerged from the "depths of consciousness."[56]

These men helped form the regional dimensions of Olson's environmental ethic. As his friend Buck Sletton once told him, "Remember, young fellow, remember, no matter how cold and wet you are, you're always warm and dry." This contradictory statement meant everything to Olson, for in it "was embodied a philosophy of life and a way of accepting the bush and all that it could mean. It involved not only a basic attitude, but the skills required to live comfortably under any and all conditions of weather."[57] Indeed, these were the men with whom Olson would put his developing environmental ethic into practice. Once when Olson's group made camp above the famous Pictured Rocks on Crooked Lake, Olson recalled their nighttime ritual: "Each night we sat there looking down the waterway, listening to the loons filling the darkening narrows with wild reverberating music, but it was when they stopped that the quiet descended, an all-pervading stillness that absorbed all the sounds that had ever been. No one spoke. We sat there so removed from the rest of the world and with such a sense of complete remoteness that any sound would have been a sacrilege."

Breaking that silence was "sacrilege," and an act that obscured its "true meaning."[58] With men like these, Olson developed his "deep awareness of ancient rhythms and the attunement men seek but seldom find," which he undoubtedly attempted to share with his son.[59] For Olson, such activities captured the "quiet" of the "distant past."[60] Moreover, in the men engaging this "distant past" alongside Olson, he often saw the crystalized connection between their respective inheritance and contemporary practice.

Indeed, Olson once described a brook-trout fishing friend as the culmination of a "heritage of countless centuries of the hunter and fisherman," a man who "became the quarry he sought."[61] For Olson, his environmental ethic was self-evident, observable nearly everywhere he stood, in everything he saw. In recalling a trip to Fort Churchill on the Hudson Bay in September, he wrote of the turning foliage "all around" him as "whirling, enveloping, carrying me with them." Being enveloped in this way led Olson to feel "part of all the beauty, the tiny sounds, and everything around me."[62] The men who accompanied him were no different; they, too, exhibited the connection between the land and its history that Olson so cherished.

Furthermore, it was through activities like trout fishing that Olson thought that the "distant past" could be engaged. In writing of a spring fishing excursion with his son, Olson described the act of pulling a fish out of the water as "what we had gone in for—the feel of spring." With a few trout as their "proof," Olson and his son had briefly "known the thrill of exploring forgotten country together, and had seen it at its best."[63]

With these men in the wilderness of Minnesota's boundary waters and the Quetico-Superior wilderness, Olson developed the "broad perspective" that became his environmental ethic, the specifics of which he disregarded as unimportant: "Whether I talk of timelessness, cosmic rhythms, and the slow cycles of seasonal change; or look at such personal things as aliveness, wonder, and

wholeness; or attempt to enter the dark infinities of mystery and the unknown—
it makes little difference." What mattered to Olson was "the grand symphony
of that land that I have known"—the region and wellspring of his intellectual
and spiritual life.[64] Similarly, when Olson described how "the sounds of wild
geese on the move haunted" him, his reaction was to capture in writing "some
of their mystery, some of their freedom and of the blue distances into which
they disappeared," and the lands in and upon which they lived.[65]

Olson's engagement with these men, those alive and the deceased legends like
Daniel Boone, of whom he could only read, brought on a dawning awareness
of an inherited culture of wilderness and its appreciation. "In looking back," he
wrote, "there was a growing appreciation of deeper meanings." As his engagement continued, "the primeval scene, its solitude and sense of removal, was
becoming part of my consciousness."[66]

Olson came to know this region, in part, through his years as a guide in the
Quetico-Superior, which instilled a "sense of timelessness and order." Looking
back on that sense's development, Olson recognized "its first intimations" in the
slow "speed" of the voyageur life that he attempted to live.[67] Here again, Minnesota's landscape is the medium through which the foundational experiences
of Olson's environmental ethic were "filtered," a landscape on which Olson
learned to slow down and observe the "coming of day and night, the eternal
watching of the skies, sunrises and sunsets, the telltale story of winds in the
maneuvering of clouds, the interwoven pattern of rain and mist, cycles of cold
and warmth, even the changing vegetation."[68]

Put simply, Minnesota's North Country and the broader region of which it is
part are inextricable from Olson's environmental ethic. This link is repeatedly
made explicit in Olson's writing about how his experiences as a boy connected
to his life as an adult: "Fifty years later I stood at the marshy entrance to the old
Lake Superior slough I had known as a boy. The dirt road and wooden bridge
were replaced by a modern highway skirting Chequamegon Bay, cars and trucks
whizzed by, but miraculously there was no other change. [. . .] As I looked back
from this long-remembered place, I realized that without my vast complex of
treasured experiences, the work of preservation of all wild creatures and their
native habitats might not have been as vital to me were my dreams not haunted
by their beauty."[69]

In a similarly reflective mood, Olson observed the fundamental relationship
between his ethic and Minnesotan experience in the preface to *Of Time and
Place,* where he described the "broad pattern" of his life as a fascination with

the wilderness. He went on to state that each memory recalled was "colored" by his "imagination," "fantasy," and "attachment to the land and a feeling for its antiquity."[70] That land was Minnesota's Quetico-Superior and Boundary Waters.

■　■　■

As Olson matured into this awareness of the region's beauty and history, he came to feel a strong sense of "gladness" each time he heard the "song of the north" or the call of the wilderness. In his own words, it called him "in its general direction as naturally as a migrating bird is by unseen lines of force, or a salmon by some invisible power toward the stream where it was spawned."[71]

So clear was the reality of interconnectedness and interdependence that Olson likened it to a feeling of world-inspired childhood wonder, "a knowing beyond intelligence, reason, or instinct, a blending of thoughts and hopes." This feeling, however, had become alien to "modern man," who had lost touch with it "through the welter of impressions that have bombarded his senses from the time he was born."[72] Reviewers of Olson's work often reflected on this theme in his writing—that of the "modern man" alienated from his natural position of embeddedness with nature. Indeed, in Michigan, Olson's *Open Horizons* was described as a book about "a Midwesterner, a scholar and a naturalist" who knew "the feeling of space and silence as no city dweller ever could."[73] A reviewer in Vermont wrote that the book held that same "sensitive, almost lyric response to nature" so characteristic of Olson's writing. The reviewer continued to note that "throughout his book runs the thread of a deepening understanding and appreciation of the spiritual value of the wilderness—a gift and a heritage we are now in danger of destroying."[74]

What Olson perceived as modern man's problems occupied space in many of his books and, as he wrote in *Minnesota History,* he was "under no illusions about the problems of this period," but these problems did not dominate the books themselves.[75] Indeed, as Philip Cafaro wrote upon the University of Minnesota Press rerelease of Olson's first four books, "the Minnesota Thoreau" focuses on modern, mechanical encroachments upon the sanctified woods and streams of the North Country." Cafaro continues, but "bulldozers make few appearances in these books: loons and ice, dancing waters and the northern lights, many."[76]

Olson believed that an antidote to many of these problems might be found in nature. Building on his own experience in the environs of Northern Minnesota and the Quetico-Superior, Olson argued that engagement with wilderness could instill in others a "dawning awareness of beauty" and "reverence for the living world," which are too often confined to childhood but might reawaken by reintroduction to the natural world.[77] Speaking of his early engagement with wilderness, Olson described a process of gradual enlightenment, a slow, steady attunement to what he often called the "music" of the "Pipes of Pan," or the concert of natural sounds one hears in the wilderness. "The days of wide-eyed wonder merged gradually into a new era of growing physical activity and exploration of the countryside. Awe and surprise were still there, but now it was coupled with a hunger for new experiences, indulging my senses, absorbing smells, sights, and sounds as a sponge absorbs water."[78]

For Olson, this sense of "wide-eyed wonder" was not extinguished naturally, like a wick burning out at the end of childhood's candlestick. "Man does not suddenly become aware or infused with wonder," he wrote in *Reflections from the North Country*, "it is something we are born with."[79]

Modern Minnesotans and, indeed, all Midwesterners and Americans would do well to heed these lessons, the core tenets of Olson's environmental ethic. For reading the Minnesota Thoreau's writings today can encourage a critical examination of or recommitment to a region's identities and histories, however flawed. Furthermore, it might catalyze public commitment to conservation in environmental action. Olson's ethic, it seems, is more needed than ever.

NOTES

1. David Backes, *A Wilderness Within: The Life of Sigurd F. Olson* (Minneapolis: University of Minnesota Press, 1999), 48–49.

2. Backes, 51.

3. Bill McAllister, "Songwriter Celebrates Nature's Gifts," *St. Cloud Times* (St. Cloud, Minnesota), August 25, 1983, 9.

4. For an overview of this use, see Deirdre N. McCloskey, *The Bourgeois Virtues: Ethics for an Age of Commerce* (Chicago: University of Chicago Press, 2006).

5. Mary Lethert Wingerd, *North Country: The Making of Minnesota* (Minneapolis: University of Minnesota Press, 2010), 40, 65.

6. Backes, *A Wilderness Within*, 328.

7. Backes, 316. Olson received these awards in 1967, 1969, 1981, 1991, and 1974, respectively.

8. See Kevin Proescholdt, "Untrammeled Wilderness," *Minnesota History* 61, no. 3 (Fall 2008): 114–23 and 117 especially.

9. Will Sarvis, "A Difficult Legacy: Creation of the Ozark National Scenic Riverways," *The Public Historian* 24, no. 1 (2002): 40–41.

10. Ken Ross, "Charles Sheldon and Mt. McKinley National Park," in *Pioneering Conservation in Alaska* (Boulder: University Press of Colorado, 2006.), 149.

11. Kevin R. Marsh, "'This Is Just the First Round': Designating Wilderness in the Central Oregon Cascades, 1950–1964," *Oregon Historical Quarterly* 103, no. 2 (2002): 224.

12. Mark W. T. Harvey, "Battle for Dinosaur: Echo Park Dam and the Birth of the Modern Wilderness Movement," *Montana: The Magazine of Western History* 45, no. 1 (1995): 34.

13. Hank Hassell and R. Sean Evans, "The Sierra Club Goes to War," in *Rainbow Bridge* (Logan: Utah State University Press, 1999), 129.

14. For a more robust summary and examination of Olson's conservation activities, see Backes, *A Wilderness Within,* ch. 10, "A Professional Conservationist, 1946–1949," 181–207, and ch. 11, "Widening Horizons, 1950–1954," 209–33.

15. The Quetico-Superior region encompasses the Boundary Water Canoe Area Wilderness (BWCAW), Voyageurs National Park, Grand Portage National Monument, and Quetico Provincial Park. For more on the region, see R. Newell Searle, *Saving Quetico-Superior: A Land Set Apart* (Saint Paul: Minnesota Historical Society Press, 1977), xi.

16. For an overview of these legislative battles, see Kevin Proescholdt, "First Fight: Bud Heinselman and the Boundary Waters Canoe Area, 1964–65," *Minnesota History* 64, no. 2 (2014): 70–84; and Kevin Proescholdt, Rip Rapson, and Miron L. Heinselman, *Troubled Waters: The Fight for the Boundary Waters Canoe Area Wilderness* (St. Cloud: North Star Press, 1995). As Eric Freedman has shown, the legacy of this fight is not simply one of conservation. At stake were "competing interests" (379), such as those of the Native American community, whose treaty-based property rights and tribal practices conflicted with congressional intent to minimize disruption in the Boundary Waters Canoe Area. To engage with Freedman's full account, see Freedman, "When Indigenous Rights and Wilderness Collide: Prosecution of Native Americans for Using Motors in Minnesota's Boundary Waters Canoe Wilderness Area," *American Indian Quarterly* 26, no. 3 (2002): 378–92.

17. For an excellent overview, see Fred T. Witzig, *Voyageurs National Park: The Battle to Create Minnesota's National Park* (Minneapolis: University of Minneapolis Press, 2004).

18. Backes, *A Wilderness Within,* 126. On the Quetico-Superior Committee, see Backes, *A Wilderness Within,* 125–62. On Oberholtzer, see Joe Paddock, *Keeper of the Wild: The Life of Ernest Oberholtzer* (Minneapolis: Minnesota Historical Society Press, 2001).

19. For the best work on this border and its history, first see William E. Lass's corpus, including *Minnesota's Boundary with Canada: Its Evolution since 1783* (St. Paul: Minnesota Historical Society Press, 1980); Lass, "Minnesota: An American Siberia?," *Minnesota History* 49, no. 4 (Winter 1984): 149–55; and Lass, "Enlarging Minnesota," *Minnesota History* 61, no. 7 (Fall 2009): 306–11. Additionally, see Richard W. Ojakangas and Charles L. Matsch, "Northwestern Minnesota," in Ojakangas and Matsch, *Minnesota's Geology* (Minneapolis: University of Minnesota Press, 1982), 199–209.

20. Sigurd F. Olson, "A Study in Predatory Relationship with Particular Reference to the Wolf," *Scientific Monthly* 46, no. 4 (1938): 323–36; Sigurd F. Olson, "Organization and Range of the Pack," *Ecology* 19, no. 1 (January 1938): 168–70; V. E. Shelford and Sigurd F.

Olson, "Sere, Climax and Influent Animals with Special Reference to the Transcontinental Coniferous Forest of North America," *Ecology* 16, no. 3 (July 1935): 375–402; see Sigurd F. Olson in "General Notes," *Journal of Mammalogy* 13, no. 1 (1932): 70–82.

21. For this chapter, I rely on the University of Minnesota Press editions of Olson's work: Sigurd F. Olson, *The Singing Wilderness* (Minneapolis: University of Minnesota Press, 1997); *Listening Point* (Minneapolis: University of Minnesota Press, 1997); *The Lonely Land* (Minneapolis: University of Minnesota Press, 1997); *Runes of the North* (Minneapolis: University of Minnesota Press, 1997); *Open Horizons* (Minneapolis: University of Minnesota Press, 1998); *Wilderness Days* (Minneapolis: University of Minnesota Press, 2012); *Reflections from the North Country* (Minneapolis: University of Minnesota Press, 1998); and *Of Time and Place* (Minneapolis: University of Minnesota Press, 1998).

22. Mark Harvey, "Sound Politics: Wilderness, Recreation, and Motors in the Boundary Waters, 1945–1964," *Minnesota History* 58, no. 3 (2002): 134.

23. Backes, *A Wilderness Within*, 316.

24. Backes, 3.

25. Michael C. Steiner, "The Birth of the Midwest and the Rise of Regional Theory," in *Finding a New Midwestern History*, eds. Jon K. Lauck, Gleaves Whitney, and Joseph Hogan (Lincoln: University of Nebraska Press, 2018), 9; Jon K. Lauck, "Soft, Democratic, and Universalist: In Search of the Main Currents of Traditional Midwestern Identity and a Grand Historiographic Synthesis," *Middle West Review* 6, no. 1–2 (Fall–Spring 2019–2020): 83.

26. William Cronon, "Landscape and Home: Environmental Traditions in Wisconsin," *Wisconsin Magazine of History* 74 (Winter 1990–91): 93.

27. See Backes, "From Contemplation to Action: Sigurd Olson's Wilderness Theology, 1959–1964," in *A Wilderness Within*, 286–313, 292.

28. Backes, 312.

29. See Roger S. Gottlieb, "Environmentalism as Spirituality," in Gottlieb, *A Greener Faith: Religious Environmentalism and Our Plant's Future* (Oxford: Oxford University Press, 2000), 147–72.

30. Candace Stuart, "Sigurd Olson's Memoirs Convey Appreciation of Unspoiled Lands," *South Bend Tribune* (South Bend, Indiana), October 3, 1982, 94.

31. Olson, *Of Time and Place*, 4.

32. Jon K. Lauck, *The Lost Region: Toward a Revival of Midwestern History* (Iowa City: University of Iowa Press, 2013); Jon K. Lauck, *From Warm Center to Ragged Edge: The Erosion of Midwestern Literary and Historical Regionalism, 1920–1965* (Iowa City: University of Iowa Press, 2017); Mark Athitakis, *The New Midwest: A Guide to Contemporary Fiction of the Great Lakes, Great Plains, and Rust Belt* (Cleveland, OH: Belt Publishing, 2016).

33. David Blackbourn complained about this tendency, writing "are all topographies in the mind, is every river nothing more than a flowing symbol?" in his book, *The Conquest of Nature: Water, Landscape, and the Making of Modern Germany* (New York: W. W. Norton, 2005), 16.

34. William H. Sewell Jr., *Logics of History: Social Theory and Social Transformation* (Chicago: University of Chicago Press, 2005), 156.

35. C. Wright Mills, *The Sociological Imagination* (Oxford: Oxford University Press, 2000).

36. As Backes brilliantly observes, Olson was a pioneer in thinking about the onset of the Anthropocene. Indeed, Olson's worldview held that engagement with nature could dislodge "a purely anthropocentric worldview." See Backes, *A Wilderness Within*, 292.

37. See Christian Knoeller, *Reimagining Environmental History: Ecological Memory in the Wake of Landscape Change* (Reno: University of Nevada Press, 2017).

38. Sigurd F. Olson, "The Quetico-Superior Wilderness Laboratory," *Science Teacher* 18, no. 5 (November 1951): 229, 231.

39. Olson, *Of Time and Place*, 31,18.

40. Sigurd F. Olson, "Canoe Paddle vs. Chain Saw," *Milwaukee Journal*, July 2, 1977, pt. 1, 6.

41. For more on the relationship between ecological consciousness and ecological resistance, see William Devall and Bill Devall, "Ecological Consciousness and Ecological Resisting: Guidelines for Comprehension and Research," *Humboldt Journal of Social Relations* 9, no. 2 (1982): 185.

42. Aldo Leopold, *A Sand County Almanac: With Essays on Conservation from Round River* (New York: Ballantine Books, 1966), 177, 244–47.

43. Olson, *Open Horizons*, 13.

44. Olson, 24.

45. Olson, 29.

46. Olson, 35.

47. Olson, 62.

48. Olson, 84.

49. Olson, 84.

50. Robert C. Wheeler, "History below the Rapids," *Minnesota History* 38, no. 1 (1962): 29.

51. "In Minnesota Border Country: Cold Streams Yield Historic Relics," *The Winona Daily News* (Winona, MN), September 1, 1963, 36.

52. Olson, *Reflections from the North Country*, 17.

53. Olson, *Open Horizons*, 84.

54. Olson, 87.

55. Olson, 97–98.

56. Olson, *Reflections from the North Country*, 24.

57. Olson, *Open Horizons*, 101.

58. Olson, *Wilderness Days*, 53.

59. Olson, *Open Horizons*, 102.

60. Olson, 103.

61. Olson, *Reflections from the North Country*, 76.

62. Olson, *Open Horizons*, 3–4, 5.

63. Olson, *Wilderness Days*, 30.

64. Olson, *Reflections from the North Country*, xi–xii.

65. Olson, *The Singing Wilderness*, 147.

66. Olson, *Open Horizons*, 30.

67. Olson, 10.

68. Olson, 104.

69. Olson, 33–34.

70. Olson, *Of Time and Place*, xi.

71. Olson, *Open Horizons*, 61.

72. Olson, 10.

73. C. Kouba, "A Book for the Mind and Spirit," *Battle Creek Enquirer* (Battle Creek, MI), May 11, 1969, 21.

74. Marjorie Howe, "Lifelong Love Affair with Nature Explored in Olson's 'Open Horizons,'" *Burlington Free Press* (Burlington, VT), April 10, 1969, 8.

75. Sigurd F. Olson, "Review: We Made It Through Winter by Walter O'Meara," *Minnesota History* 44, no. 5 (Spring 1975): 190.

76. Philip Cafaro, "Review: Sigurd Olson: Environmentalist and Writer," *Conservation Biology* 12, no. 1 (February 1998): 257.

77. Olson, *Open Horizons*, xiv.

78. Olson, 21.

79. Olson, *Reflections from the North Country*, 69.

7

FOUR HUNDRED MILES SOUTH OF BLACKDUCK

A View of Northern Minnesota from below the State's Mason-Dixon Line

My cross-country coach, Kent Viesselman, told us to answer the question, "Where's Wells, Minnesota?" not with "two hours south of Minneapolis" but rather "four hundred miles south of Blackduck." Blackduck, Minnesota, of course, was a small town known to anglers and deer hunters way up in Beltrami County. My hometown, Wells, was at the state's other end, an old rail stop. At seventeen, I saw *some* humor in our curmudgeonly coach's bitterness toward a "Twin Cities"-centric Minnesota perspective. But only later in life did I discover the saying's usefulness for illustrating my hometown's marginalized spot in the state's geography.

Where're you from?

Wells?

Isn't that down south?

It's four hundred miles south of Blackduck.

Saying I grew up in "Minnesota" still rings of some unearned pride. I sense in others' eyes, especially—though my wife (from South Dakota) assures me this is partly projection—that saying "I'm from Minnesota" connotes pine trees and blue lakes, happy schools and public libraries, professional sports teams, red-eyed loons, and quilted moose. But that's not Wells.

Southern Minnesota is flat. It's combines and strip malls, water towers, and baseball. People whisper about hockey. Walleyes are a hundred miles away.

An interviewer once asked Bob Dylan whether he could trace his music to something "unique" in Minnesota, but Dylan declined the question's framing, saying "Minnesota has its own Mason-Dixon line":

> I come from the north, and that's different from southern Minnesota. If you're there you could be in Iowa or Georgia. Up north the weather is more extreme—frostbite in the winter, mosquito-ridden in the summer, no air conditioning when I grew up, steam heat in the winter and you had to wear a lot of clothes when you went outdoors. Your blood gets thick. It's the land of 10,000 lakes—a lot of hunting and fishing. Indian country, Ojibwe, Chippewa, Lakota, birch trees, open pit mines, bears and wolves—the air is raw. Southern Minnesota is farming country, wheat fields and hay stacks, lots of cornfields, horses and milk cows.[1]

When I read this, to paraphrase Annie Dillard from *Pilgrim at Tinker Creek*,[2] it was as if I hadn't realized I was a southerner until Dylan said so. Sure, I'd been wrapped in a puffy winter coat with a scarf lassoed around my face to shuffle in waist-deep snow around the block as a ghost the night of the Great Halloween Blizzard of 1991, so maybe I disagreed with Dylan's weather remarks. But my homeland *was* cornfields, carp-filled lakes, towering grain bins, and a flat demeanor more befitting a hay wagon than the berserk irreverence of a chilled ride on a logging sled.

The novelist Jon Hassler, in fact, called my hometown—a train town—a "godforsaken place."[3] When I read that in the ninth grade, I barely winced at the suggestion. I was just pleased to get in on the conversation. *Of course, it was forsaken,* I nodded quietly. *All the good stuff was up north.*

■　■　■

Northern and southern Minnesotans have differences, though not as many as people think. A friend from the Iron Range talks about babies being born out

of the back seat of Corsicas out on lake country gravel roads and deer hanging from pine trees, draining blood, but none of that sounds out of place for
Faribault County, either.

I suppose the dissipating hockey syndrome—the farther south, the fewer
teams—is a real thing. I once told Duluth's congressman Rep. Pete Stauber
where I grew up as a way of apologizing for my lack of hockey knowledge, and
he said, "Faribault B.A.'s[4] got a good club."

"No, Faribault *County*," I replied, drawing a useful distinction between my
county and the private school an hour north of us in Faribault *the town*.

Frankly, about the only "Minnesota" qualities of Wells are the county's French
surname—*Faribault*—and the high teacher pay (which brought my Nebraska
father and South Dakota mother east). Otherwise, we didn't resemble *Lake
Woebegone,* but rather *Dull Plains.* Our town celebrated "Kernel Days," capital-
izing on both the cannery that shut down a year after we moved there in 1992
and the Civil War–era, carpetbagging "Colonel" who founded our town. We
claimed a Dairy Queen, one stoplight (when the elementary school posted a
"caution" signal), and about two thousand people. Our concrete company (where
I worked two weeks before tendering my resignation on a typed letter) built the
beams for the Metrodome and U.S. Bank Stadium. But the leading "southern"
quality of my town was our high school's mascot: The Rebels.

I wish I could say I had no idea why, when the towns of Kiester, Wells,
Bricelyn, Freeborn, and Walters banded together in the early 1990s, they
opted for "The Rebels." But they sought to both commemorate our "southern"
status in the state as well as capitalize on the University of Nevada–Las Vegas
"Running Rebels"—a popular basketball team at the time. The name should
probably be changed, but I can also say that for over a decade I yelled out, "Let's
go, Rebels!" (initial drawings by Coach Viesselman featuring a gray uniform
and a gun were replaced by the Union blue, a wide-brimmed cowboy hat, and
a saber), only occasionally feeling like I was speaking about anything other
than a sports team.

Nevertheless, I actually owe one of those sports teams—cross-country—for
my tenderfoot awakening to place within my state. We traversed Minnesota's
geographical ecosystem in a bus or a van. To travel to Mountain Lake about
two hours west was to visit cowboy country, out there on Buffalo Ridge, where
wide-open skies and tall blue stem grass look more like South Dakota. Traveling east to Lanesboro, the coulees and cold, cave-emitting streams resembled

the hollers of Appalachia or the little villages buried at the foot of the White Mountains where Frost bumbled around with a notepad. And we yearly ran a race on Swain Hill overlooking the harbor in Duluth. It was only four or five hours by interstate, but it was my introduction to the North Country.

■　■　■

We'd leave early on a Friday afternoon, skipping the pep rally and the football game, and connect up with Interstate 35 in Albert Lea. Driving northward, a dread filled my stomach. I despised races but enjoyed the camaraderie. North of Hinckley, as we came upon the Saint Louis River basin, my headphones played Chicago Transit Authority's greatest hits, and I saw something that would change my life in that moment: the sea. A blue wall rose, somehow reaching me there in the middle of the country. Not the ocean, nor saltwater, but Lake Superior, Gitchi-Gami, and the impossibility of maritime life reaching here into the middle of the continent suddenly opened me up to an epistemological vulnerability that people on the coast take for granted: that at any moment, anyone on a boat from faraway lands can come ashore and say hello, can greet you, can mingle, can stay awhile and mix in with the locals.

That night, we ran up the hill from our hotel, staring at the harbor, with wooden masts and container ships floating at eye level with us from those tumble-down wooden homes. This was the year of that 6-foot-8-inch basketball phenom Rick Rickerts, from Duluth East High School, who was tearing up zones. I thought every angular-jawed kid I ran into on a bike might be his kid brother or a cousin. We ate a big dinner at Perkins—milkshakes, hamburgers—and walked the harbor, seeing the lift bridge, the lights of Superior twinkling, and then we retired to our hotel room, anxiously awaiting our sentence in a few hours.

In the morning, I woke with a dread. *Race day.* We put on our sweats and, bleary-eyed, boarded our van and drove up to the golf course. People from southern Minnesota certainly vacationed up north. That was a term, "up north." I didn't know a separate term to describe where I was from. "Down south?" It seemed oxymoronic to be from the "south" of the North Star State. But that was my case. Heading up the pigtailed roads on the bus, the light from the rising sun curving up over western Michigan striking my eyes, I wanted to be visiting this place with leisure on my mind, not racing.

"Where are all the buses?" remarked one of the seniors. As we summited to where the race would happen, only golfers dotted the hill. Coach—who for decades counted on the race occupying the last weekend in September—shifted uneasily in his seat.

"I'll find out what's going on."

He walked into the clubhouse, and none of us runners moved. A small delirium sparked inside me.

"Coach could be *angry* when he gets back in the car," cautioned his wife, holding the fluffy collie in her lap.

Within a minute, Viesselman, in his blue windbreaker jacket and gray beard, like some misplaced crab fisherman on the prairie, lumbered back into the van.

"Welp, I screwed up," he said, eerily calm. "The meet is next week."

I was momentarily ecstatic. *No race.*

But then a cold washed over the van.

Coach Viesselman—"Vies" for short—terrified us. He threw kids caught walking in the back of his Astro Van and drove out to the airport west of town, making them run into town, following them like a warden in his van. He'd take down the show-offs, the homecoming kings, the cheerleading captain, the honor roll kids, with a simple *cluck* of his tongue and a damning line that cut out the heart of fragile egos. "Are you done now?" he'd ask, clearing the idle chatter and gossip hovering over our stretching pods like a field of locusts stripping the last living green from a field.

We cruised away in deathly silence. I said goodbye to the gray harbor passing from view; the royal blue St. Louis River cutting through an autumn forest fell to our feet as we climbed westward up the bluff, and I braced for the other shoe to menacingly drop. We hadn't done anything wrong. But we knew, all six of us, we'd seen our coach in a low moment. The real hell would come when he got back to town and explained it to our parents, to his bosses in the activities director's office, maybe even to the school board, and that mounting anxiety on *his part,* we knew intuitively, would mean all the more hamstring-burning pain for us.

After an hour, we reached a trail outside Hinckley, where I'd learned from sixth grade state history that the big fire had burned. Vies parked, and we dutifully stepped out of the van.

"Run that way for thirty minutes and turn around," Coach said.

No one argued. We turned around and started jogging. A few paces in, we quickly did the math, our legs buckling. *Sixty minutes of running.* For all intents and purposes, we would spend the next hour merely as heads attached to stationary bikes. After an hour of pines and birch as our wallpaper, we returned, sweaty, panting, hands atop knees, ribcages sharp, our minds numb from the tedium, and Vies pointed in the other direction.

"Now run that way for ten minutes."

There have been Saturday mornings in autumn later in life when I leisurely drove up to Duluth from the Twin Cities, stopping off for blueberry pie and coffee at a bakery in Pine City or Hinckley, only to get back into the car to speed through forests of red and yellow, with a breeze slipping through the window, giving just enough chill to justify a jean jacket and a nostalgic state of mind, and I've almost been envious of my former stamina. But on that Saturday morning in 2000, teenage sarcasm sapped, we climbed exhaustedly back into the van to drive south on Interstate 35. Slumped in my seat, sweat caked into my brow, I watched the pine trees fade to billboards of the northern suburbs, then the silver skyscrapers downtown to the billboards of the southern suburbs, before the pockets of big woods remaining around the dells of Northfield fed into those golden cornfields of my boring homeland opened up around Owatonna. Only briefly is there a stretch of remarkable trees. Somewhere, north of Owatonna and south of Faribault, the north and southbound lanes bifurcate, enveloping a stand of deciduous trees, and there, perhaps guilty for his punitive action, Vies told us a bizarre, slightly chilling thought to humor our last hour together.

"I always thought this was a good place to bury a body," said our coach.

Trees in southern Minnesota insinuated sure danger. Concealment. *Distrust.* Our little van filled with teenagers from southern Minnesota, from practically Georgia in Dylan's words, nodded our heads and rode in the back of that van rolling down the interstate toward that prairie sea.

■ ■ ■

Unlike a lot of kids in Wells who had cabins but in the so-called premier lakes north and east of Mankato, where speedboats pulled divorcees in bikinis and lakeside tiki bars resembled something you might find on the Gulf, I always felt seasonably comfortable in Minnesota's Vacationland, farther west of Duluth. My Nebraskan great-grandfather held a government job as a postman during the Great Depression and scrounged together savings and purchased a tract of land from Weyerhauser Lumber Company along Little Mantrap Lake in Hubbard County in the 1930s. Loggers had clear-cut the place, just two miles south of Itasca State Park, where a few stands of old-growth trees were mercifully spared. But the pine had grown back by my generation. So during summers, we fished and swam and dried out on the diving platform listening for bass to electrically pop the bottoms of green lily pads on Little Mantrap. We drove to the Pizza Hut in Detroit Lakes and ended up at the forest museum in Grand Rapids, watching the pillowing smoke from the Blandin Mill issuing over the virgin Mississippi. On fall weekends, when my brother and I ran in the Swain Cross Country Meet, my parents hopped in the car and drove north to watch us and then drove two hours west to spend the night in the cabin—with the silver gas heater turned up high—and they'd close the cabin for the season before driving back down on Sunday.

Northern Minnesota was a white northland, a blanket of silence from October through May, though. I knew people were up there. We'd cheer for the pizza parlor owner from Bemidji during the curling events at the Winter Olympics. The Minnesota Vikings got in trouble at a snowmobile retreat up near Lake Mille Lacs. In sixth grade, we even took a class trip up to Ely and the lighthouse. We canoed in the Boundary Waters and pulled over near Happy Wanderer on Highway 1 so a number of us, nauseous, could vomit in the ditch. It was invigorating.

Sure, we'd see kids from Moorhead or Warroad or Virginia or Staples at sporting events. They'd look like normal teens. They seemed as clueless as us. But you just couldn't be sure they weren't a little more grown-up, either, a stoicism growing over kids a little farther from the city.

■ ■ ■

But I'm wary enumerating too many differences between "North" and "South" because it feels like the wrong geographical fraction in Minnesota.

A lot of southerners make their way north. When an elderly woman partially ran over my brother's foot while he went for a run in northeast Minneapolis, I drove him into urgent care, where—in a surprise to everyone—the mother of Leo's hometown friend, Dane Giese, Deb, was working as a part-time nurse.

"I'm seeing a guy up here now," she said, "I split my time between here and Wells."

When I lived in Winona, a barista I knew drove up to see her father, who lived in a memory care unit in Duluth.

"It's four hours up, four hours there, and four hours back down," she said.

The other day on the phone I spoke with a city manager in East Grand Forks, just across the Red River from North Dakota, who told me that he used to work down in Belle Plaine, a team we played in basketball.

"It was just the next logical step," said the manager, "a little bigger town."

Moreover, Minnesota's regions aren't that different geographically and agronomically anymore, either. Curiously, the north is starting to look like the south, and the south, the north.

■   ■   ■

According to a 2012 article from the *Scientific American,* moose are leaving northern Minnesota.[5] "Moose may disappear from boreal woods as circumpolar regions warm and transform," reads the ominous subhead. Apparently moose—with the delightfully Scandinavian-hockey-player of a scientific name: *Alces alces andersoni*—aren't doing too well with the climate. Beginning in 2002, wildlife resource officials put radio collars on 150 moose. Nearly 120 subsequently died. Cars and train collisions got some. Others pointed to the rise in gray wolves, taking calves. But warmer summers mean the key ingredients in moose's diet—oak and maple leaves—are migrating northward. And moose aren't the only titular Minnesotans on the run. According to a recent story in the *Minneapolis Star Tribune,* pine trees are under the scourge of increasingly warm summers, thanks to CO_2.[6] Another headline declared loons may soon be leaving thanks to the hotter summers.[7] Lastly, corn has expanded into northern Minnesota.

This last summer, when my brother and I and Mom drove from the cabin to Dorset, self-proclaimed restaurant capital of the world, we stopped off at a four-way stop, and Leo, who hadn't been up to the family place in a while, looked in astonishment at the corn crop coming up.

"Whoa," he uttered. "There's corn up here?"

■   ■   ■

A spokesperson for the University of Minnesota Extension Service cautioned me that corn's growth into northern counties is largely due to improved hybrids, hard-shelled seeds for shorter growing seasons.[8] Moreover, there's been a hiccup on the longer trend. Between 2012 and 2017, the numbers of acres harvested for corn in Minnesota actually *dropped* by over half a million acres. But in 1978, Faribault County—my home in the south, along the Iowa border—boasted nearly three times as many farms and almost 400,000 acres used for crops. Meanwhile, of the 71,000 acres used for crops in Hubbard County, only 700 acres of *corn* were planted. Today, however, corn dots 11,000 acres in Hubbard County, a geometric jump.[9]

So maybe distinctions like "northern" and "southern" Minnesota are increasingly tenuous. Maybe someday "northern" Minnesota will mostly exist in our imagination as climate change alters distinctive topographical and agricultural products.

In 2015, Governor Mark Dayton closed down walleye fishing in Lake Mille Lacs due to impacts from overfishing,[10] and the other day, I walked past the clothing store owned by the Dayton Brothers, Askov Finlayson (named for two towns dotting an exit sign off Interstate 94), and it was closed, with a sign posted that read: "We'll soon be reopening with climate-positive winter-wear." Their campaign—to turn Minnesota from the "Midwest" to "the Bold North"—stirs chit-chat over pints but is also an antecedent with a fuzzy pronoun. The North is only in our minds. Or brands. As pine country recedes, the pine trees continue to appear on Minnesota branding, such as Caribou Coffee or in the advertising of the local hockey team or in the image of the Super Bowl crew.

Maybe none of these distinctions are as foundational as we make them out to be, as Dylan says in the rest of his "Mason-Dixon" quote.

"In the north, it's more hardscrabble," he said. "It's a rugged environment—people lead simple lives, but they lead simple lives in other parts of the country, too. People are pretty much the same wherever you go."

■ ■ ■

According to Google, my hometown is not 400 miles but actually 308 miles south of Blackduck, a town northeast of Bemidji in Beltrami County. I've never visited Blackduck. But at a population of 745, Blackduck is probably like the town where I spent most of my first seven years: Kiester, a softball's throw north of the Iowa border. I doubt I would feel out of place in Blackduck. Because the older I've gotten, the more I sense Minnesota's real contours.

I once heard Louise Erdrich say she viewed "I-94" as a belt splitting the state between northern and southern halves. Garrison Keillor wrote that he used to daydream about driving west on Highway 212, down that stretch of towns that leads out to the Dakotas.[11] When I lived for a summer in Willmar, interning at the *West Central Tribune,* I learned about that great nexus of Highway 23 (which could take you to South Dakota), Highway 12 (which could ferry you into the western suburbs), and Highway 71 (which could shoot you straight into the North Country). Kandiyohi County branded itself as "The Gateway to the Lakes." I'd never heard the Coen brothers–esque accent in Wells, but when I walked into the newsroom at the *West Central Tribune* in the summer of 2006, a man with a pink, popped-collar polo and spiked hair welcomed me with a hearty, "Oh ya, we're sure glad to have ya here." I'd also never seen a man with hockey hair until I met the paper's editor, Kelly Boldan, whose gray locks—like the tail feathers of a bird cruising over a lake—fluttered as he rushed through the newsroom to grab a printer or another cup of coffee.

But what I'm getting at is if we're going to craft a border in Minnesota, it's not horizontal. In Maine, the schism pits "The County" and the eastern, coastal communities from Portland on up into Bar Harbor. In California, the "Inland Empire" is made up of trailers dropped off in deserts hundreds of miles east of Los Angeles. It's "West and East River" in South Dakota. And in Minnesota, if we want to talk regions, it's "out-state" and "in-state."

Or—as the *Minneapolis Star Tribune* once invoked—the "retro" and the "metro."

■ ■ ■

I'd often *sensed* I belonged to a "retro" class. During my middle school years, Mom left teaching English in Blue Earth to attend law school at William Mitchell in St. Paul, and my brother and I accompanied her to classes during the summer, journeying from Wells into the heart of the Cities. I remember walking around St. Paul, wearing my out-of-style sneakers and straight-legged jeans, feeling like I had missed a memo.

But kudos to the editorial board at the *Minneapolis Star Tribune* for saying it aloud.[12]

The editors actually pulled the thesis from a book authored by John Sperling, who would later found the University of Phoenix. "Retro states," they wrote, "descend from the Old South. They are largely white, religious, rural in their values and individualistic in their politics. Metro states descend from the commercial North. They are multi-ethnic, secular, metropolitan in their values and collaborative in their politics."

The editors argued that "retro" was creeping into the Twin Cities suburbs, with calls for "disinvestment, intolerance, and retreat." This was all in 2004, during the reign of Republicans Michelle Bachman and Tim Pawlenty, a conservative brand soon to be diminished with three successive elections of a Democratic-Farmer-Labor governor, the legalization of gay marriage in the state legislature, and the like.

Nevertheless, reading the *Strib*'s analysis, even in a clumsy way, I remember feeling caricatured by the argument and miffed. That coming fall, I voted—in my first presidential election—for the Republican ticket (so far, the only time in my life) of George W. Bush and Dick Cheney, not perhaps entirely *uninfluenced* by that editorial. Even today, the argument bothers me, makes me feel that my town was somehow *retrograde,* backward. Even if the *Strib*'s editorial board was right, I didn't want someone *saying that.*

■ ■ ■

But there are concentric circles of culture emanating out from the Twin Cities. Those of us living on the periphery of this vortex (Wells is ninety-four miles from the Lakeville McStop, which constitutes the southern breakwater of the Twin Cities Metro area) share in a commonality of reference to those *within Greater Minnesota*—though I sort of prefer "out-state."

And the first time I *really* felt *it* was in the Blue Earth gymnasium at a basketball game, circa 2002, seeing kids wearing blaze orange clothing. One guy even donned a cowboy hat and twirled a lasso. I was totally stumped. *Why would you lean into that stereotype?*, I thought. *Why would you want to look like a hick?*

I suppose they'd learned to do so on television. The *Blue Collar Comedy Tour* was popular on Comedy Central. Moreover, in 2000, the Minnesota Wild—with its mascot of an amorphous beast—became the state's hockey team, projecting a *wildness* with rurality.

But, regardless, I see now that in that gymnasium in Blue Earth was the first time I ever saw a Trump supporter. No one (outside him, maybe) knew he was running yet. Not many outside Illinois had even heard the name "Barack Obama." But staring at those guys in blaze orange and western tack down on the Blue Earth sideline felt like I was watching my neighbors run toward a depiction of themselves leveraged by someone *not from here.* We'd lost our ability to even imagine for ourselves something beyond what we'd been told. The hospitals in rural America closed. The schools consolidated. Even the dance hall down the highway—The Golden Bubble—shut down. *Oh,* seemed to be the thought, *we should now just be rednecks. That's what everyone says we are, anyway.*

■ ■ ■

In 2012, I stood in my kitchen in Winona and listened to the Minnesota Public Radio report on the vote in the legislature to legalize gay marriage and perked up when the reporter noted that not only liberal Twin Cities legislators supported the bill.

"First-term Rep. Shannon Savick, DFL Wells, said she's voting for the bill," said the reporter Tom Scheck. "She said her brother is gay, and she didn't think twice about the vote."[13]

I brimmed with pride, listening as she talked about her brother fight discrimination growing up. But I also felt wary about what she said next.

"It could cost me the election because I come from a really conservative area," said Savick, "but I'm hoping I do enough good in other areas that they will overlook that."

Shannon did do enough good. But voters did, as she predicted, send her home that next cycle.

■ ■ ■

Politics is only part of the puzzle, but for whatever reason, I've rarely felt out of place in the Cities. They're too much like home. I doubt Blackduckers would feel out of place in Minneapolis or St. Paul, either. When I lived off of East Lake Street, jogging the two miles to the Mississippi, I'd run past Mexican bakeries, an old Swedish grocery store, some quiet Irish taphouses, a service station or two—all venues you might find in Wells or Blackduck in their heydays. Where I—and I'm guessing someone from Blackduck, too—have always felt alienated was in the suburbs.

■ ■ ■

On my first day teaching writing at Normandale Community College, I asked students to share a favorite book, band, etcetera, and I was blown away by how many students who grew up surrounded by the rolling green soccer fields of Eden Prairie, and who'd never seen a sprayer, with its insect-like tires spreading out over three-fourths of a two-lane county paved road, told me they loved country music: Zac Brown Band, Trace Adkins, something eye-raisingly called Lady Antebellum. And in that moment I realized what those kids back at the gymnasium in Blue Earth had realized, that the place I was from, the place where I grew up, was also no longer a place, but an idea, an imaginative scene of hay bales and Chevy S-10s and girls in cut-off denims down at the gravel pit swimming hole, and it would never, ever matter if I said otherwise. Just like the North Country, just like the Range, or the North Shore, brought to life in a mini-putt golf course high up on the fourth floor of the Mall of America, with its waterfall spilling over artificial granite rocks strewn with spiny pine trees reaching up toward heaven, intermixed with the cry of children screaming on the Camp Snoopy rollercoaster, Wells, Kiester, Southern Minnesota, the Country were now, also, as Willa Cather always said they would become, when she spoke of pioneers—a *place of ideas*. We were beholden to suburbanites' image of us.

■ ■ ■

So I worry about the gray mass of homogenizing outlet malls and fast-food chains bulging in the middle of our state. It's our new map, neither North nor South, but simply *there*.

This summer, my wife and I visited my sister-in-law, commissioned by Rosemont, a southeastern suburb along Highway 52, to paint a water-themed mural outside the splash pool in what remains of the old town's heart. A child stood over Laura in her floppy hat and asked her, "What are you doing?"

"I'm painting about the water, an otter, a person singing in the rain, an octopus, to show how water is life, how what we flush or dump or drain all goes somewhere," Laura said, with a teacher's patience.

"But did they want that? Did they ask for that?" the kid responded.

"Yes!" Laura said. "They wanted this!"

It was the tepid first steps of a suburb wishing to go green, to at least imagine for itself a spot on the map.

■ ■ ■

Late in the cross-country season, when the combines cleaved brown husks in clumps in muddy fields; when the men in green seed caps and baggy denim sipped coffee with one leg on the steel steps of their grain trucks, creating a small-town traffic jam outside the grain elevators, the tallest buildings in town; our varsity runners—six boys in baggy blue windbreakers and bare legs, running along the country roads outside of town—were greeted by Coach lounging next to his bicycle in a patch of grass adjacent the gun range and the lagoon. As we stretched, he told us a story we'd never heard.

"I was out running south of town on one of these late-autumn afternoons," Vies said, picking at bits of his afternoon cigarette in his teeth with a panatela of grass, "It was probably 1982, the season over. Winds from up north were cold, but still no snow. And off up near the Schmitz place, rounding a sectional, I saw this big dog off its leash, munching corn husks in the field. It was odd, for the size of the dog. But then, I looked closer, saw the size of this big black animal, and realized, '*That's no dog. That's a wolf.*'"

■ ■ ■

Would it be *as odd* for my coach in Faribault County, down along the southern border, to see a gray wolf as for my thirty-one-year-old brother to react in surprise to seeing corn north of Dorset, tucked along a pine meadow? It's a natural melody for Minnesotans: the prairie to the forest, the river to the lakes. Maybe Dylan was wrong. We all know the geography. There is no "Mason-Dixon Line" in Minnesota. We are *one Minnesota,* to borrow the language of the current governor.

But there is a southern incursion, no doubt, into the Northland, at least at its southern border. And I've seen it firsthand, as my hometown of late has, well, encountered a problem with Confederate flags.

■ ■ ■

Close to half a dozen Confederate flags popped up in Wells during the summer of 2015, when South Carolina pulled that flag from atop their statehouse after a mass shooting at a black church. The flag wasn't entirely *unprecedented* in southern Minnesota. A Confederate flag haunted the window of a home in nearby Janesville. Another in New Richland. In addition to its racism, the standard of the seceded states bugs me as a Minnesotan, who learned in our state history class in sixth grade that Minnesota—newly a state in 1858—was the first in the Union to volunteer troops for the North's cause to bring those rebellious states back into a single nation. The 1st Minnesota Infantry Regiment lost over 80 percent of its soldiers at Gettysburg, fighting with the stars-and-stripes, not the stars-and-bars.

And the flag's appearance in Wells was not a "retro" act. In 1861, my hometown wouldn't be born for another decade. The farmers in the area certainly wouldn't have sent their sons off to fight for some senator at the other end of the Mississippi. No, the Union recruited heavily along the river towns of Winona, Wabasha, Red Wing, Hastings,[14] but those who came back spread out, to mill cities or the timber camps up north. One Civil War veteran rumored to have made his way north was Thomas P. "Boston" Corbett, the assassin of John Wilkes Booth. They don't know how he died for sure, but his last known residence was outside Hinckley during the fire of 1894, and a "Thomas Corbett" was among the dead.[15]

Coach Viesselman liked to stop off in Hinckley, at Tobies Restaurant and Bakery. But we never ventured into the museum about the Great Hinckley Fire. There, displays show how the spread of smoke cast soot on windows of buildings in downtown Duluth or Green Bay. They say the light went four miles high. You could see the flames as far away as Mason City, Iowa, on that day in 1894, just a century before I was born in Albert Lea. Wells was standing then, too. A lot of German farmers had moved to the area already, out there in Dunbar Township, north of the railroad, north of the creamery and grain elevator. Already they had a sense for this state that had been taken for them from the Dakota and the Ojibwe. Already, they knew town and city. East was the Mississippi and west, the Big Sioux, the Red River up north, and somewhere Superior. A consciousness had been imposed by artificial lines in black dirt. But there was a sense of their neighbors, who lived beyond them. And they knew the fishing was better up north, maybe the beer a little colder, and to pack a flannel if you were going. That's always been my sense of the North, anyway. And I can't help but wonder if a farmer, maybe a Rollenhagen or a Staloch, in my hometown in the oxymoronic southern county of the North Star State, would've doffed his cap after riding out on a wagon to check the crops, to see an orange line hovering in the sky and maybe wonder, *What's going on up there now? What kind of trouble have they got up north?*

NOTES

1. Bob Dylan, "Q&A with Bill Flanagan," Bob Dylan.com, March 22, 2017. https://www.bobdylan.com/news/qa-with-bill-flanagan/, accessed October 10, 2019.

2. "I had been a bell my whole life, and never knew it until at the moment I was lifted and struck." Dillard, Annie. *Pilgrim at Tinker Creek*. New York: Harper's Magazine Press, 1974, 36.

3. Hassler, Jon. *Grand Opening*. New York: William Morrow, 1987, 42.

4. Bethlehem Academy.

5. Daniel Cusick, "Rapid Climate Changes Turn North Woods into Moose Graveyard," *Scientific American*, May 18, 2012, https://www.scientificamerican.com/article/rapid-climate-changes-turn-north-woods-into-moose-graveyard/, accessed October 10, 2019.

6. Mark Boswell, "Climate Change Threatens Our Forests," *Minneapolis Star Tribune*, February 3, 2019, https://www.startribune.com/climate-change-threatens-minnesotas-forests/600042780/, accessed October 10, 2019.

7. Jennifer Bjorhus, "Loons Likely to Disappear from Minnesota Due to Climate Change, New Report Warns," *Minneapolis Star Tribune*, October 12, 2019, www.startribune.com/loons-likely-to-disappear-from-minnesota-due-to-climate-change-new-report-warns/562874132/, accessed October 16, 2019.

8. Bongard, Phyllis. "Inquiry on Corn Patterns." Email to the author, 2019.

9. U.S. Department of Agriculture, "Census of Agriculture." https://www.nass.usda
.gov/AgCensus/index.php. Accessed October 10, 2019.

10. John Reinan and Jennifer Brooks, "Dayton Says Walleye Restrictions on Lake Mille
Lacs Could Be Eased," *Minneapolis Star Tribune*, July, 11 2017, https://www.startribune
.com/dayton-says-walleye-restrictions-on-lake-mille-lacs -could-be-eased/433706493/,
accessed October 10, 2019.

11. Garrison Keillor, "Just Follow the Map," GarrisonKeillor.com, December 31,
2007, http://www.garrisonkeillor.com/just-follow-the-map/, accessed October 10, 2019.

12. Editorial board, "A Great Divide: Where Does Minnesota Belong?," *Minneapolis
Star Tribune*, August 23, 2004.

13. Tom Scheck, "Same-Sex Marriage Bill Heads to House Floor, Supporters Con-
fident," MPRNews, May 7, 2013, https://www.mprnews.org/amp/story/2013/05/07
/same-sex-marriage-bill-heads-to-house-floor-supporters-confident, accessed October 10, 2019.

14. "Minnesota and the Civil War," Minnesota Historical Society, http://sites.mnhs
.org/civil-war.

15. Swenson, Grace Stageberg. *From the Ashes: The Story of the Hinckley Fire of 1894.*
St. Croix, MN: Croixside Press, 1979, 165–68.

8

RUSSELL KIRK OF MICHIGAN

Citizen of Plymouth, Sage of Mecosta

Michigan lays claim to a raft of renowned writers—Ernest Hemingway, Bruce Catton, and Jim Harrison among them—but one overlooked author of estimable repute is Russell Kirk. By the time Kirk was in his mid thirties, he had become a towering figure in Western political thought. Little appreciated is the extent to which his philosophical sensibilities were formed in a youth spent in two Michigan towns, one in a leafy suburb of Detroit in the southeast Lower Peninsula, the other in a glaciated sand county "up north."

In the 1950s, the United States was grappling with its new status as the world's preeminent power. The nation had emerged victorious in World War II and now found itself leading the free world against militant communist regimes in Russia and China. But how would the United States lead—through hard-bitten *Realpolitik,* tender-minded idealism, or prudent historical experience?

The historian, philosopher, and novelist Russell Amos Kirk of Michigan offered a remarkable answer to that question in 1953 with the publication of

The Conservative Mind, a best seller that the *New York Times* called "an intellectual bible of the conservative movement." In its pages were penetrating
biographies of John Adams, Alexis de Tocqueville, James Fenimore Cooper,
Nathaniel Hawthorne, George Santayana, T.S. Eliot, and other guardians of
"the permanent things"—a rich vein of conservative beliefs and institutions
that anchored American culture and politics to solid bedrock amid the swirl
of modernity's shifting sands.[1]

It is indicative of *The Conservative Mind*'s staying power that it would go
through seven editions in Kirk's lifetime, thus making its author a much-sought-
after public intellectual. Over the next four decades, Kirk—called the "American Cicero"—would become an advisor to presidents, a syndicated columnist,
a founder of scholarly journals, the author of thirty additional books, and a
speaker on more than five hundred college campuses. For his many labors, he
was awarded the Presidential Medal of Freedom by Ronald Reagan in 1989.[2]

Since his passing in 1994, Kirk's esteem has continued to grow. His work
has been translated into more than one dozen languages. New editions of his
books continue to roll off the presses, not just in the United States but also in
Eastern Europe, South America, and Asia. C-SPAN dedicated the better part
of an entire program to him in its series on America's most important public
intellectuals. Hillsdale College endowed a chair in his name. An award-winning
biography by Bradley Birzer in 2015 explored everything from Kirk's political
philosophy to his ghost stories, which have been favorably compared to those
of Stephen King.[3] Admirers retrace his youthful steps in the wonderfully quaint
environs of his childhood hometown, Plymouth, Michigan, while scholars
mine his archives at Central Michigan University and the Russell Kirk Center
for Cultural Renewal in Mecosta, Michigan.

I will come back to the significance of Kirk's work on those two settlements,
Plymouth and Mecosta, in short order, for the geography of these two places
shaped Kirk's imagination and informed his work. In a globalizing world, Kirk
took his place in the international republic of letters, persisting in time and growing in repute. Yet it should not be forgotten that he was, in the end, a Michigan
man. He grew up dividing his childhood between Plymouth, on the outskirts
of Detroit, and Mecosta, a "stump-country" village at the geographic center of
the Old Northwest. As a young adult, he worked in Henry Ford's Greenfield Village and went to the state land-grant college in East Lansing. After completing
doctoral studies in Scotland, he settled "up north," in Mecosta, where he spent the
better part of four decades writing and lecturing from his family's ancestral home.

Kirk was a Michigan man not just because he had a Michigan street address. Kirk was a Michigan man because he loved the Great Lakes State and its place in the Old Northwest. He loved its stories. He was especially interested in the region's early historical geography and intellectual history. Thus, it was in Michigan that Kirk's moral imagination, philosophic reason, and historical sensibilities were nurtured. And it is in Michigan that the opportunity to explore his physical and imaginative geography exists.

TIME, PLACE, AND FAMILY

Russell Amos Kirk was born in Plymouth, Michigan, on October 19, 1918. From his autobiographical writings, we can glean that while he was still a youth in the 1920s and 1930s, Kirk developed the capacity to understand the Great Lakes State through transformative modern forces—industrialization, urbanization, canals, railroads, westward expansion, and the like. He was attracted even more to the state's earlier history, back through Michigan Territory's exploration, settlement, and founding. Why, already at a young age, was he aware of his affinity for older rather than newer things? He readily acknowledged that he did not fully understand why he possessed a historical awareness that combined powerfully with a conservative temperament. "In ways mysterious our political preferences are formed," he once wrote.[4] But he had memories of conversations, feelings of communion with loved ones in places that became formative to the future man of letters.

One such conversation occurred with his maternal grandfather, Frank Pierce, in his hometown of Plymouth, some twenty miles west of Detroit. Wrote Kirk, "I think of walking with my grandfather, a sagacious and courageous man, along a railway cut through a glacial moraine." The old man and the young boy were speaking of the living presence of the past. "That communion with an old gentleman I admired infinitely, and our reflections that day upon the living past, were among the influences that prevented me from becoming an evangel of Modernity."[5] That powerful statement suggests why Kirk was drawn to the early stories of the places he loved.

Kirk recalled a similarly formative event with his father. The scene, also in Plymouth, captured his awakening to the mysteries of time and place: "I think," Kirk wrote, "of a Sunday afternoon in my father's company, resting on a slope high above the village millpond, I a little boy. We lay in the shade of great trees; and I recall reflecting on the peace and beauty of the scene, and the great age of the trees—and wishing that everything about us that day might never change."[6]

It cannot be overstated: Kirk's capacity to imagine the deeper history of a place first emerged in Michigan, in the crucible of Plymouth, a community that he looked back upon fondly. That was where he learned about his family roots. Many of his relatives, he reported, were from Plymouth Colony and elsewhere in Massachusetts and New Hampshire, and it excited his imagination to grow up in a locale that had cultural connections to his hardy New England forebears, even those long deceased. As Kirk liked to say, quoting the French psychologist Gustave Le Bon, "The dead alone give us energy."[7]

ADAMS, HAMILTON, AND JEFFERSON

Plymouth, Michigan, a western outpost of New England, was initially settled by people of European stock in 1825, not by Kirk's relatives but by Connecticut Yankees. It was the same year the Erie Canal opened up the Northwest to the Northeast, and settlers poured into what would become the Upper Midwest. The Michigan town where Kirk grew up was called Plymouth in honor of the first Pilgrim settlement along the shore of Massachusetts Bay. Illustrative of the town's self-conscious roots in New England was the fact that it was built around a New England–style village green that today is called Kellogg Park. Kirk noted the cultural significance of the town square in his autobiography—it provided a sense of place, a cohesive element in an otherwise modern community that struggled against the centrifugal forces of the industrial age.[8]

A precocious and observant child, Kirk absorbed the values of his "pilgrim and Bible-reading ancestry." He learned the civic virtues that a New England culture valued. Classical republican virtues of self-sacrifice were seen in the Civil War and Spanish American War memorials in town. Moral earnestness was apparent in the Depression-era charities he saw growing up. Religious observance was evident in the various churches in Plymouth. Community cohesion was symbolized by the town square where residents gathered. Humane learning was experienced in the public schools he attended and in the personal libraries of his grandfather and mother. Those childhood influences in Plymouth would later contribute to Kirk's abiding respect for the most prominent New Englander among the founders, John Adams—the one American who figures large in the opening chapters of Kirk's later best seller, *The Conservative Mind*. Adams, who had a dour view of human nature, nevertheless harbored the hope that America might be a virtuous republic.[9]

Yet Plymouth, Michigan, pleasant as it was in Kirk's memory, was not the idyllic New England village of autumn-splashed postcards. In the late nineteenth and early twentieth centuries, the town took a modern turn due to the railroads and industries it attracted. Kirk's father worked as an engineman for a railroad, and the family lived in a prefabricated Sears, Roebuck, and Co. house. Kirk described his start in life as "a boyhood beside the railroad yards." But he was not drawn to the industries that built modern-day Plymouth. To him, industrial growth represented the triumph of Alexander Hamilton's vision for America, the vision of a commercial republic that too often resulted in ugly, hurried, and dehumanizing landscapes. Just twenty miles to the east, Kirk had seen Detroit's grim streets—the very image of what modern industrial growth often looked like. It was the outcome of an enterprising people who tolerated or even valued the "creative destruction" of capitalism as the path to a better future.[10]

Not all Americans shared the Hamiltonian vision of the future or its relentless gunning for profit. Kirk never viewed human beings as merely *Homo economicus,* and his autobiography includes a telling passage about his father's side of the family, who embraced the Jeffersonian vision of an agrarian republic. Those "farmers and farm laborers in Southeastern Michigan contended unsuccessfully against the tide of industrialism that swept out of Detroit. Gradually their landmarks were effaced." The hopeless clash of values between yeomen Jeffersonian farmers and Hamiltonian industrialists gave young Russell Kirk a civilizational confrontation to ponder. Writing proudly of his father's family, Kirk noted, "They were the salt of the earth . . . unmachined." More, they "were attached to old houses, old trees, old country roads; for the old bucolic ways they expressed a piety almost Roman. But theirs was a setting of moribund farms, barns sagging to their ruin, fields grown up to brush—rural America in retreat," like the Jeffersonian vision that inspired it.[11]

Kirk kept something of these Scottish ancestors throughout his life. He cut against the grain of modernity by describing himself as a "Northern Agrarian."[12]

In his autobiography, Kirk shared his lively imagination with readers, illuminating for them a great civilizational drama. Its stage was Michigan and the Midwest. And its five acts stretched from America's founding generation to the early twentieth century. It was a drama whose heroes included Adams, Hamilton, and Jefferson. As Kirk's reading and schooling expanded, he learned to integrate the story of his family and hometown into the broader story of the Midwest. In turn, the broader story of the Midwest morphed into the founding of the nation.

Until 1783, the land that would become Michigan and the Upper Midwest was considered an extension of the Commonwealth of Virginia mostly, but also of a smattering of other states along the Eastern Seaboard. Because the founders did not want to lose that contested territory to either the Native Americans or the British, they made the region the Northwestern Theater of the War for Independence. To secure such a prize would more than double the territorial extent of the nation.

The race to control the vast interior of North America was understandable. The Northwest was a land of forest and prairie parklands, of glacial till scored by good rivers that made a superb transportation network linked by short portages. Voyageurs from Canada as well as explorers such as Étienne Brûlé and Henry Schoolcraft all remarked on the Northwest's abundant resources: its diverse timber and wildlife; its copper, coal, limestone, and salt deposits; and its rivers with enough elevation change to generate the energy to operate sawmills and flour mills. Nor should the unexpected beauty of the region go overlooked. From the wild shores of Lake Superior to the gentle bluffs over the Great River Country where the Mississippi, Illinois, Missouri, and Ohio converge, the land was considered some of the best on Earth.

It is no surprise, then, that George Washington viewed the Northwest as the stage for an empire of liberty. During the Revolutionary War, he dispatched George Rogers Clark to the Northwest to wage fierce military campaigns from 1778 to 1782 to weaken the British claim to the region. Clark's victories over the British at Kaskaskia and Vincennes meant that the 1783 peace settlement would be favorable to American ambitions in the West. The ink on the Treaty of Paris had hardly dried when Washington began referring to the Northwest as the "second promised land," where Americans could make a better life for themselves for generations to come.[13] That land was the new republic. And the new republic represented America's experiment with ordered liberty. One of the architects of the new republic, James Madison, thought of the future Midwest as a living tutorial in how to make a large republic succeed where previous republics had failed.

It all sounds so analytically neat, so narratively coherent, so pedagogically tidy—but then, Mecosta has not yet been considered.

MECOSTA, CENTER OF THE OLD NORTHWEST

The village of Mecosta may initially seem like an unlikely place to cultivate literary talent. This run-down shadow of a town was where Kirk often went as a child in summer. There, he spent time with his mother's side of the family and enjoyed the lakes and cooler weather away from the occasionally oppressive heat of southeastern Michigan.

At an elevation of 1,000 feet, the village is located near Lake Mecosta and the Canadian Lakes—right in the middle of the old Northwest Territory. Growing up in Michigan, Kirk knew the North Country to be a land of many struggles—between people and the land; between various American Indian tribes; between the aboriginal inhabitants and European intruders; between the British and French; between the British and Americans; between those who tried to establish a Jeffersonian agrarian republic and those who favored a Hamiltonian commercial republic; and between those who clung to something from the past and those who chose to move on. "Up north" describes deceptively rich layers of historical geography interwoven with the region's intellectual history. And Kirk, over the course of his lifetime, unleashed many of the secrets of that contested land.

Of his summer home in Mecosta, which in adulthood became his full-time residence, Kirk wrote:

> My mother's family lived, most of them, nearly two hundred miles to the north and west [of Detroit], in Mecosta County; and about them stretched to the horizon and beyond, the stump country—the cut-over lands that the lumbermen of the 'seventies and 'eighties had left desolate behind them. Often I went there in summer; from my earliest recollection of the region, I loved its bleak ridges and its scrubby second-growth woods, its remote lakes and its sand trails, its poverty-racked farmsteads and the silent village of Mecosta itself, shrunk to a tenth of its early population . . . a village of one great broad street a mile long, white clapboard shops with false fronts scattered along it. The village would have suited Wyoming or Colorado well enough; the country round it, however, belonged peculiarly to the lake states. Glaciated and ravaged, Mecosta County was like the empty land that peers out of the pages of the Mabinogian [*sic*]. Here I came to know the world of silence.[14]

Note the terms Kirk used in the above passage to describe this place "up north." Glaciated land, ravaged hillsides, bleak ridges, cut-over forests, stump country, remote desolation, abandoned property—all paint Mecosta in heavy dark shades that contrast to the light hues of Plymouth. It is the difference between a J. M. W. Turner painting and a Tiffany lamp—as though Mecosta and Plymouth represent two interior states of Kirk's mind.

Bradley J. Birzer, the biographer of Russell Kirk, undertook extensive research in the Kirk archive at the Russell Kirk Center for Cultural Renewal in Mecosta. Birzer discovered that his subject believed something about Mecosta was mysterious, haunted, even touched with some remnant evil. Certainly, many of the short stories and ghostly tales Kirk wrote are set in the remote desolation of the stump country. Through his gothic fiction, he seemed able to pierce the silence of the land and give its people and spirits a voice.[15]

And what was that voice? Many times, it was a spirit that defied Jefferson's Enlightenment, with its Cartesian survey lines that relentlessly divided an untamed landscape into the straitjacket of baselines and meridians. Other times, it was a spirit that pushed back against Hamilton's materialism, recalling an ancient adage about man not living by bread alone. At still other times, it was a spirit warning that Adams's vision of a virtuous republic was too difficult to attain or, if attained, to maintain. The crooked timber of humanity would not permit it. Ultimately, the voice "up north" was a spirit that rebuked even the great Washington himself, who overreached when he proclaimed the Northwest to be the "second promised land." Kirk believed no person could say such a thing with assurance, for it is an exceedingly great mystery that belongs ultimately to the divine.

In Kirk's understanding of the human condition, the lighter shades of Plymouth were a necessary complement to the darker tones of Mecosta. Neither could exist without the other. Neither could be understood without the other. Kirk's imagination thrived in the tension between the two. To read his work is to trace paths into that ineffable mystery.

NOTES

1. William H. Honan, "Russell Kirk Is Dead at 75; Seminal Conservative Author," *New York Times*, April 30, 1994, 13.

2. For a brief biography of Kirk, see the preface by George Panichas, ed., in *The Essential Russell Kirk: Selected Essays* (Wilmington, DE: ISI Books, 2007), xi–xxv.

3. Bradley J. Birzer, *Russell Kirk: American Conservative* (Lexington: University Press of Kentucky, 2015), 292.

4. Russell Kirk, "The Exemplary Conservatives," in *The Essential Russell Kirk: Selected Essays*, ed. George Panichas (Wilmington, DE: ISI Books, 2007), 33.

5. Kirk, "The Exemplary Conservatives," 32–33; Russell Kirk, *The Sword of Imagination: Memoirs of a Half-Century of Literary Conflict* (Grand Rapids, MI: Eerdmans, 1995), 10.

6. Kirk, "The Exemplary Conservatives," 32; Kirk, "Reflections of a Gothic Mind," in *The Essential Russell Kirk*, 289.

7. Kirk, *The Sword of Imagination*, 2.

8. Kirk, 3.

9. Kirk, 4–5; Russell Kirk, "Reflections of a Gothic Mind," in *The Essential Russell Kirk*, 288; Kirk, *The Conservative Mind*, 71–113.

10. Kirk, *The Sword of Imagination*, 2–3.

11. Kirk, 5–6.

12. Kirk, 178.

13. George Washington, quoted in Gleaves Whitney, "The Upper Midwest as the Second Promised Land," in *Finding a New Midwestern History*, eds. Jon K. Lauck, Gleaves Whitney, and Joseph Hogan (Lincoln: University of Nebraska Press, 2018), 281, 297.

14. Kirk, "Reflections of a Gothic Mind," in *The Essential Russell Kirk*, 290.

15. Birzer, *Russell Kirk*, 292–93, 387.

9

ALL ONE THING

Seeking the Source of the Mississippi

A thin January sun spills through the pines as Itasca State Park supervisor Robert Chance shuttles my friend Andy and me through the northern Minnesota park, famous as the headwaters of the Mississippi River.[1] The roadsides are heaped in freshly plowed snow. The air is a crisp but hardly intense 10 degrees above zero.

At a boat landing not far from the headwaters, Robert swings the SUV around and muses, "These places that we find desirable have been desired by others before us." He is recalling the occasion—years earlier in his Minnesota Department of Natural Resources (DNR) career—when his vision of adding public access to a remote lake ran headlong into the archaeological remains of a Native American village at the site. But he could just as easily have been referring to Itasca itself, where the layering of landscape, the Mississippi River, and the human story are thickly intertwined.

A drive through the North Country where Lake Itasca resides quickly reveals that we're not in Kansas anymore, nor anywhere else in someone's impression of the Midwest. To Fly-Over scoffers, the Midwest is a long stretch of air flight reading, but here on the ground in northern Minnesota the landscape is pocked with glacial lakes hidden behind deep swaths of Northwoods pines or poking out from wide stretches where farms have replaced the prairie. The farms are less dense here, though, than in much of the Midwest, sharing the landscape with reeds and wetlands and long stretches without homes.

Andy and I have come to Itasca from Dubuque, Iowa, where the Mississippi passes 800 river miles downstream from the headwaters and 1,600 miles before it spills into the Gulf of Mexico. Here, too, the human story is tied tightly to the great river.

My home in Dubuque lies in the Driftless Area, another unique region of the Upper Midwest. The land is called "Driftless" because there is no glacial drift here—the glaciers repeatedly bypassed and even encircled the landscape, leaving it rugged amid the glacially sculpted Midwest. With its rugged, steep valleys, rock towers, and river bluffs, the Driftless has always struck me as a region of mystery. But I'd always thought that this great river must link as well to another place of equal, if different, mystery at its North Country source. Both the Driftless and the headwaters, it seemed to me, lay in contrast to the straight corn-rowed plains of the greater Midwest.

We'd both been to Lake Itasca before (Andy is Robert's brother-in-law) and in more inviting summer weather, but the timing worked out for a couple of teachers on semester break, so we loaded our snowshoes and overnight bags into my car and set off on a January road trip to the Mississippi headwaters.

Itasca is a thousand-acre northern Minnesota lake shaped like a wishbone, an inverted Y, with two lobes pronging off to the south. Or like inverted antlers, which may have led to its Ojibwe name, Omushkos, Elk Lake in English, called Lac Le Biche by the French before it was renamed Itasca.

A fledgling Mississippi River pours from the north end of the lake through a thirty-foot boulder-strewn outlet. The river here is knee deep, clear, and achingly cold in contrast to the giant that lumbers through the Driftless. Canoeists who ply their way from the headwaters to the Gulf of Mexico will, near Itasca, bump their crafts' noses on either side of the shore on any of the numerous bends in the river and may find themselves tugging their boats over the shallows. The river will grow by leaps and bounds from here. Lake Itasca lies 2,400 miles[2] above the Gulf of Mexico. By the time it reaches Louisiana, the Mississippi often exceeds a mile in width and runs almost two hundred feet deep near the French Quarter of New Orleans. At the Delta it will pour 420 billion gallons of water into the Gulf of Mexico each day.[3]

Located just two hundred miles south of the Canadian border as it exits Lake Itasca, the tiny Mississippi meanders north and east for sixty river miles till it is turned aside by a three-way continental divide on the Giants Range, a highlands plain. First the Laurentian Divide diverts waters on its north face to the Hudson Bay, then the St. Lawrence Divide diverts water east to the nearby Great Lakes and the St. Lawrence Seaway. Almost in recompense for rerouting the still-young river southward, the divides direct all waters on their southern and western flanks to the Mississippi, and on to a long journey through the Driftless and to the Gulf. In all, the Mississippi River, with help from the Missouri and Ohio Rivers, will drain 40 percent of the continental United States.[4]

The mystique of America's central river draws half a million tourists—domestic and international—to the headwaters each year. On a typical summer's day, young and old will totter across the slippery glacial boulders where the Mississippi pours forth. Dozens at a time wade across the pebbly-bottomed bed of the infant river.

Robert's wife, Kathy, tells us later that she remembers their young daughter playing in the newly birthed river with a girl her same age from another country who spoke no English. "The river was their common language," Kathy says.

■   ■   ■

Although the glaciers never reached the Driftless Area, their meltwaters carved and deepened the Mississippi Valley against a backdrop of cliff-like river bluffs. By contrast, those same mile-high glaciers deposited a maze of hills and ridges onto the Itasca landscape. The repeated advances and retreats of the mile-high ice left behind moraines, kames, eskers, and drumlins formed when the glaciers dropped their payloads of soil, sand, pebbly rubble, and well-polished boulders in their final melting retreat 12,000 years ago.

The fingerprints of glaciers are everywhere in the region. A hundred marshy glacial lakes dot the 33,000-acre Itasca State Park, many of which are kettle ponds formed from huge ice blocks that broke off from the retreating glaciers and then sank from their great weight into the still-soft glacial outwash. South of Lake Itasca, near Park Rapids, the land flattens out again, having first been bulldozed flat beneath an advancing glacier and then overlaid with outwash rubble from its meltwaters.

The Lake Itasca basin itself is a glacial tunnel valley, formed by a rushing river at the bottom of the ice that scoured out the land beneath the glacier. Today's lake covers 1,065 acres at an average depth of seventeen feet and a maximum of forty.

■ ■ ■

I am a lover of textured, layered landscapes and the stories of the peoples who settle there. From the Mississippi bluffs near my home I ponder sunrise mists loitering just above the river. Elsewhere in the Driftless, rock towers rear up unexpectedly where a country road descends and twists into a stream valley. Springs erupt mysteriously from the bedrock and disappear again into the karst landscape.

The human story in the Driftless is deeply connected to the landscape and the Mississippi River. Native Americans first called the Driftless Area home 12,000 years ago as they hunted just south of the glaciers. Later, Woodland period peoples built burial mounds, many in the shape of great bears and birds, above the Mississippi. The Meskwaki, Sauk, and Ho-Chunk witnessed the arrival of French Canadian trappers and miners such as my own town's Julien Dubuque, who came to mine lead in 1788. The 1832 massacre of the Sauk on the Mississippi, ending the so-called Black Hawk War, brought Euro-Americans, who established cities, towns, and farms along the river.

The human story at Itasca followed similar patterns, lagging somewhat in time as the ice retreated. Ancient peoples followed the melting glaciers northward, hunting megafauna just beyond the retreating ice. An 8,500-year-old bison kill site in the boggy landscape near the headwaters was unearthed in 1937. At the site, archaeologists found knives, scrapers, and arrow points used by the people, as well as bison, deer, bird, and fish bones. Later peoples built burial mounds not far from the headwaters.[5]

The Ojibwe populated the region beginning in the 1500s, having migrated westward from the Great Lakes and St. Lawrence River. Supported by the French, they battled and displaced the Dakota in the Itasca region by the early 1700s.[6]

French Canadian fur trappers began arriving in the 1600s, and Euro-American intrigue for locating the headwaters of the Mississippi River followed within a century. The Paris Treaty of 1783 ending the War of Independence established the Mississippi River as the western boundary of the United States, igniting a rush to locate the headwaters and firmly establish the border.[7] But the ganglia of northern Minnesota lakes and connecting rivers, as well as the lack of an established definition of a "headwaters," made exploration of, and agreement about, the true headwaters problematic. It would prove difficult to settle on a single source.

The British Canadian fur trader and surveyor David Thompson was among the earliest headwaters explorers, claiming Turtle Lake as the river's source in 1798.[8] But while that lake's waters flow into the Mississippi River, cartographers today call its inlet and outlet the Turtle River. The Mississippi lies south of Turtle Lake.

After the Louisiana Purchase moved the national border westward, General Zebulon Pike was commissioned by the U.S. government in 1805 to map the upper Mississippi River, study its plant and mineral resources, select locations for forts, and establish contacts with Native Americans. But Pike and his twenty soldiers set off too late in the year from St. Louis,[9] and by the time they reached Leech Lake, about 150 miles downstream from Itasca, deep winter had set in, and his men were ill fit for further travel. Pike knew of Thompson's earlier findings but declared the waters above Leech Lake too insubstantial to be called the Mississippi, and dubbed Leech Lake the headwaters instead. But Pike also took a small group of his men northward on a side expedition and simultaneously declared Red Cedar Lake, 30 miles upstream, a "minor upper source."[10] The "source" was moving upstream, and was perhaps not singular after all.

Next up was Lewis Cass, who in 1820 retraced Pike's journey as far as Upper Red Cedar Lake (today named Cass Lake) before turning around. Unlike Pike, however, he knew he hadn't reached the headwaters, having heard that the Mississippi could be traced to Lac Le Beche.[11]

In 1832—the same year that the Sauk were massacred at the Mississippi River a few hours north of my home in the Driftless—Henry Schoolcraft, a crewman from the Cass expedition, was commissioned by the U.S. government to visit the northern Minnesota region to settle disputes among tribes and inoculate them against smallpox. He set out toward Leech Lake with a crew of thirty-five to conduct his business. Schoolcraft made it his own separate and unannounced goal to reach the headwaters once and for all.[12]

Having completed much of his commissioned work, Schoolcraft left most of his men behind at Cass Lake in early July and set off with a smaller crew in search of the headwaters. Unlike previous explorers, Schoolcraft relied heavily on Ojibwe guides, most prominent among them Ozawindib, an Ojibwe chief. Each boat in the five-canoe flotilla also included Ojibwe guides and paddlers.[13]

As they neared Lac Le Beche,[14] Schoolcraft lamented the marshy ground wherever they had to portage: "A man who is called on for the first time, to debark, in such a place, will look about him to discover some dry spot to put his feet upon. No such spot however existed here. We stepped into rather warm pond water, with a miry bottom."[15]

Closer to Lac Le Biche, though, lay firmer ground, and Schoolcraft's mood lifted. He noted that others had once occupied this land: "The carbonaceous remains of former fires, the bones of birds and scattered camp poles, proved it to be a spot which had previous been occupied by the Indians."[16]

Portaging farther, they came at last upon Lac Le Beche on July 13. The lake, Schoolcraft writes, was "in every respect, a beautiful sheet of water seven or eight miles in extent. . . . The waters are transparent and bright, and reflect a foliage produced by the elm, lynn, maple, and cherry, together with other species more abundant in northern latitudes."[17]

Finally, he describes the outlet, the beginning of the Mississippi River, "perhaps ten to twelve feet broad, with an apparent depth of twelve to eighteen inches. The discharge of water appears to be copious, compared to its inlet," the lake's volume and discharge having been accentuated by numerous springs beneath its surface.[18]

On borrowed time away from his sanctioned and commissioned tasks, Schoolcraft and his party quickly planted a flag on the lake's only island and held a brief service whereupon Schoolcraft renamed Lac Le Biche by combining parts of the Latin words for "truth" and "head," verITAS CAput, or ITASCA.[19]

The name Elk Lake was later re-bestowed on another lake directly upstream from Itasca, thus depriving it, too, of its Ojibwe name.

It was all one thing, this loss of land and life, and even of names.

In 1836, the French geographer Joseph Nicolett poked a few holes in Schoolcraft's headwaters exploration—inlet holes, to be exact. After charting several inlet streams and upper lakes that fed into Itasca, Nicolett graciously claimed, "I come only after these gentlemen [Schoolcraft and his crew], but I may be permitted to claim some merit for having completed what was wanting for a full geographical account."[20] But he had opened the door to considering whether the Mississippi could be traced to a single source.

Fifty years later, in 1881, the Civil War leader and travel writer Captain Willard Glazier laid out his rationale as to why Itasca *was not* the headwaters. Glazier pointed to a small creek flowing into Itasca from an upstream lake he claimed to have found. In the tradition of headwaters explorers before him, Glazier published a narrative of his discovery and promptly named the new lake after himself. But suspicion soon arose when the public noticed Glazier's plagiarisms from Schoolcraft's text (e.g., "the beautiful sheet of water").[21] The newly discovered Glazier Lake turned out to be the already-discovered Elk Lake.[22]

Glazier eventually admitted his fraudulent writings and discoveries. But the question still remained: if Elk Lake lay upstream from Lake Itasca, which one *was* the headwaters of the Mississippi? Was there even a single source?

In 1888–89, the Minnesota Historical Society commissioned the surveyor Jacob Brower to settle once and for all the debate over the headwaters. Brower split the difference, so to speak. He acknowledged that upper lakes and streams contributed flowage to Lake Itasca and in that sense might be considered *as a region* to constitute the headwaters. But these streams and flowages were small (he called them the "infant Mississippi"), and even occasionally dried up in the heat of summer. Only the stream leaving Lake Itasca was constant, significant, and long enough to be called a *river,* and thus he declared Lake Itasca the headwaters of the Mississippi.[23]

In the end, it was Western linear thinking *par excellence*—or *par obsession*—that insisted there be an identifiable single headwaters to the Mississippi.

The Ojibwe, despite participating as guides, were overall bemused by this obsession. According to the Leech Lake Reservation Historian Larry Aitken, to the Ojibwe "it was amusing, that aggressive effort. . . . Because it was not important where it started—the whole river was of central importance."[24]

It was all one thing.

■ ■ ■

Robert, Andy, and I abandon the relative comfort of the SUV to hike the quarter-mile trail down to the headwaters. Soon the Mississippi lies in front of us: a narrow and shallow stream tumbling energetically over glacially rounded boulders, emptying from the lake in a swath about thirty feet wide. The lake itself is iced over, but the stream bubbles with such vivacity that it flows unobstructed for some distance.

We watch the tiny Mississippi emerge for a while. I consider edging down to the shore to stick my hand into the bubbling waters to say that I had *touched* the river that will flow past my home, but, having moments earlier almost slid into the water across the ice-encrusted snow, I decide otherwise.

Robert has other things to show us, so after a short while, we retrace our steps. About thirty feet downstream, Robert pivots and shows us erosional damage occurring as the exuberant stream collides with the shoreline, the damage accentuated by millions of tourist feet over time. Robert would like to rearrange the glacial boulders at the outlet to channel the flow more to the center, but the idea is receiving some flak from historical societies, he tells us, which is ironic because in the 1930s, the Civilian Conservation Corps (CCC) moved the river's outlet some distance from where Schoolcraft had encountered it, to create better tourist access away from the marshes.[25] Robert points out a dearth of trees in the distant marsh where the Mississippi had formerly emerged. To say that *this one place* has always been the headwaters flies in the face of history.

■ ■ ■

The logging industry followed exploration of the headwaters almost immediately. In 1837, the U.S. government wrested possession of northern Minnesota and northern Wisconsin from the Ojibwe, and 1838 brought the first entrepreneurs with eyes set on the expansive northern forests. The first northern Minnesota sawmill commenced ripping trunks into floatable logs the following year.[26] These logs would be bound together and floated down the Mississippi to sawmills in Driftless Area river towns like my own.

Massive old-growth pines fueled the drive, with 3.5 million acres of northern Minnesota dominated by white pines up to four hundred years old. A single such tree, according to the Minnesota forester Chuck Wingard, could "build a small barn, a farmhouse, a church."[27] By 1900, over 30,000 lumberjacks worked the northern Minnesota forests, harvesting $1 billion worth of trees annually. Although awareness was already growing that the great forests were dwindling, the industry continued felling pines, seeing deforestation as merely the first step to opening up the land to agriculture.[28]

Having established Lake Itasca as the Mississippi River headwaters, Jacob Brower and a small group of conservationists lobbied to preserve the last stands of native pines in the vicinity of the lake. In 1891, by a one-vote majority of the state legislature, Itasca became Minnesota's first state park, and the second-oldest state park in the nation. But the law only provided the state with a patchwork ownership of lands surrounding the lake. It provided even fewer resources for regulating the logging industry.[29] Some areas of the intended park boundaries were still privately owned and open to logging, and the lake and river remained available to loggers to float their product. Loggers and the early park commissioners quarreled over how much the loggers could dam the lake and flood the river to float their logs downstream.

One of the most important figures in the battle with loggers was Mary Gibbs, named Interim Commissioner in 1903 at age twenty-four when her father, the park's fourth commissioner, died unexpectedly. Objecting that logging dams threatened the survival of shoreline trees by raising the water level of the lake, Gibbs famously confronted loggers who threatened to shoot if she so much as touched their headwaters dam. Gibbs retorted, "I will, too, put my hand on [the dam levers], and you will not shoot it off."[30] The loggers sat by as Gibbs raised the dam gate and lowered the water level on the lake. Gibbs's persistence established that Lake Itasca would not be destroyed for the sake of logging.

By the 1920s, all logging had ceased at Itasca State Park.

Despite—or because of—her success, Mary Gibbs's tenure as Interim Park Commissioner lasted only four months before she was replaced.

■ ■ ■

A sign back at the Itasca State Park interpretive center reads "Come for the river, return for the pines." It is all one thing. But Robert reminds us that the pines, not the river, were the reason for the park's inception. Indeed, the park today harbors 20 percent of Minnesota's remaining old-growth forest.

We are back on the park roads again in Robert's SUV, and he is commenting on the current state of the forest. The few remaining old-growth red pines date roughly back to the 1700s. Along the road we see numerous downed trees and stumps whose trunks snapped about three feet off the ground during wind storms in 2012 and 2016. Robert explains that the blown-over trees had been weakened or already killed by age, disease, pests, and past wind storms. Foresters are reseeding with white pine where possible.

The forest also harbors deciduous trees typical of the Northwoods, like aspen and birch, as well as hardwood oak and maple. Some of these, too, are battling infestations, like the emerald ash borer. Climate change exacerbates the problems. Robert, who grew up in northeast Minnesota's Iron Range, remembers long winter stretches when night-time temperatures plummeted to –40 degrees. Such long, intense cold spells were integral to knocking back pest populations.

■ ■ ■

The Mississippi River had already become a highway of floating logs before Itasca began harvesting its forests. By 1836, the first of several steam sawmills began operating in Dubuque to cut the logs that had been floated downstream in massive lumber rafts.

And though Mary Gibbs put a stop to a logging dam that endangered the Itasca shoreline, the downstream Mississippi River would later be harnessed with twenty-seven locks and dams from the Twin Cities to southern Illinois in a 1930s Works Progress Administration (WPA) project to ensure a nine-foot-deep channel for barges. Lock and Dam #11 stretches across the Mississippi River at Dubuque.

The environmental impact of the lock-and-dam system is complicated. A typical fifteen-barge tow can move as much grain as a thousand semi trucks. But large amounts of silt are trapped behind the dams, slowly filling up back-water habitats.

Then again, in winter the agitation below the dam gates provides open water that attracts bald eagles scoping for fish in the otherwise frozen river.

■ ■ ■

This is wolf country, Robert says, back on the road at Itasca. A wolf pack is known to live in the southern end of the park. Its alpha male occasionally strays south of the park, but not too far, because another pack's boundary lies nearby. Similarly, a wolf pack to the north avoids the park. "It's as if they've adopted the park boundaries as their own," Robert says.

The vast Itasca forest, bog, and meadow habitats harbor a Northern Midwest wildlife oasis. A 2003 publication of the Minnesota Department of Natural Resources listed *canis lupis*—the Gray Wolf—as "Common,"[31] not so many years after a 1959 report had indicated the once-prolific species was "no longer present in the park."[32] In addition to the usual Northlands roster of mammals (shrews, rabbits, rodents, beavers, raccoons, foxes, coyotes, squirrels, and the like), Itasca is home to black bears and minks (Common) and bobcats and mountain lions (Rare). The Woodland Jumping Mouse is "Rare," but would be really cool to see.[33]

The quality of lake habitat is under duress, however. Upstream from Lake Itasca, Elk Lake may finally be getting its due attention—from biologists, at least—after having been denied status as the headwaters. Elk Lake is one of twenty-four "sentinel lakes" scattered throughout Minnesota being studied to determine "how major drivers of change, such as development, agriculture, climate change, and invasive species, can affect lake habitats. Elk Lake was selected to represent a deep, mesotrophic lake in the Northern Lakes and Forests

(NLF) ecoregion. With the exception of a group campsite and a paved nature trail, there is no development on Elk Lake."[34] In addition, "approximately two thirds of Elk Lake's watershed was never logged."[35]

That said, the health of Elk Lake is still at risk. Despite not being directly touched by human habitation, it hasn't escaped the latent effects of humans on the environment at large. Elk Lake saw an increase in lake temperature of 1–2 degrees from 1985 to 2010, with resultant declines in native fish species.[36]

Nearly lost amid the fifty-four-page biological study is a quick line stating "[Elk Lake] represents the headwaters of the Mississippi River."[37]

■ ■ ■

The river that exits the North Country develops a whole new set of environmental issues as it lumbers through the rest of the Midwest and beyond. The Mississippi is much maligned for carrying erosional silt, as well as fertilizer, pesticides, and other chemicals from agricultural, industrial, and residential runoff—a drainage ditch, its detractors call it. The critics are as right as they are wrong. The Mississippi River, for example, carries so much fertilizer that it annually creates a 6,500-square-mile dead zone in the Gulf of Mexico.

But at the same time, the Upper Mississippi National Wildlife and Fish Refuge offers one of the largest havens for wildlife in the nation. Established in 1924, the refuge covers 240,000 acres along 261 river miles from Wabasha, Minnesota (250 as-the-crow-flies miles from Lake Itasca), to Rock Island, Illinois. The refuge, with its forested bluffs jutting up to six hundred feet above the river, hosts 306 bird species, 250 bald eagle nests, 5,000 heron and egret nests, 50 percent of the world's canvasback ducks, 51 mammal species, 42 mussel species, and 111 species of fish. Forty percent of the nation's waterfowl use the Mississippi, including the refuge, as their migration highway in spring and fall.[38]

As for me, I lament the departure of Canada geese each fall and greet their return in the spring as they follow the Mississippi River and its watershed tributaries, collecting from and returning to the east and the west and the north, forming a vast overhead network like the veins of a single, overarching leaf in the sky.

■ ■ ■

Robert and Kathy invite Andy and me to dinner at their rural home outside of Bemidji the evening after we've surveyed the park with Robert. Robert's kenneled hunting dogs greet us as we pull in, the January sun waning in the frigid western sky. We tell stories well into the night. Kathy has wrapped up a fund-raising position at Bemidji Public Television and is about to embark on a new position fund-raising for the Page Education Foundation. Their daughter has made Itasca-themed presents out of popsicle sticks and paper for her uncle Andy and me. Robert, who abounded with information and stories earlier in the day at Itasca, is quieter now in the evening. We learn, though, that his retirement—originally intended just weeks away—is on a short delay so that their daughter can bring her classmates to the park in May, to be introduced to Daddy's park.

The house is warm against a cold night.

When Andy and I return to Itasca, to the Four Seasons cabin complex, under a starlit sky and in biting cold, another occupant has settled in at the four-plex—probably an ice fisherman.

We settle in for the night.

Itasca State Park has a long tradition of hosting visitors, whether in grand style or in primitive sites. A mere decade after the park's founding, the Itasca Park Lodge was built, later to be renamed the Douglas Lodge after Minnesota Attorney General Wallace B. Douglas, who had fought fiercely to establish the park. The lodge was constructed with rustic downed pine timber from the Itasca forest. It was designed to house the Park Commissioner and more than two dozen guests, "with sixteen rooms and numerous and commodious closets," a 36-by-22-foot "great room" walled with oiled and shellacked "rough logs," and a large stone fireplace.[39]

Since then, of course, additional cabins have been constructed at Itasca, some of them rustic and some more elaborate, but none with the grand elegance of the Douglas Lodge. And the park offers over two hundred campsites for tents, trailers, and RVs.

■ ■ ■

I am writing at 7:00 a.m. from the kitchenette of the Four Seasons cabin on the morning of January 10, just a single light on above me near the stove where I have heated up some coffee. It's still dark outside, but the day begins to lighten around 7:30. Andy is still asleep. Outside it is 5 degrees, already up from -5 when we returned to the cabin last night. The Weather Channel announces that the Lake Itasca region will be warmer than normal in the thirty-day forecast.

Our time with Robert having been completed the day before, Andy and I retrieve our snowshoes from the car and head north along the eastern lobe—or antler—of Lake Itasca. We'll "discover" the headwaters on snowshoes, we figure.

But as an hour or more ticks off and our progress has been slight, we cede the headwaters discovery back to Schoolcraft and set a new goal. We'll cross Lake Itasca on snowshoes. After all, there are numerous pickup trucks parked on the ice in the middle of the lake while their owners fish from an assortment of huts.

Twenty feet out onto the lake, our shoeprints fill with water. This is not good. We try another spot, and again our tracks fill with water about twenty feet from the shore. It could be that the underlying ice is solid and a thin layer of slush has accumulated in the insulating snow cover. After all, those pickup trucks out in the center of the lake. . . . But then, I have read (from Schoolcraft among others) that Lake Itasca is fed by lake-bottom springs, and perhaps at certain places the spring water weakens the ice cover from underneath. The ice fishermen may know the safe route onto the ice. We are not ice fishermen.

We abandon the hike. Our wives and colleagues, via Facebook, think it a wise choice. Our adult children are delirious with derision. We're too embarrassed to ask Robert. That night, back at the cabin, I Google the matter. Slush on top of the ice may be normal and entirely safe. Unless there are springs underneath.

■ ■ ■

The cold follows us back to Dubuque the next day, traveling faster than the river waters. The winter has been mild so far back home, but within a few days of our arrival a six-inch snowfall pummels the town. A day after the snowfall I am on the road again, this time with nine Loras College students en route to the other end of the Mississippi, to New Orleans, for a Gulf Coast environmental restoration service trip. The delta is sinking relative to rising sea levels, in part because the channelized and dammed river no longer spreads its replenishing hoard of silt out over the bayou. It is all one connected thing.

■ ■ ■

My wife and I return to Lake Itasca six months later, in June. Our family is vacationing at a Minnesota lake two hours away, and one rainy day we ditch the cabin and head north to the headwaters.

We won't call it an idyllic day. The mosquitoes bite us ravenously. The headwaters trail is crowded. But we play for a while, as we should, in the infant Mississippi waters.

Driving home later in the week, we watch the landscape change before us. The North Country's vast flatland forests and eyeball lakes give way to rolling hills, and then to steeper and steeper rock towers in the Driftless. We have exited one region of mystery and reentered another.

But as unique as these regions are—how utterly unlike some Fly-Over airflight passenger's vision of the Midwest—it occurs to me on our drive home how much is connected in some way to this river. We cross the Minnesota River, which joins the Mississippi at the Twin Cities. Then the Root River, the Zumbro, the Upper Iowa—all flowing to the great river.

The Mississippi River enters the Driftless Area just south of the Twin Cities. If river lengths have a life, the Mississippi leaves its youth behind in the North Country. By the time it reaches the Driftless it has entered its prime, bisecting steep river bluffs. Every drop of water in every Midwest stream (and well beyond) wends a path to the Mississippi. By New Orleans, the river has aged but carries with it the weight and power of wisdom.

But here at Itasca begins our Mississippi River, clean, clear, and tumbling forth over a cascade of rounded stones.

And here in the thirty-foot-wide river with its glacially pebbled bottom play the children from various lands, all speaking a common language.

■   ■   ■

The Ojibwe did not understand the white men's obsession with finding the headwaters. All the river's waters and tributaries played a role in watering the earth.

Jacob Brower echoed the Ojibwe in at least one small way. While he declared once and for all that the Mississippi River began at and flowed from Lake Itasca, he conceded that the waters flowing into Itasca from several upstream lakes and creeks contributed to the Mississippi River as well. He called these upstream sources the "Greater Ultimate Reservoir."[40]

He almost said it, but not quite: *It is all one thing.*

NOTES

1. Robert Chance served as Itasca State Park (Minnesota) Supervisor from 2012 to 2019, and began his service with the Minnesota Department of Natural Resources (DNR) in 1977. He retired six months after the date of this interview. Special thanks as well to Connie Cox, lead interpretive naturalist at Itasca State Park, who gave me a primer on all things Itasca and directed me to several key sources.

2. River miles are notoriously hard to measure. Calvin R. Fremling, in *Immortal River: The Upper Mississippi in Ancient and Modern Times* (Madison: University of Wisconsin Press, 2005), puts the length at 2,301 miles. A signpost at the headwaters states 2,551. I'll split the difference at 2,400 miles.

3. Fremling, 16.

4. Fremling, 12.

5. Paul S. Martin, "Extinct Bison in Minnesota," *Ecology* 52, no. 6 (1971): 1137–1137, www.jstor.org/stable/1933829, accessed April 6, 2020.

6. "The History of the Ojibwe People," an excerpt from *The Land of the Ojbwe*, booklet (St. Paul: Minnesota Historical Society, 1973).

7. "Exploring the Mississippi Headwaters," Read the Plaque, https://readtheplaque .com/plaque/exploring-the-mississippi-headwaters, accessed April 6, 2020.

8. Joseph Tyrell, *David Thompson, Explorer* (n.p., 1900, digitized by the University of Toronto), https://archive.org/stream/davidthompsonexpootyrr/davidthompson expootyrr_djvu.txt.

9. Pike passed through the Driftless on his way north and visited Julien Dubuque to gather information about the lead mines in the region that would later become my hometown.

10. Zebulon Montgomery Pike, *Exploratory Travels Through the Western Territories of North America* (London: Longman, Hurst, Rees, Orme, and Brown, 1811), 75.

11. *The Search for the Great River's Source*, booklet (Park Rapids, MN: Itasca State Park, n.d.), 6.

12. Philip P. Mason, ed., *Schoolcraft's Expedition to Lake Itasca* (East Lansing: Michigan State University Press, 1958), xii–xiv.

13. Norah Deakin Davis, *The Father of Waters: A Mississippi River Chronicle* (San Francisco: Sierra Club Books, 1982), 15.

14. Schoolcraft uses the name Lac Le Biche, rather than Omushkas or Elk Lake, in his memoir. Thus, I use that name here.

15. Henry Rowe Schoolcraft, *Schoolcraft's Narrative of an Expedition Through the Upper Mississippi, to Itasca Lake, in Schoolcraft's Expedition to Lake Itasca*, ed. Philip P. Mason (East Lansing: Michigan State University Press, 1958), 33.

16. Schoolcraft, 33.

17. Schoolcraft, 36.

18. Schoolcraft, 36.

19. *The Search for the Great River's Source*, 6.

20. Timothy Severin, *Explorers of the Mississippi* (New York: Alfred A. Knopf, 1967), 282.

21. Captain Willard Glazier, *Headwaters of the Mississippi* (Chicago: Rand, McNally, 1893), 339.

22. Severin, *Explorers of the Mississippi*, 283–88.

23. Jacob Brower, The Report of the Commissioner of the Itasca State Park, May 9, 1891 to December 8, 1892 (Minneapolis: Harrison and Smith, 1893), 18.

24. Itasca State Park Information Center, June 29, 2016.

25. Robert Chance, interview with the author, January 9, 2019.

26. Joe Steck, "Logging Boom and the Birthplace of Minnesota," *Mankato Times*, March 14, 2017, http://mankatotimes.com/2017/03/14/a-moment-in-time-logging-boom -and-the-birthplace-of-minnesota/.

27. Leif Enger, "A History of Timbering in Minnesota," Minnesota Public Radio, November 16, 1998, http://news.minnesota.publicradio.org/features/199811/16_engerl_history-m/.

28. Enger, "A History of Timbering in Minnesota."

29. Connie Cox, *Mary Gibbs: A Shining Light for Itasca* (Park Rapids, MN: Itasca State Park, 2008), 10–12.

30. Cox, 23.

31. Robert S. Sikes, John R. Tester, and Ben Thoma, *Mammals of Itasca State Park* (Park Rapids, MN: Itasca State Park, Minnesota Department of Natural Resources, 2003), 5.

32. Sikes, Tester, and Thoma, 28.

33. Sikes, Tester, and Thoma, 4.

34. Sentinel Lake Assessment Report, Elk Lake (15-0010), Clearwater County, Minnesota (St. Paul: Minnesota Department of Natural Resources, 2011), 1.

35. Sentinel Lake Assessment Report, 3.

36. Sentinel Lake Assessment Report, 12 and 32.

37. Sentinel Lake Assessment Report, 1.

38. U.S. Fish and Wildlife Service, "Upper Mississippi River National Wildlife and Fish Refuge," www.fws.gov/refuge/upper_mississippi_river, accessed June 17, 2016.

39. Connie Cox, *Douglas Lodge: Minnesota's Own Resort* (Park Rapids, MN: Itasca State Park, n.d.), 7–8.

40. Brower, *Report of the Commissioner*, 18.

10

THE MYSTERIOUS MIGRATION
OF A MARVELOUS MASTODON

I

Think of this as the story of the extinct elephant in the room—and a creature whose journey suggests an upper boundary for the Midwest. The room is the gleaming lobby of the North Dakota Heritage Center, next door to the state capitol in Bismarck. Visitors are greeted by what has become the state's iconic American mastodon. The bones of this long-extinct beast emerged in the late nineteenth century from the muck of lowlands in southern Ontario. Then, after fleeting fame and an unlikely westward odyssey, they went missing again, only to be rediscovered almost a century later.

"It is well known," wrote Thomas Jefferson in 1787, "that on the Ohio and in many parts of America further north, tusks, grinders, and skeletons of unparalleled magnitude, are found in great numbers, some lying on the surface of the earth, and some a little below it."[1] Jefferson never traveled so far west or north himself, but he studied reports of these legendary beasts. The mastodons were cousins of mammoths and ancestral kin to elephants. And Jefferson knew of Native American myths suggesting that beyond the seaboard settlements of the infant republic great beasts still might roam.

Ancestors of mastodons emigrated from Eurasia across the Bering Strait land bridge maybe two million years ago. Their habitat? Primarily the Midwest: Michigan, Ohio, Indiana, Illinois, Wisconsin, Minnesota, and into the Dakotas—and southern Ontario (Canada's Midwest?). While remains have been found elsewhere in North America, they are most abundant in an area once covered by the Laurentide Ice Sheet. And they have often been uncovered accidentally by farmers or construction crews.

American mastodons lived on the needles of spruce and tamarack trees common to what paleontologists call a spruce parkland or sedge wetland environment. As the glaciers receded, newly exposed land was colonized by new plants and animals. Mastodons found themselves in closed forests, with fewer spruce and far more abundant deciduous trees. By 13,000 years ago, their population had dwindled. And their demise was likely hastened by humans, Paleo-Indian hunters whose spear points were found with mastodon bones.

Mastodons "north of the Ohio" migrated farther north as the glacier retreated. Their northern limit was traced in the 1950s by a pair of University of Michigan archaeologists, R. J. Mason and G. I. Quimby. Mason and Quimby discerned a pattern as they mapped mastodon discoveries in the bogs, ponds, and lakes that dotted the Michigan landscape—plentiful traps for these "megaherbivores." In addition, salt deposits and saline water in southern Lower Michigan drew mastodons from throughout the Great Lakes who needed to replenish their salt.[2]

The largest-known trail of mastodon footprints was found near Ann Arbor, and the University of Michigan's Natural History Museum is the only place in the United States where both male and female skeletons are displayed. Michigan legislators more recently named the mastodon their state fossil. Nor were mastodon finds such a rarity elsewhere in the Upper Midwest. Bones were often, as Jefferson suggested, "a little below" the surface, and thus readily discovered along a line arcing from southern Ontario into the Dakotas.

Later researchers would call this curving edge of the ice sheet the Mason-Quimby Line (map 5). Mason-Quimby suggests a plausible northern boundary, stretching back to prehistory, for what is commonly considered the Midwest. By a coincidence of names, it offers a complement to the Mason-Dixon Line, which, extending west, followed the Ohio River to the Mississippi and then back up that

Map 5. The Mason-Quimby Line denotes the northern limit of the region in which mastodon and mammoth remains have been discovered around the Great Lakes.

river to become the southern boundary of Iowa. The mysterious northwesterly trail that led the Canadian mastodon to Bismarck followed the general course of the Mason-Quimby Line. Another coincidence, to be sure, but thereon hangs a tale.

II

In 1886, a century after Jefferson's account, three young men were digging a drainage ditch on William Reycraft's farm near Highgate, in southern Ontario. By then the frontier was fading. The great beasts were understood to be long extinct. Their habitat had yielded to forests, to man, and then to agriculture. North of the Ohio, and farther west, lay North America's richest soils, often edged by swamp and swale. As Reycraft's nephew, John Reycraft, dug in such soft earth, his shovel struck something hard. Not a rock, he discovered, but a massive bone. And there were more.

Word spread through the little farm community just north of Lake Erie, although a bone or two was not such an extraordinary find. Mastodon as well as mammoth fragments turned up in the area with some frequency. William Reycraft regarded his as little more than a curiosity. Still, he decided to exhibit them in the Kent County agricultural hall. Eventually reports of the discovery piqued the interest of a pair of enterprising promoters, John Jelly and his nephew, William Hillhouse. Jelly had earlier profited from the display of mammoth bones in his hometown of Shelburne, Ontario.[3]

In 1890, the two men paid William Reycraft the considerable sum of $25 Canadian for the rights to dig deeper in his swale. Jelly put a crew to work. By nightfall on the second day of digging they had filled two wagons with what the *Chatham Tri-Weekly Planet* described as "ancient ossifications." There was a jawbone more than two feet across, a shinbone four and a half feet long, a shoulder blade "as large as the top of a No. 9 stove." All the bones were found within a radius of fifteen yards, at a depth of four to five feet.[4] "The cavity of the eye, from whence the fire of a mastodon eye shone around the swamps of Kent in prehistoric times," the *Planet* noted, "is almost large enough to admit a man's head."[5]

News accounts speculated on a creature reaching twenty feet in height with a weight four times that of Jumbo, the famous elephant of Barnum and Bailey's Circus, who was said to weigh five tons. Although the lower jawbone alone weighed upward of one hundred pounds, the "Highgate Monster," as it happened, was not quite as grand as originally claimed. The skeleton, probably that of a young adult male, actually proved closer in size to an Indian elephant, standing about ten feet tall at the shoulder. The discovery nonetheless became a media sensation. Reycraft soon regretted his $25 sale. How much would Jelly take to "forego his bargain?" Said the *Planet,* "the answer was that $3,000 couldn't do it."[6]

Why such a high price? Because the remains were so extensive that they could become a lucrative curiosity. The beast was estimated to be 95 percent intact, making it one of the most complete fossilized skeletons ever found in North America. The bones were photographed in the presence of correspondents "of all the leading papers of Canada and the U. S.," the *Planet* reported. The *Toronto Globe* described the discovery, in terms worthy of an age of hyperbole, as "equaling, if not surpassing, anything yet known to science."[7] Jelly and Hillhouse cleaned the bones, then strengthened them with layers of hot white glue. One tusk was all that was missing. The other, Hillhouse reported, was "a perfect beauty"—until one of the workmen slipped while carrying it to the ditch to wash it. The "perfect beauty" was broken in two places and had to be glued back together.

Jelly and Hillhouse mounted a display in a Highgate storefront, then began touring neighboring towns and festivals (a tooth disappeared while the skeleton was on exhibit in Guelph, Ontario). The fossils would be laid out on a platform, or atop the big chests in which they were transported. They drew crowds. A Shelburne resident recalled the excitement when the bones came to his city. "They were nine days a wonder," he wrote, "and a countryside of people called to see them."[8]

In this Victorian age, before mass communication, the discovery of such remains promised entertainment as well as education. The arrival of radio was a generation away, phonographs were still rare, and travel beyond the nearest farm town depended on a carriage or, at best, a rail line. In the rural Midwest, the circus came to bigger towns. Maybe an orator gave a lecture or a performer found a local stage. But a mass culture of entertainment was just dawning.

In Chicago, the hub of the Midwest, the great Columbian Exhibition opened in 1893. This was the beginning of mass entertainment of a sort. From the White City of temporary exhibits, to exotic scenes from around the world, to Buffalo Bill Cody's Wild West Show, this was entertainment on a scale beyond anything tried before. Hundreds of thousands of Americans converged on a single venue. Otherwise, this was the era of Barnum and Bailey. And in smaller towns, it was the era of *The Music Man*. On its Ontario tour, the Highgate Mastodon was accompanied by Jelly's "Mastodon Brass Band." (Mastodons were in vogue south of the border as well, with at least two troupes of "mastodon minstrels" also on tour.) In that same year of 1893, Jelly and Hillhouse turned to another promoter, Robert Essery, to widen the reach of their prize bones. They apparently leased the skeleton to Essery to take "The World's Greatest Wonder" on the road. Transporting the bones required six padded crates, weighing in at 1,200 pounds.[9] Essery ventured west, putting up posters in the Midwest and western Canada proclaiming "a monster unearthed! Do not fail to see the Highgate Mastodon!" When the promoter reached Edmonton, Alberta, however, he was stricken with typhoid fever and died.

Essery and the mastodon had followed the vanishing frontier. In the 1890s, new railroads were luring settlers. In the upper Midwest, immigrant farmers, many from Germany or Scandinavia, built settlements that often felt provisional. The loss by Native Americans of their "Indian Lands," which the railroads offered cheaply to new arrivals, was in many ways an open wound. Just three years earlier, in 1890, a U.S. Seventh Cavalry detachment in South Dakota massacred Lakota families attending a ghost dance at Wounded Knee. North Dakota had become a state only the year before.

III

The mastodon lost its lowland lake-plain habitat 13,000 years ago. Canada lost its Highgate Mastodon in 1893 with the death of Robert Essery, when someone else took the fossils south of the border. They were exhibited in towns that lay along rail lines, and rather coincidentally along the Mason-Quimby Line. Neche,

North Dakota, was one village where handbills went up, under the charge of a pair of promoters named Thompson and Glover.

Sometime soon after, for reasons no one has discovered, the bones ended up as unclaimed freight in storage at the Bibb Broom Corn Company, on Third Street North in Minneapolis. In 1896, Harry Dickinson, a Great Northern Railway fireman who may have been familiar with the heavy crates from their transit along Great Northern routes, bought the mastodon from Bibb Broom Corn and paid $11 to ship it to his father, a railroad man in Barnesville, Minnesota. There, father and son unpacked and carefully reassembled the numbered bones.[10]

The Dickinsons exhibited the mastodon around Minnesota, from St. Cloud to Willmar to Moorhead, with forays into South Dakota, all presumably on stops served by the recently organized Great Northern Line. In 1896, a prominent physician, James Grassick, was apparently among the visitors when the Dickinsons spread out the bones in Grand Forks, North Dakota. In 1898, the mastodon was displayed in Minneapolis, at 213 Nicollet Avenue. But young Harry Dickinson was ready to set out farther west, and in 1899 decided to sell the bones. He placed a newspaper ad and also contacted Doctor Grassick. "I have traveled with this skeleton through a part of Minn. and S. D.—two yrs. ago, and showed for over a year," he wrote, "and as I have no use for it would sooner take $10 for it now then to keep it any longer."[11]

The value of the mastodon had always been the revenue it could generate on display. Now the Minneapolis exhibit was closing. Dickinson was anxious. Would Grassick like to buy it? "I intend to leave the city next Monday or Tuesday so if you wish these massive bones," Dickinson told the doctor, "let me hear from you by return mail for if not sold by Sunday I will not let it go for that price." Grassick paid the $10, becoming the third or fourth owner. Dickinson hauled the crates to the Great Northern depot in Minneapolis and had them shipped, along with a sample of handbills and a print of the mastodon, to Grand Forks. (The freight bill of $27.84 suggests where the greater cost lay.)[12]

Back in Ontario, Hillhouse and Jelly had been at pains for years to recover their great discovery. When Essery died, however, they were at a loss. Then a packet arrived in the mail for Hillhouse. It included a handbill from an exhibition of the mastodon, probably sent by a niece who lived in Neche, in the northeastern corner of North Dakota. So the bones were still on tour, although Glover and Thompson never turned up again. Jelly had died in 1895, his wonder of nature unrecovered.

But Hillhouse held out hope. In 1902, Grassick loaned the bones to the University of North Dakota in Grand Forks. The curator of the young university's fledgling museum, the biology professor M. A. Brannon, was excited to display such significant fossils. He proudly boasted of the loan to a reporter from the *Grand Forks Herald*.[13] The news soon reached Hillhouse. The Canadian quickly tried to reassert his claim to ownership of the Highgate Mastodon. A flurry of correspondence ensued.

In June 1902, Hillhouse wrote to the president of the university. His stationery bore the ornate letterhead of his Ontario hardware store. "I have just read in an American newspaper an article that excites my curiosity," he reported. He described the original excavation, and his care for the remains. "We lost track of them for some time," he continued, "until one day a friend of mine sent a handbill from Neche, N. D. announcing the showing of a mastodon skeleton." The handbill mentioned Jelly and on the back was a picture of the crew at the excavation site. "I am in that photo," Hillhouse said, "and we paid for that photo to be taken."[14]

The university forwarded Hillhouse's letter to Grassick, who lived in nearby Buxton. The doctor offered Hillhouse a cordial, if cautious, reply. He conceded that the skeleton he had purchased in Minneapolis three years earlier "corresponds in some points [he had written "a good many" but crossed that out to say "some"] to the description you give of your specimen—and if originally the same—it certainly has had quite a romantic history."[15] Meanwhile, Grassick wrote to Harry Dickinson, who replied that when he owned the bones, "at least two different parties claimed they had a right to claim the skeleton . . . but nothing was ever done about it." These two parties were likely Hillhouse and the executor for the estate of John Jelly.

Hillhouse, for his part, was not about to be put off by Grassick's airy reference to "a romantic history." He hired a lawyer to pursue his claim with the university, citing the "strange and fortuitous chance" by which the mastodon had arrived on campus. "The skeleton," attorney John W. Douglas wrote, ". . . is THE finest ever discovered." He hoped the question of ownership could be settled amicably. "It may be that Mr. Hillhouse may personally call to arrange the matter as he once carried on business near Devils Lake [ninety miles west of Grand Forks], and has yet quite an interest in your state. . . . He hopes that the college authorities will aid him in regaining possession of so unique a piece of property."

Douglas also wrote to Grassick. There was not "the ghost of a doubt" that the bones were those that belonged to Jelly and Hillhouse, he declared. Indeed, "Justice at once demands that you be paid all outlay [his client would do that] . . . I presume that you will be equally willing to surrender the skeleton. . . . With two parties actuated by justice the matter can soon be arranged." Douglas offered Grassick swift reimbursement so that his client could regain possession "of these long preserved relics of a bygone time." Grassick replied that he would "carefully consider" the proposition.[16]

The doctor was unsettled—and upset that the university had publicized his loan of the skeleton. Brannon, the museum curator, offered a hasty defense against Grassick's charge of "talking too much." "I told the reporter of the *Grand Forks Herald* in order to advertise the loan, and give publication to the possession of such a rare thing," he wrote. While admitting he was no lawyer, Brannon told Grassick, "it seems to me that your title is absolute and unquestionable."[17]

The curator suggested that Hillhouse was trying to regain possession "years after the natural right has expired." But he also talked to the chair of the university's board of trustees, William Budge: "He said that if you could give the university a bill of sale for the mastodon that the state of N.D. would see to it that it was kept here."[18]

So, the university would buy the skeleton, and the state would defend the acquisition. Grassick was feeling the pressure. He soon received a letter from the relatives of Jelly as well. They vowed to "investigate the matter fully." He wrote to the Bibb Broom Corn Company in Minneapolis to see if they knew anything of the claims Dickinson had alluded to. C. W. Bibb replied that the sale and title were valid from his end. After consulting a judge, Grassick agreed to sell the bones to the university for his total "outlay" of $100.

Hillhouse was not giving up. He, too, had to contend with Jelly's executors, who claimed sole possession for their clients. ("But they are mistaken," he wrote Grassick.) He had to admit that his time to press a claim may have expired, but asked Grassick to respond "freely." "You will find me fair and square in this matter," wrote the prominent hardware merchant. He appealed to Grassick as a fellow Midwesterner: "I might say I am an old Dakota boy. I ran the first hardware store in Devils Lake and built the first building in Bottineau."[19]

Grassick explained that the skeleton was too large for his private collection, hence his decision in the spring to deposit it with the university. But his further explanation sounds somewhat dubious. "Had we got together at an earlier date," he wrote, "doubtless mutually satisfactory arrangements could have been made as to its identity, etc., but having waived my rights in it before knowing of you I am very sorry indeed to state that I can do nothing for you in the matter."[20]

Grassick had not responded to Simon Jelly. Now he received a telegram from the Jelly heir in Shelburne: "Hold bones until I arrive or letter from me answer paid." Grassick's reply was immediate, without the temporizing he offered Hillhouse: "Bones are owned by the University of North Dakota and in their possession."[21]

IV

Professor Brannon had secured this splendid find for the university. But the mastodon exhibit was temporary. Then the remains disappeared from view, a treasure in limbo. Not until 1947 did a North Dakota history professor notice old crates in the rafters of Macnie Hall tagged "partial mastodon skeleton."

Having let this storied specimen languish for forty-five years, the university transferred ownership to the North Dakota State Historical Society. The care-taker in charge of the society's storage was told to expect a number of donations from the university: "A Washington hand printing press, a double ox yolk, mastodon skeleton, three spinning wheels, a steam boat pilot wheel and prob-ably some other smaller pieces of equipment." The majestic mastodon had been reduced to one item on a list of neglected pioneer relics. Another four decades would elapse, with Highgate's "Wonder of the World" once more forgotten.[22]

In 1991, however, came the moment for a mighty mastodon miracle. The historical society determined that its new glass and steel heritage center—the "Smithsonian of the Plains"—ought to feature an exhibit devoted to the state's first people. These humans were presumed to be Paleo-Indians, whose hunting, coupled with habitat loss, likely helped seal the mastodon's extinction.

North Dakota Heritage Center designers envisioned a reconstructed mega-fauna skeleton for their display. An ancient mammoth or bison as the opening exhibit would convey the drama and majesty of the era. The curator, Mark Halvorson, spoke up: "Will a mastodon do?" The reply was an enthusiastic yes. Said Halvorson, "Okay, I'll pull out our mastodon." The state paleontologist, John Hoganson, was startled. "You have a *mastodon*?" he asked. "Sure," said Halvorson, "beside the '61 Lincoln Continental out in the warehouse." It had happened again, the mighty mastodon had been consigned to a collection of storage crates. Hoganson found the Lincoln and found the crates. Inside was a skeleton in waiting, the bones smooth and white, close to perfect.[23]

In 1992, the reassembled Highgate Mastodon was unveiled, more than a century after a farmhand's shovel struck something hard on the Reycraft farm in Ontario. The bones had made their circuitous way along the line R. J. Mason and George Quimby first described—a line approximating a northern boundary of the Midwest's prime agricultural lands. Farther north, a harsher climate and the absence of rich topsoil demarcate a region that depended less on farming and more on timber and extractive mineral wealth. Duluth and Marquette are Midwestern cities by political definition, but may have as much in common with Bangor, Maine, or Bozeman, Montana, as they do with the more fertile regions of Michigan and Minnesota and lands farther south in what is commonly called the Midwest.

Perhaps as much as any political boundary, the Mason-Quimby Line defines the northern reach of those attributes of climate, soil, and livelihood most associated with the region. It is a fluid border, this habitat of the Highgate Mastodon, blurring states and even nations, but it might also reflect the upper limits of the Midwest state of mind.

And what of William Reycraft, on whose farm the bones were found? In his later years, he moved to Petoskey, in northwestern Michigan, on the northern edge of the Great Lakes just above the Mason-Quimby Line. New railroads drew visitors to the region's cool, pine-scented air. Nearby was Bay View, a Methodist summer colony on the shores of Lake Michigan. Reycraft, who died in 1923, built a house in this Midwestern Chautauqua, where an array of activities, both educational and entertaining, offered a more settled cultural successor to the excitement of a traveling mastodon.

NOTES

1. Lee A. Dugatkin, *Mr. Jefferson and the Giant Moose: Natural History in Early America* (Chicago: University of Chicago Press, 2009), 87.

2. Catherine H. Yansa and Kristin M. Adams, "Mastodons and Mammoths in the Great Lakes Region, USA and Canada: New Insights into Their Diets as They Neared Extinction," *Geography Compass* 6, no. 4 (April 2012): 175–88.

3. Peter Russell, John Hoganson, Paul Karrow, and John Motz, *A Mastodon in a Biscuit Box* (Waterloo, Canada: Earth Sciences Museum of University of Waterloo, 2010), 20.

4. "Excitement at Highgate," *Chatham Tri-Weekly Planet*, May 19, 1890.

5. "An Extinct Monster," *Chatham Tri-Weekly Planet*, May 23, 1890.

6. "Excitement at Highgate," *Chatham Tri-Weekly Planet*, May 16, 1890.

7. Jim and Lisa Gilbert, "Gilberts: Highgate Mastodon Was a Huge Find—and Large Loss—for Chatham-Kent," *Chatham Daily News*, February 26, 2021.

8. John W. Douglas to James Grassick, July 5, 1902, James Grassick Papers, North Dakota State Historical Society, Bismarck; hereafter cited as Grassick Papers.

9. Russell et al., *A Mastodon in a Biscuit Box*, 8.

10. Merry Helm, *"Journey of the Highgate Mastodon,"* Dakota Datebook, Prairie Public Broadcasting, July 23, 2004.

11. Harry Dickinson to James Grassick, undated, Grassick Papers.

12. Receipt, November 8, 1899, Grassick Papers.

13. M. A. Brannon to James Grassick, July 9, 1902, Grassick Papers.

14. William Hillhouse to President, University of North Dakota, June 23, 1902, Grassick Papers.

15. James Grassick to William Hillhouse, July 7, 1902, Grassick Papers.

16. John W. Douglas to James Grassick, July 5, 1902.

17. M. A. Brannon to James Grassick, July 9, 1902.

18. Brannon to Grassick, July 9, 1902.

19. William Hillhouse to James Grassick, July 28, 1902, Grassick Papers.

20. James Grassick to William Hillhouse, August 1, 1902, Grassick Papers.

21. James Grassick to Simon Jelly, July 28, 1902, Grassick Papers.

22. Russell et al., *A Mastodon in a Biscuit Box*, 14.

23. Russell et al., 15.

11

GREAT LAKES GOTHIC

John Voelker's *Anatomy of a Murder*, Robert Bloch's *Psycho*, and the Haunt of the Northern Borderlands

In April 2019, nostalgic fans crowded Detroit's historic Redford Theatre for a twin bill uniquely apropos to the Great Lakes State: a sixtieth-anniversary screening of Otto Preminger's 1959 psychological thriller set on Lake Superior, *Anatomy of a Murder,* and a new documentary chronicling its making, *Anatomy of Anatomy,* made by the Michigan-based documentarian David C. Jones. "The movie is full of Michigan flavor and color and stands as the greatest of all movies filmed entirely in the Great Lakes State," John Monaghan wrote of a film that was nominated for seven Oscars in 1960, including best picture, actor, and director.[1]

Based on a real-life murder trial, *Anatomy of a Murder* was adapted from a best-selling 1958 novel by Michigan Supreme Court Justice John D. Voelker, who served as defense attorney in the trial on which the novel is based. The titular murder took place in Big Bay, Michigan, in the early morning of July 31, 1952, and shortly thereafter, Coleman A. Peterson, a lieutenant in the U.S. Army, was charged with killing Michael Chenoweth, owner of the local Lumberjack

Tavern. The presumed motive was revenge for the alleged rape of Peterson's wife, Charlotte, and the underdog attorney Voelker shocked big-city lawyers by successfully defending Peterson, who was found not guilty by reason of insanity.

At his documentary's debut, Jones recalled for the *Detroit Free Press* how *Anatomy* first captured him with its black-and-white "noir look" and unsettling interest in events happening "on the edge of the frame."[2] The film possessed a unique style," he noted, mingling classic noir with psychological thriller set on the forested shores of a body of water that wasn't the North Sea or the Irish Sea or even San Francisco Bay, but Superior, the "Lake Gitche Gumme" of Henry Wadsworth Longfellow fame, the Ojibwe's "shining big-sea-water" or simply "big sea."[3] *Anatomy*'s setting wasn't the famously foggy Bay Area of film noir classics, but a formidable body of freshwater—the largest in the world—one that the singer-songwriter Gordon Lightfoot reminded a nation, in his chart-topping song "The Wreck of the Edmund Fitzgerald," never "gives up her dead."

Lightfoot's number-one song was a surprise hit, an ominous folk tune in a minor chord. In fact, the unexpectedly popular song was only the latest in a decades-long run of Great Lakes Gothic hits that began with the publication of Voelker's *New York Times* best-selling novel of 1958, gathered momentum with Wisconsin resident Robert Bloch's 1959 novel *Psycho,* and culminated in the darker notes, the duende, of Lightfoot's chart-topping single of 1976. Although critics in New York and Los Angeles failed to connect the dots, the pronounced literary and cinematic interest in the region across two decades popularized a cultural milieu that continues into the twenty-first century: a phenomenon I call the Great Lakes Gothic.

GREAT LAKES TERROIR

Readers naturally associate the iconic settings of English literature with the word "gothic," conjuring places such as the Yorkshire moors of Emily Brontë's *Wuthering Heights* or the haunting Dartmoor of Arthur Conan Doyle's *The Hound of the Baskervilles.* But while the genre emanates from the United Kingdom and northern Europe, it refuses to be confined to Old World locations. Instead, its trademark "wild and desolate landscapes"[4] possessed of "an atmosphere of brooding gloom"[5] can and do occur in analogous climates and topographies around the world. The genre's earliest practitioners fashioned their mystery-imbued settings from the intemperate or inhospitable climes around them—for example, from the chilly, windswept, maritime climate of Dr. Jekyll's London or Lord Manfred's English countryside in *The Castle of Otranto,* the 1764 fiction widely considered the first gothic novel.[6] And yet the gothic critic Jerrold E. Hogle rightly points out that it long ago ceased to be a "fixed genre," having "crept, throughout the world . . . with many of its initial features still visible."[7] He asserts that the gothic can be "transported out of . . . past contexts, despite some harkenings back."[8] Precisely because the aesthetic is so portable, it is possible to locate for it an alternative "terroir," defined as "the complete natural environment in which a particular wine is produced, including factors such as the soil, topography, and climate." Applied broadly, "terroir" attempts to define the indefinable: the factors both tangible and intangible that grow a product, whether that product is a commodity crop, a human resource crop, or a cultural geography. If the gothic in its purest form is indeed produced by a comingling of a northern climate mitigated by the presence of a large body of water and the often erratic and inclement weather such bodies whip up, it stands to reason that the gothic, like the wine grape, could grow anywhere where its most basic requirements are met, though it is more likely to sink roots in places similar to those from whence it sprang: places marked by short days; long, stormy winters; and inconstant, fitful sunlight.

Unsurprisingly, the early American gothic first took root in New England, a region whose geography, topography, and climate closely matched the mother country's. Many if not most of the early American writers classified as gothic, including such canonical authors as Nathaniel Hawthorne, Herman Melville, and Emily Dickinson, drew inspiration from the region's brooding climate and broken topography. In "The Picture in the House," H. P. Lovecraft reminds readers of the New World's rightful claim to the phantasmagoric: "Searchers after horror haunt strange, far places. . . . They climb to the moonlit towers of ruined Rhine castles, and falter down black cobwebbed steps beneath the scattered stones of forgotten cities in Asia. . . . But the true epicure in the terrible, to whom a new thrill of unutterable ghastliness is the chief end and justification of existence, esteems most of all the ancient, lonely farmhouse of backwoods New England; for there the dark elements of strength, solitude, grotesqueness, and ignorance combine to form the perfection of the hideous."[9]

For all his exuberance, Lovecraft misses a crucial point in his advocacy for America's homegrown gothic settings: as New England became more urban and less forested in the late nineteenth and early twentieth century, it grew less amenable to the borderline, borderlands psychology on which the gothic thrives. As the region gentrified and urbanized, the gothic spirit flew south—to become the Southern Gothic of Flannery O'Connor's "Christ-haunted" region—and west along the northern tier to settle along and near the Great Lakes, where the novelist Constance Fenimore Woolson turned the fortress-like quality of many Great Lakes islands into the settings of short fictions with gothic themes featuring storms, shipwrecks, lighthouses, and lover's quarrels. By the late nineteenth century, the moribund tastes of the "true epicure in the terrible" had expanded to include the states of the old Northwest Territory, with a new gothic ground zero emerging in Woolson's Michigan.

Woolson's literary canon begins with 1873's "Ballast Island," wherein the spinster Miss Jonah gives voice to a sentiment that serves as an early *esprit de corps* for the evolving Great Lakes Gothic, telling those who would take her from her forlorn outpost back to the comforts of civilization: "Here I'm going to stay. I like it here. It's lonely, but I'm best alone. . . . I have a fancy I shall not live long, and I want to be buried on Ballast."[10] Woolson would go on to set at least nine more stories on Great Lakes islands, including three on Lake Superior's Apostle Islands, blazing a literary trail for others to follow, most notably fellow Midwesterner Mary Hartwell Catherwood. Catherwood's 1893 novel *The White Islander* captured the mystery of a region that inspired more than a dozen of her short stories set on the lakes, including those included in the 1899 collection *Mackinac and Lake Stories*. Catherwood's preface to *The White Islander* references a panoply of gothic themes, including "the eternal glitter of the lake" and the remains of an "old tragedy" on the aptly named Skull Island. The author's invocation of the alluring and sometimes dreadful beauty of Mackinac comes with a defiant warning to those who would seek to tame the island: "No landscape-gardening and placarding of commercial man can ever quite spoil its wild beauty," Catherwood writes in the preface. "The white cliffs and the shaggy wilderness defy him."[11]

While a new generation of native writers such as Woolson and Catherwood, both born and raised in Great Lakes states, helped sow the seeds for a Great Lakes Gothic, other factors conspired to move the literary locus of an evolving Midwestern Gothic north from its 1920s and 1930s regionalist headquarters in Corn Belt states such as Ohio, Illinois, Iowa, and Kansas to the northern borderlands. Like New England before it, the agrarian Midwest had become too thoroughly settled, some said, to grow and nurture the strange fruits of the gothic. The expanding cultivation of corn, whose farming served to domesticate and to civilize, offered little quarter for the darker strains of the gothic, which all but required proximity to woods, wilds, dunes, or barrens. For a literary style centered on remote places, deep forests, and mist-shrouded shorelines, a place like Iowa could, at best, serve as an imperfect if not ironic host, since by 1940, the Hawkeye State was among the most thoroughly cultivated and domesticated places in America.

Encroached on by clear-cutting and commodity crop agriculture, the deep, brooding forests so characteristic of the Midwestern Gothic had retreated northward into Minnesota, Wisconsin, and Michigan by the time Voelker's breakthrough novel *Anatomy of a Murder* was published in 1958. While corn had pushed its dominion dramatically northward into the southern and central parts of the Great Lakes states by the 1940s,[12] in the far northern borderlands, second-growth pines and conifers had reestablished themselves in formerly clear-cut areas, aided by government conservation programs and forest management. Another expanding crop—automobile tourists—brought a surfeit of seasonal visitors north from more settled, populous areas in the Corn Belt and Rust Belt to a still remote, and rapidly reforesting, Great Lakes region whose isolated vistas metropolitan Midwesterners found strangely alluring.

With its copper and timber industries in steady decline, Michigan's Upper Peninsula, in particular, looked to replace lost revenue by exoticizing native lands and cultures little understood by urbanites in the region. Advertisers made hay by harkening back to Ojibwe legends adapted and anglicized by writers such as Henry Wadsworth Longfellow, whose *Song of Hiawatha* became a kind of anthem in northern Michigan. By the early 1950s, railroad marketers of the Upper Great Lakes had "successfully linked literature with landscape," dubbing the Upper Peninsula the Land of Hiawatha, while convincing seasonal visitors to the region's lodges of the unique mix of geographical and cultural factors that made this place seem "more natural as well as more primitive."[13] Visitors from regional industrial centers such as Chicago, Detroit, and Minneapolis–St. Paul readily bought into the air of romantic escape and exoticism on offer in hunting lodges, national forests, and craggy shores redolent of the gothic.

The forest-loving tourists who flocked to northern Michigan in the 1950s could thank the Civilian Conservation Corps (CCC) for many of the densely wooded settings that served as scenic backdrops for their outdoor vacations. Between 1933 and the start of World War II the CCC planted approximately 485 million trees in Michigan alone[14]—more than three trees for every man, woman, and child alive in America in 1930. During the same period, Michigan reacquired significant amounts of land from failed homestead and timber claims and from acres sold by defunct or downsizing lumber companies, consolidating more than 5 million acres under the management of the state's Department of

Conservation.[15] Unwittingly, the conservationists of the 1930s were regrowing a climate in which a regional gothic might flourish. Writing for the Newberry Library in Chicago, Kara Johnson posits that wilderness, rather than the small town or the city, is North America's definitive setting, pointing out that the earliest writers of the American Gothic "articulated the need to adjust a Gothic tale to America's particular setting."[16] Hogle asserts the centrality of "primitive wilderness" to fictional narratives with a gothic flair.[17]

Before the European settlers arrived, nearly 35,000,000 acres of what would become the state of Michigan were covered in wilderness, a dense northern hardwood, pine, and conifer forest.[18] Rooted in the state's glacial moraine soils, trees encroached on nearly every corner of the landscape, in many cases growing right to the water's edge. The heavily wooded and windswept lake shores of Wisconsin and Michigan, in particular, made them a natural seedbed for the development of a Midwestern Gothic, as the northern half of both states remained conspicuously depopulated. For example, in 1950, the population of Michigan's Upper Peninsula (UP) totaled just 300,000, a figure that was nearly ten thousand less than the population of St. Paul, Minnesota.[19] By the late 1940s, the myriad factors contributing to the UP's singular terroir made it ripe for the advent of a neo–American Gothic. Dark forests, shuttered factories and timber mills, abandoned mines, ragged black-rock shorelines, tempestuous weather, and the rapidly expanding presence of a cultural Other—seasonal visitors and other transients who troubled, worried, or otherwise preoccupied the long-settled—bubbled up brooding undercurrents that ran just beneath the sunnier narratives proffered by the region's marketers.

In 1950, 80 percent of the UP's 10.5 million acres were covered in forests.[20] Into this natural resource–based economy had flowed a steady stream of in-migrators to fill jobs in local industry coupled with a steady influx of war service personnel, including Korean War veterans such as Coleman A. Peterson, who, prior to committing the gruesome murder at the center of John Voelker's legal thriller, had set up temporary residence at Perkins Park outside of town. At the time of the killing, Lieutenant Peterson was permanently based at Camp McCoy in Wisconsin, but had come to Big Bay, thirty miles northwest of Marquette, for mandatory officer training and target practice. When his wife, Charlotte, returned from a night playing pinball at the nearby Lumberjack Tavern, bruised and battered and alleging she had been raped by Chenoweth, Peterson loaded the German Luger pistol he used in World War II, and returned to the bar to confront his wife's alleged rapist.[21] Days later, Peterson hired Voelker to defend him against charges of first-degree murder in what evidence suggested had been a revenge killing. Tried in Marquette in September 1952, *People versus Coleman Peterson* encapsulated the gothic trope of insider versus outsider. The trial featured Voelker—defense attorney, author of true crime fictions set on the shores of Superior, and consummate UP insider—attempting to defend Peterson, a transient resident and ultimate outsider said to have murdered in cold blood a decorated marksman and former state patrolman who owned a local watering hole.

The subsequent trial shocked those unaware of the escalating tensions between insiders and outsiders in Marquette County and across the Upper Great Lakes region, where postwar prosperity had been uneven. The Petersons were outsiders, temporary residents living in a mobile home community whose patrons were transient by nature. Some locals regarded the park residents as drains on the system, making of them the "Other" present in so many gothic narratives. In the novels of Mary Shelly and Robert Louis Stevenson, the Other is often monstrous. In the work of Horace Walpole, the Other is typically supernatural. But in the American Gothic, the Other is often cultural—the one whose unexplained, unlikely, or unwanted presence becomes the subject of gossip, rumor, conjecture, or fear. In Big Bay, Lieutenant Peterson; his wife, Charlotte; and the many seasonal visitors and transient residents who swelled Marquette County's population in the summer months served as a cultural Other, simultaneously representing both an economic boon and a perceived threat to a tenuous status quo. The haunt of the *People versus Coleman Peterson* wasn't the undead or a ghost as in the gothic tales of old, but the inner workings of the mind that could kill a man in cold blood without any outward signs of remorse, and the skeletons in the closet kept by a community struggling to alleviate socioeconomic disparities among its residents while protecting the rights of its most vulnerable citizens.

Doctors were called in to assess Peterson's sanity, with one ultimately concluding that Peterson, in what amounted to a dissociative state, had acted on an "irresistible impulse" he could not possibly control. The same week the *Holland Evening Sentinel* in Holland, Michigan, ran the headline "Army Lieutenant Slays Bar Owner as Patrons Watch," the front page contained a series of headlines that hinted at the inimitable mix of gothic elements at work in the state. In one story, a mysterious fleet of ships had been seen off the shores of Lake Michigan and also reported off Saugatuck. In another, police and hospital authorities in Grand Rapids were attempting to locate a man, Robert H.

Henderson, twenty-two, who was said to be "running around with a fractured skull."[22] The police detective Captain Walter Coe reported that Henderson had been hit on the head with an axe by his neighbor. While the axe had presumably been dislodged, Henderson had disappeared and was now at large. Meanwhile, Arthur Graham Jr., sixteen, had drowned in the Saginaw River after developing a cramp while swimming. So read the headlines on a single day in July of 1952, a typical day, in many ways, at the height of a busy tourist season. While tragedies such as these—murders, skull fractures, accidental deaths by drowning—can and do happen across America on a winsome summer day, the unique terroir of the northern Great Lakes states—their thousands of miles of shoreline, their many millions of acres of woodlands, their seasonal influx of new residents and recreators determined to seek pleasure or escape—make them, perhaps, more likely to occur in a region whose darker notes had lately caused novelists and filmmakers to stand up and listen.

When the actor Jimmy Stewart learned that the director Otto Preminger planned to film on location in northern Michigan near the site of the murder of Chenoweth, he was said to have been displeased at the prospect of the frigid weather awaiting the cast and crew.[23] The average daytime high in Marquette, where Preminger proposed to shoot the majority of the courtroom scenes, was a chilly 35 degrees in March, and Stewart was better accustomed to the benign climes of southern California. Shot in black and white during months when the northern hardwoods had yet to leaf out, the film was awash in the monochromatic grays characteristic of other, more iconic film noir locations. While the dappled light of Gitche Gumme catches the camera's eye occasionally, it offers only temporary illumination, for, as Hogle reminds, "any 'light' of rational revelation in the Gothic is always countered by a fearsome chiaroscuro that mixed illumination with ominous and mysterious darkness."[24]

The film presented a series of unique challenges to veteran director Preminger, who proposed to adapt to the big screen Voelker's novelization of the real-life Michigan murder trial of 1952, one in which there was no clear protagonist. Army lieutenant Peterson had murdered bar owner Chenoweth after the alleged rape of Peterson's wife, Charlotte, at the Lumberjack Tavern, and the Associated Press coverage of the event described Lieutenant Peterson as a cool-headed, cold-blooded killer who "pumped five bullets" into his victim before turning himself in to a patrolman at the trailer park where he lived. "I shot him," Peterson was quoted as saying, "it's as simple as that."[25] Preminger hoped to reconstruct the dramatic courtroom scenes as recounted in the 1958 novel written by Voelker, who, since his first novel in 1943, had been writing under the pen name Robert Traver. The director's task was further complicated by Voelker's crowded schedule as a sitting justice on the Michigan Supreme Court when the film began shooting in the late winter of 1959.

Voelker himself was haunted by an Upper Peninsula on whose topography and terroir he had deeply imprinted as a young man, a place where big dreams were both earnestly made and tragically thwarted. His father, a prosperous saloon owner in Ishpeming, discouraged his son from leaving home to attend college, believing that he should take over the family business. Voelker followed his mother's wishes instead, graduating first from the Northern Michigan Normal School (later to become Northern Michigan University) and, later, from the University of Michigan Law School in 1928. Shortly thereafter, the newly married attorney moved to Chicago, nearer to his wife's family in Oak Park, Illinois. The young lawyer accustomed to the woods and wilds of his native northern Michigan loathed life in the metropolis, telling his wife, Grace, that "it was better to starve in Ishpeming than to wear emeralds in Chicago."[26] In "Backwoods Barrister," the Michigan historian Richard D. Shaul describes the young attorney's life in Chicago as one of creeping despair. Even the pen name Voelker chose for his fiction writing, Robert Traver, reflected the particular sadnesses of the author's young adulthood: Robert was both the first name of Voelker's brother who had died of influenza while serving in the U.S. Navy in World War I, and the first name of the author's only son, who died at eighteen months.[27] Voelker borrowed his mother's maiden name, Traver, to complete the family-inspired nom de plume. Voelker's mother, Annie, had encouraged her son's writing habit when he was a boy, leading to his earliest story, the decidedly gothic "Lost All Night in a Swamp with a Bear."[28]

While Voelker learned his love of writing from his mother, it was his father who introduced him to the wilderness of the Upper Peninsula, encouraging his son to go forth and explore the darker recesses in and around Ishpeming, a place surrounded by lakes, ponds, and timber that inculcated in the aspiring writer a keen appreciation for the beauty and danger of nature.[29] Later, years spent as a county prosecutor in nearby Marquette, on the shores of Lake Superior, taught him something about the darker human impulses born of a place in dynamic socioeconomic flux. By the time Voelker was hired to serve as defense attorney in what would become the most famous court trial in the Upper Peninsula, the

People versus Coleman Peterson, he had left his county attorney post to set up his own private practice, styling himself a country lawyer or backwoods barrister who drew the majority of his clients from within Marquette County.

A MIDWESTERN *PSYCHO*

One year after St. Martin's Press published Voelker's novel *Anatomy of a Murder* in 1958, in nearby Wisconsin another budding Great Lakes novelist, Robert Bloch, published *Psycho.* The novel tells the story of Norman Bates, a mother-obsessed motel caretaker living a secret life as a serial killer. Like Voelker, the Chicago-born, Milwaukee-raised Bloch had grown up along the Great Lakes, drawing inspiration not just from the city's dramatic, ever-changing weather, but also from its endless cavalcade of musicals and movies. The first film the young writer viewed solo, *The Phantom of the Opera,* starring Lon Chaney, captured his attention as no other had before, with a quintessential gothic setting Bloch described as "a gloomy, dungeon-like stone chamber dominated by a massive organ on which he played the proclamation of his love" and a "distraught heroine" imprisoned in an adjoining chamber.[30]

Mentored early in his career by H. P. Lovecraft, Bloch published a number of pulp fantasy and science fiction books before the arrest of the serial killer Ed Gein in Plainfield, Wisconsin, inspired him to write *Psycho.* Indeed, Bloch and Sauk City, Wisconsin, writer August Derleth became Lovecraft's most promising disciples and protégés, giving Lovecraft's gothic tales a new next-generation home in the upper Great Lakes. In Derleth's short story "Beyond the Threshold," the narrator's pilgrimage embodies the migration of a regional haunt from its traditional home in New England to the Upper Midwest. Summoned from his comfortable post at a university library in Massachusetts back to a "lonely house deep in the forest places of northern Wisconsin,"[31] Derleth's narrator falls under the spell of "the north country Indian legends: the belief in a monstrous, supernatural being . . . the haunter of the great forest silences."[32]

While Derleth hybridized his own obsession with northern borderlands folklore with Lovecraft's interest in the occult and the supernatural, Bloch drew inspiration from real-life horrors happening in the Great Lakes region. Though he claimed at the time to be only distantly aware of the sensational story of a small-town serial murderer in his midst, news of the gruesome slaying was splashed across the front page of nearly every newspaper in the state, and at the time of Gein's arrest in 1957, Bloch was living less than forty miles from Plainfield in nearby Weyauwega, Wisconsin. Regardless, the author later recalled the premise for his novel *Psycho* in expressly gothic terms, writing: "At the time I decided to write a novel based on the notion that the man next door may be a monster, unsuspected even in the gossip-ridden microcosm of small-town life."[33] While Dr. Jekyll and Dorian Gray could terrorize densely populated London with impunity and relative anonymity, the social dynamics of small-town Wisconsin seemed to militate against a maniac or a madman setting up shop in their midst. In his true-crime essay of 1962, "The Shambles of Ed Gein," Bloch spoke directly to what drew him to the story of the man known as the Butcher of Plainfield or the Plainfield Ghoul. The author sets the stage: "On the evening of November 16, 1957, visitors entered an ancient, lonely farmhouse—not in backwoods New England but in rural Wisconsin. Hanging in an adjacent shed was the nude, butchered body of a woman. She had been suspended by the heels and decapitated, then disemboweled like a steer. In the kitchen next to the shed, fire flickered in an old-fashioned potbellied stove. A pan set on top of it contained a human heart."[34] Gein, Bloch concluded, "may or may not have been a cannibal and a necrophile, [but] was—by his own admission—a ghoul, a murderer, and a transvestite. Due process of law has also adjudged him to be criminally insane."

The real-life story of Gein fit the American Gothic formula perfectly. Near the small town of Plainfield, Wisconsin, where he lived, Gein was well known and, as much as a man who kept mostly to himself could be, well liked. On the day of his arrest, the fifty-one-year-old was babysitting two children of a local family, the Hills, who subsequently invited him to dinner. When the children arrived to call on their dinner guest, Gein emerged from his woodshed to say he would be ready as soon as he was finished dressing the deer hanging inside. The kids knew their babysitter didn't hunt deer, so they laughed at what they assumed was a joke and peered inside to see "the butchered body of a middle-aged business-woman."[35] Bernice Worden had disappeared recently from the hardware store she owned on Main Street in Plainfield. As if adhering to some gothic script, the same week word of Gein's grisly murders broke in Wisconsin newspapers, a lethal snowstorm hit the state, mingling the macabre headlines "Youth Tells of Seeing Gein's Heads" with "Some Schools Still Closed; Five Dead."[36] Meanwhile, Eau Claire citizens were all but imprisoned, with all roads in and out, including U.S. Highway 12, blocked by heavy snow.[37]

Gein's macabre crime proved eerily similar to the 1952 murder of Michael Chenoweth hundreds of miles away in Michigan's Upper Peninsula. As had been the case in Michigan, the victim in Wisconsin was a well-known owner of a popular local business. Like Peterson before him, Gein had been friendly with his victim prior to the homicide, buying products from her store and making social visits. Similarly, on the night Peterson murdered Chenoweth, his wife, Charlotte, had been happily buying drinks and feeding quarters into the pinball machine at the tavern Chenoweth owned. On the day of the murder, November 16, 1957, Gein had chatted easily with his eventual victim, Worden, across the counter at the hardware store, where he reportedly purchased a 99-cent bottle of antifreeze.[38] Later it would be revealed that Gein had also killed another local woman, tavern-keeper Mary Hogan, who had been missing since December 8, 1954.[39] In gothic fashion, each of the three heinous murders combined familiarization (Gein and Peterson were known in the communities in which they killed) with defamiliarization (the community of Plainfield knew little of what the bachelor, Gein, did on his remote Wisconsin farm). Similarly, Big Bay, Michigan, knew little of what went on inside the insular mobile home where Lieutenant Peterson and his wife shared an intensely private, some said psychologically abusive, relationship, or behind the scenes at the Lumberjack Tavern where the victim, Chenoweth, was alleged to have been unfaithful to his wife. For many readers and observers, the idea that a madman or a murderer could be among them all along seemed more plausible in the small towns and villages of the Great Lakes states, where the simultaneous tendency to familiarize and defamiliarize produced dramatic tension.

While the idea of a killer living a double life was as familiar as Stevenson's *Dr. Jekyll and Mr. Hyde* or Bram Stoker's *Dracula,* the stories of the two murders depended for their national resonance on tropes associated with life in the rural Upper Midwest. Gein was routinely dubbed a bachelor farmer, though more accurately he was a "bachelor handyman." He lived by himself in what was alternately described as a "rickety old farmhouse" and a "secluded farmhouse,"[40] piquing the fears of an increasingly urban America that had, by the late 1950s, largely left its rural roots behind. The press cast Gein as a kind of wolf in sheep's clothing, referring to him as "a bachelor whose career as part-time handyman and part-time ghoul covered nearly two decades."[41] The method of Gein's murders—decapitations, butchering, and disembowelings—doubly horrified Americans for whom such methods seemed shockingly provincial and uncivilized. It was no accident that Gein had told the children whom he had been babysitting that he had been dressing a deer in his woodshed; in his case, the rural serial killer hunted his town-dwelling prey as he might have stalked a deer. The story of the Plainfield Ghoul forced readers in the rest of a rapidly urbanizing nation to reconsider a long-held stereotype of small-town life: that the gruesome and the macabre couldn't happen in places where nothing much happened at all. As Bloch himself observed after the tragedy, "A pity Grace Metalious wasn't aware of our graying, shy little-town handyman when she wrote *Peyton Place!* But, of course, nobody would have believed her. New England or Wisconsin are hardly the proper settings for such characters; we might accept them in Transylvania, but Pennsylvania—never! And yet, he [Gein] lived. And women died."[42]

Though the town's response to the tragedy isn't featured in either Bloch's novel or Alfred Hitchcock's blockbuster 1960 film adaptation of the same name, Plainfield's reaction to the horror in its midst also struck many readers as quintessentially Middle American in its combination of repression, denial, and frontier justice. Committed to the Central State Hospital for the Criminal Insane, Gein was effectively barred from his home community for life. District attorney Earl Killeen promised the town that "Ed Gein never will walk the streets of Plainfield again."[43] When the Associated Press returned to Plainfield one year after Gein's commitment to the insane asylum, it found "Nothing but fire-blackened debris . . . left where the old house stood." The AP reported that "outsiders" had proposed to buy the property to "set it up as a bizarre museum," until someone in the community had enacted a kind of frontier justice, burning the house and its contents to the ground, presumably in hopes that the gruesome memories contained therein would burn along with it. "It seems to be the general feeling that the fire was no accident," Plainfield's village president, Harold Collins, told the press.[44] By November 1958, one year after the hardware store owner Bernice Worden was butchered, all the buildings on what had been the Gein farm had been razed, and the new owner had planted the sandy, marginal soils in a new crop of pine trees. The town's desire to move on was a profoundly human one, though its eagerness to repress the memories, and to raze the physical structures that had housed them, seemed to some quintessentially Midwestern. The AP concluded its retrospective on a sanguine note: "There is little discussion nowadays in Plainfield of the story that touched all the literate world with horror. They did not even open all the graves Ed Gein said he robbed. In a community of fewer than 700 persons, there are things better not known. And some things known too well already."[45]

In interviews, Bloch maintained "reclusivity" was necessary for a serial murderer, whether fictional or real, operating in a close-knit rural community like Plainfield. And he marveled at the level of good-natured neighborly acceptance—or was it, instead, near criminal disengagement—that had allowed the Butcher of Plainfield to grow into such a monster over a period of two decades. In "The Shambles of Ed Gein," Bloch reflects at length on the extreme denial that fostered the development of the perpetrator's unprecedented barbarism: "Yet for decades he roamed free and unhindered, a well-known figure in a little community of 700 people. Now small towns everywhere are notoriously hotbeds of gossip, conjecture, and rumor, and Gein himself joked about his "collection of shrunken heads" and laughingly admitted that he'd been responsible for the disappearance of many women in the area. He was known to be a recluse and never entertained visitors; children believed his house to be "haunted." But somehow the gossip never developed beyond the point of idle, frivolous speculation, and nobody took Ed Gein seriously."[46]

CONTEMPORARY GREAT LAKES GOTHIC

Hollywood capitalized quickly on the developing Great Lakes Gothic, adapting both Voelker's and Bloch's novels less than seven years after the respective murders that inspired them rocked the region. *Psycho* was made into a film of the same name within two years of Gein's commitment to the state hospital, and debuted at theaters nationwide one year after Otto Preminger's *Anatomy of a Murder*. The story of such provocative murders in the nation's northern borderlands compelled audiences to reconsider the quiet, don't-rock-the-boat domesticities they had previously imagined as the region's calling card. Though Hitchcock would set his film adaptation in the lonesome deserts of Arizona and southern California, the storyboard retained the haunt of the remote places and reclusive rural characters embodied by Ed Gein's Plainfield, Wisconsin. And while the film version of *Psycho* debuted to mixed critical reviews in 1960, in the decades that followed, its estimation in the eyes of critics has steadily grown, with the film listed as the fourteenth greatest American film by the American Film Institute in 2007, ranking one spot behind *Star Wars*.[47] Meanwhile, in 2012, *Anatomy of a Murder* was declared "culturally, historically, or aesthetically significant" and selected for preservation in the United States National Film Registry by the Library of Congress.[48]

Psychological thrillers with distinctly gothic themes, the blockbuster novels by Great Lakes natives Voelker and Bloch depicted the region as the source of darker notes, of duende, played in a region whose rural remoteness, shuttered industries, and dynamic migration patterns inspired native writers and filmmakers seeking homegrown drama.

Bloch would go on to publish many horror stories, including his 1974 novel *American Gothic,* inspired by the true-life story of the Chicago serial killer H. H. Holmes, the homicidal doctor who would later become the subject of Erik Larson's best-selling historical nonfiction set on the shores of Lake Michigan, *The Devil in the White City.* Bloch's interest in gothic themes, especially criminal shadow selves, extended to his 1990 release, *The Jekyll Legacy,* a book written as a sequel to Stevenson's *Dr. Jekyll and Mr. Hyde,* and to two sequels of his most famous franchise, *Psycho II,* in 1982 and, in 1990, *Psycho House.*

Voelker, meanwhile, continued to write and to fish in his native Upper Peninsula, publishing a total of eleven books under the nom de plume Robert Traver. While much of his writing after *Anatomy* focused on fly fishing—so much so that he became known as the Bard of Frenchman's Pond—the lawyer-writer returned to gothic themes of murder and courtroom drama in his 1981 novel, *People Versus Kirk.* Set once more on the Upper Peninsula and penned using the Robert Traver pseudonym, the action centers on a trout-fishing Michigan lawyer hired to defend a young man, Randall Kirk, accused of drowning the beautiful Constance Spurrier, with whom Kirk was having a longtime affair. Like the accused lieutenant in *Anatomy of Murder,* Kirk claims to have no memory of the murder by drowning, his defense hinging on the question of "impaired consciousness" in much the same way that Lieutenant Coleman Peterson's successful defense depended on "irresistible impulse."[49]

While Voelker and Bloch kept the Great Lakes Gothic alive in their popular fiction throughout the 1980s, Voelker's death in 1991 followed by Bloch's in 1994 paved the way for new inheritors of the gothic style that was bottled and distilled by writers who had themselves grown up in the Great Lakes states. Writer-directors Joel and Ethan Coen, raised in the suburbs of Minneapolis, blended Garrison Keillor's dark Lutheranism with the Great Lakes Gothic style of Bloch in their 1996 film, *Fargo.* Set in a remote cabin on Moose Lake, Minnesota, the film billed as a "homespun murder story" became an instant cinematic classic. In literature, Chicagoland natives Dave Eggers and Michael Hainey carried on the Great Lakes Gothic tradition with memoirs written about the tragic early deaths of parents in the Pulitzer Prize–nominated *A Heartbreaking Work of Staggering Genius* and *After Visiting Friends: A Son's Story,* respectively. For both Eggers and Hainey, the Windy City serves as symbolic backdrop to the sting felt by the bereaved in places where long, dark winters threaten to dim the life force and snuff out would-be recoveries. Growing gothic interests spanned age demographics, too, from the runaway success of Marshall, Michigan's, John

Bellairs, author of fifteen gothic mystery novels for young adults from 1969 to 1982 (many in collaboration with Chicago's renowned gothic illustrator Edward Gorey) to Milford, Michigan's, funeral director–author Thomas Lynch, who ruminates on the funereal folkways of his native northern borderlands in his 1997 memoir, *The Undertaking: Life Studies of a Dismal Trade.*

The wider commercial success of the Great Lakes Gothic begs a larger question: what is the connection between a people, their worldview, and their weather? Are Midwesterners a fatalistic people because the weather can, and does, kill? Does the impenetrability of the millions of acres of Great Lakes forests, coupled with the deep, dark waters of Lake Michigan and Lake Superior—the same that drowned and wrecked the crew of the seemingly unsinkable *SS Edmund Fitzgerald* on Lake Superior in November of 1975—somehow translate into the collective chilly disposition of a mind-of-winter people, as well as to the real and imagined tales such a people create to entertain, to delight, and to convey deeper (darker) truths about themselves? By contrast, are Californians portrayed as the nation's sunny optimists because, to name just one example, Imperial County is the sunniest place in the lower forty-eight states according to the data compiled by the U.S. Centers for Disease Control and Prevention (CDC), compared to, for example, Kent County, Michigan, which ranks 2,847 out of 3,111 counties in terms of average daily sunlight.[50] Looking at the CDC maps, the overwhelming majority of states shaded blue to indicate the least amount of average solar radiation are also the Blue states on the political spectrum. That observation, in turn, begs a corollary question: are the artists and writers of the Great Lakes Gothic somehow bluer, too, in temperament or in worldview—the living embodiments of Keillor's characterization of a region inhabited by "God's frozen people"?[51] And of what consequence to regional tropes and traits is the fact that two of the top-ten coldest cities in America (Duluth, Minnesota, and Marquette, Michigan) are located on the shores of the Great Lakes, and seven of the remaining eight chilliest places based on minimum average temperature are found within a northern borderlands region bounded by other cities on the list of America's most frigid: Marquette on the east; Huron, South Dakota, on the west; and Williston, North Dakota, on the north.[52]

Northern borderlanders famously succumb to the so-called pathetic fallacy, projecting their own emotional state onto the weather in much-spoofed responses like "Oh, I'm fair to partly cloudy," or "I'm fair to midland." But beyond the lampooning it's worth asking if there may be a fatal attraction between the seasonal surfeit of natural calamities that befall the Upper Midwest—from drownings on Lake Superior and Lake Michigan to record polar vortices in Wisconsin, Minnesota, and Michigan—and the persistent darkly deadpan that worms its way into a region's collective disposition. It's possible to surmise that "God's frozen people" are, paradoxically, most happy when they are unhappy, most alive when faced with death.

Whether a Great Lakes gothic terroir insinuates itself into the psyche of those who alchemize it into art, or whether native artists imbue the region with the fatalism that has come to define its popular image, is destined to remain a matter of chicken-and-egg conjecture, as long-standing as the debate over the pathetic fallacy itself. What is certain is that the unique climate, weather, and topography of America's northern borderlands produce a distinctive mood that resonates in film, literature, and culture eagerly consumed far beyond the region.

NOTES

1. John Monaghan, "Freep Film Festival's 'Anatomy of "Anatomy"'" Revisits Making of a Mich. Movie Classic," *Detroit Free Press*, April 13, 2019, https://www.freep.com /story/entertainment/2019/04/13/anatomy-anatomy-revisits-making-mich-movie -classic/3443331002/.

2. Monaghan, "Freep Film Festival's 'Anatomy of "Anatomy.'"'"

3. "Why Is the Big Lake Called 'Gitche Gumee'?," *Lake Superior Magazine*, January 1, 2006, https://www.lakesuperior.com/the-lake/lake-superior/281almanac/.

4. Kip Wheeler, "Literary Terms and Definitions," Carson-Newman University, https://web.cn.edu/kwheeler/lit_terms_A.html, accessed November 1, 2019.

5. J. A. Cuddon, *A Dictionary of Literary Terms* (London: Deutsch, 1977), 381–82.

6. "The Castle of Otranto: The Creepy Tale That Launched Gothic Fiction," *BBC News Magazine*, December 13, 2014, https://www.bbc.com/news/magazine-30313775, accessed November 1, 2019.

7. Jerrold E. Hogle, "Introduction: Modernity and the Proliferation of the Gothic," in *The Cambridge Companion to the Modern Gothic*, ed. Jerrold E. Hogle (Cambridge: Cambridge University Press, 2014), 1.

8. Hogle, 5.

9. H. P. Lovecraft, "The Picture in the House," http://www.hplovecraft.com/writings /texts/fiction/ph.aspx, accessed November 1, 2019.

10. Constance Fenimore Woolson, "Ballast Island," *Appletons' Journal: A Magazine of General Literature* 9, no. 223 (June 28, 1873): 838.

11. Mary Hartwell Catherwood, *The White Islander* (New York: Century, 1900), vii.

12. Howard G. Roepke, "Changes in Corn Production on the Northern Margin of the Corn Belt," *Agricultural History* 33, no. 3 (July 1959): 126–32.

13. Camden Burd, "Imagining a Pure Michigan Landscape: Advertisers, Tourists, and the Making of Michigan's Northern Vacationlands," *Michigan Historical Review* 42, no. 2 (2016): 45.

14. Michigan.gov, "Forest History" in *2006 State Forest Management Plan*, https://www.michigan.gov/documents/2-ForestHistory_165779_7.pdf, accessed November 1, 2019.

15. Ibid.

16. Kara Johnson, "The American Gothic," Newberry Library Digital Collections for the Classroom, October 12, 2018, https://dcc.newberry.org/collections/the_american_gothic.

17. Hogle, "Introduction: Modernity and the Proliferation of the Gothic," 4.

18. Michigan.gov, "Forest History."

19. George N. Skrubb, *Marquette, Michigan City Plan*, 1951, https://marquettemi.gov/wp-content/uploads/2017/08/ENTIRE-1951-MASTER-PLAN.pdf.

20. Skrubb, *Marquette, Michigan City Plan*.

21. "Army Lieutenant Slays Bar Owner as Patrons Watch," *Holland Evening Sentinel* (Holland, MI), July 31, 1952, 1.

22. "Man Roaming Around with Fractured Skull," *Holland Evening Sentinel* (Holland, MI), July 31, 1952, 1.

23. Monaghan, "Freep Film Festival's 'Anatomy of "Anatomy.'""

24. Hogle, "Introduction: Modernity and the Proliferation of the Gothic," 5.

25. "Army Lieutenant Slays Bar Owner as Patrons Watch," 1.

26. Frederick M. Baker Jr. and Rich Vander Veen III, "Michigan Lawyers in History—John D. Voelker: Michigan's Literary Justice," *Michigan Bar Journal* 79, no. 5 (May 2000): 530–31.

27. Richard D. Shaul, "Backwoods Barrister," *Michigan History* (November/December 2001), 84.

28. Shaul.

29. Shaul.

30. Robert Bloch, *Once Around the Bloch: An Unauthorized Autobiography* (New York: Tor Books, 1993), 45.

31. August Derleth, "Beyond the Threshold," in *The Ithaqua Cycle,* ed. Robert M. Price, (Hayward, CA: Chaosium, 2006), 81.

32. Derleth, 87.

33. Gina Wisker, *Horror Fiction: An Introduction* (New York: Continuum, 2005), 126.

34. Robert Bloch, "The Shambles of Ed Gein," in *True Crime: An American Anthology*, ed. Harold Schechter (New York: Library of America, 2008), 549.

35. "Unbelievable Ed Gein Story Began to Unfold at Plainfield a Year Ago," *La Crosse Sunday Tribune* (La Crosse, WI), November 16, 1958, 12.

36. "Some Schools Still Closed; Five Dead," *Stevens Point Daily Journal* (Stevens Point, WI), November 20, 1957, 1.

37. "Bulletin, Snow Blocks Roads," *Kenosha Evening News* (Kenosha, WI), November 19, 1957, 1.

38. "Gein Facing Lie Test on Grave Thefts Story," *Kenosha Evening News* (Kenosha, WI), November 19, 1957, 1.

39. Ibid.

40. "Unbelievable Ed Gein Story Began to Unfold at Plainfield a Year Ago," 12.

41. Ibid.

42. Bloch, "The Shambles of Ed Gein," 552.

43. "Unbelievable Ed Gein Story Began to Unfold at Plainfield a Year Ago," 12.

44. Ibid.

45. Ibid.

46. Bloch, "The Shambles of Ed Gein," 552.

47. Tim Dirks, "100 Greatest American Movies," *AMC Filmsite,* https://www.filmsite .org/afi100films_2007.html, accessed November 1, 2019.

48. Susan King, "American Film Registry Selects 25 Films for Preservation," *Los Angeles Times,* December 19, 2012.

49. Robert Traver, "Review of *People Versus Kirk,*" *Kirkus Reviews,* October 20, 1981, https://www.kirkusreviews.com/book-reviews/robert-traver/people-versus-kirk/.

50. Christopher Ingraham, "Map: Where America's Sunniest and Least-Sunny Places Are," *The Washington Post,* July 13, 2015, https://www.washingtonpost.com/news/wonk /wp/2015/07/13/map-where-americas-sunniest-and-least-sunny-places-are/.

51. W. Dale Brown, *Of Fiction and Faith: Twelve American Writers Talk about Their Vision and Work* (Grand Rapids, MI: William B. Eerdmans, 1997), 202.

52. "The Coldest Cities in the U.S," *World Atlas,* https://www.worldatlas.com/articles /10-coldest-us-cities.html, accessed November 1, 2019.

TIM FRANDY

12

HOW TO MAKE A NOISE LIKE A WORM

Fishing Guides, Tourism, and Identity in the Northwoods

The Lake Superior region of the American Upper Midwest is known for its deep forests of white and red pine, paper birch, and maple, with thousands upon thousands of freshwater lakes—representing one of the greatest concentrations of lakes in the world. The region is famed for its recreational opportunities, and city dwellers from Chicago, Minneapolis, Milwaukee, and beyond use summer weekends and holidays to vacation in an area of immense natural beauty: camping, hiking, swimming, boating, and fishing. Locals—especially those with deep roots in the region—have long maintained a special relationship to hunting and fishing. For many of them, fishing, hunting, and gathering (berries, maple syrup, wild rice, wild onions, mushrooms, and more) are not done simply for pleasure. They are regarded as work, and they represent a way of life. To know the land and waters well (and the creatures that inhabit it) is a life's work of personal, intellectual, emotional, physical, and spiritual fulfillment. For many of us who grew up in this region, our heroes weren't the intellectual elite or the wealthy, they weren't musicians or artists or athletes . . . no, they were fishermen and hunters.

I was raised in a rich environment of stories involving the harvest: of my grandfather Bill, who, when out of work one summer, decided to fish for food, catching a legal muskie every day for the duration of August, a month in which it is famously difficult to catch muskies. Of my grandmother Sigrid, who was ambidextrous and could outpick everyone in the berry patch, and who fished every spring for walleye until she could no longer get into the aluminum boat at age eighty-five. Of my great auntie Saima, who had a knack for catching large eight-pound walleye through the ice in impossibly shallow water during the early winter. Of my Uncle George, who once took a fishing trip to Ontario and caught so many fish that he was immediately hired on as a guide at the resort he stayed at.

We also heard the stories of the many legendary fishing guides in the region, in particular the guides from the 1950s—like Porter Dean, Louie Spray, Bob Ellis, and Ray Kennedy. Porter Dean was called the barefoot fishing guide because he never wore shoes while guiding (neither summer nor winter). Dean was legendary for his fishing talents, his boozing, his shore lunches, and his coarseness. Louis Spray was a bootlegger and speakeasy owner, whose catching of three record-sized muskies was tainted by his reputation as a scoundrel and a cheat.[1] Bob Ellis, who now has a fishing tournament named in his honor, popularized the technique of row trolling across the region. He lost his wife to a minister because—in my mother's words—"she didn't like being second place to a fish." Ray Kennedy was a prankster who targeted anyone off his guard, and his famous fifty-pound muskie was mounted and hung in a locally owned Minocqua restaurant, where it served as a symbol of the town.

Locals sometimes differentiate these old-time guides from the guides of today, who rely heavily on technology, and who are businessmen as much as fishermen, branding themselves with their own television shows, publications, and lure lines. Old-timers generally worked for resorts or for hire, and they were brilliant outdoorsmen. They knew every bay and bar on hundreds of lakes and could catch any kind of fish at any time of year. They also occupied important liminal roles in the community. They mediated between outsiders and locals, working on the front lines of the tourist economy of the north. Ultimately, they proved crucial in the transformation and codification of a regional identity in the Northwoods.

Importantly, in spite of popular anxieties about the loss of distinctive local cultures, local cultures sometimes intensify their distinctiveness in response to the global forces that seemingly threaten them—a process termed by Roger Abrahams and others as "oppositional identity formation."[2] This subject has been explored by folklorists for decades. For instance, Amy Shuman, in her classic essay "Dismantling Local Culture," argues that "local culture is always marked and always part of a larger-than-local context."[3] Yvonne Lockwood has noted in her work on festivals that communities engaged with tourist economies have vigorously emphasized their own distinctiveness—performing it for both outsiders and themselves through special events and everyday cultural practices.[4] Erika Brady has explored how locals in the Ozarks sometimes perform external stereotypes in front of tourists to provoke reaction and leverage power.[5] And Regina Bendix, in her exploration of the emergence of tourism in nineteenth-century Switzerland, has emphasized how locals and tourists both are active agents in crafting identities that emerge from both groups' pursuit of "authentic" and "real" cultural experiences.[6] Identity formation is an ongoing process of negotiation amid a multitude of internal and external cultural factors. Though tourism did not singularly create identity in the Northwoods, it did exaggerate and intensify certain aspects of the local region, shaping local identities through interactions and cultural dialogue between locals and tourists through the first half of the twentieth century.

In 2011, I was contracted to conduct fieldwork with a dozen individuals in the Northwoods who were actively engaged in subsistence-based fishing and hunting practices. This project was funded by the Wisconsin Arts Board and used to develop both my own dissertation research as well as two exhibits at the Chippewa Valley Museum in Eau Claire, Wisconsin (*Changing Currents* and *Harvesting Traditions*). My aim was to explore the meaning of these enduring subsistence practices in the modern day, and to contextualize them within the historical evolution of these practices. I found that subsistence hunters and fisherman were engaged in a cultural performance very different from that of recreationalists or sportsmen, for whom contemporary game management is designed.[7] Part of this story intersects with the history of my own family, who were talented outdoorsmen and -women, several of whom cobbled together a living through a mix of guiding, tourism, seasonal labor, and the home harvest.

Most pertinent to this chapter, I spoke with individuals living in Vilas County, Wisconsin, like Dave Osborn, a contemporary low-tech, backwoods fishing guide and boat and canoe restorer; like my uncle Jim Frandy and father, Tom Frandy, both outdoorsmen and retired high school teachers who grew up in the mid-twentieth-century resort culture; and most important, like Forrest

"Forrie" and Olive "Ollie" Johnson. I sat down to record stories about fishing and guiding from Forrie and Ollie Johnson on September 5, 2011, in their home in Manitowish Waters, Wisconsin. My parents, Tom and Patricia Frandy, were also present, creating an ideal environment for story swapping.

Forrie was one of the best storytellers I knew growing up. Though known locally for an occasional dramatic embellishment, he had the ability to turn any ordinary occurrence into something memorable and magical. A Norwegian American from Iron Mountain, Michigan, he is married to my father's cousin, Ollie. Ollie, who passed away in May of 2020 at age ninety-two, was Finnish, French, Sámi, and Anishinaabe, and like Forrie, she worked as a high school English teacher until the late 1980s. Both were in their mid-eighties at the time of the interview. And both were deeply enmeshed in the daily operations of Ollie's family's resort between the 1940s and 1970s.

The family resort was established by Ollie's grandfather, Abe LaFave (~1860s–1930s), a French Canadian fur trapper, who walked from Canada to northern Wisconsin in the 1880s. In Wisconsin, he homesteaded land to open LaFave's Island Lake Resort. Originally, the resort was located on a small island in Island Lake (the building, which is now a private residence, is still standing), but the resort was later relocated to the mainland. Abe's son John married Saima Nelson (Ollie's parents), and they took over operation of the resort, with many of their relatives and friends serving as seasonal workers in summertime and during deer season. It's within this context of the resort that these stories occurred.

"I'VE NEVER SEEN A MOTOR THAT BIG": A BRIEF HISTORY OF NORTHWOODS TOURIST FISHING

The south shore of Lake Superior has provided abundant fisheries—rich in walleye, muskie, northern pike, trout, perch, whitefish, bass, and panfish—for the Anishinaabe, Dakota (prior to their displacement west), and other Indigenous inhabitants of the region for thousands of years, who traditionally harvested with nets, traps, and spears. The region saw waves of French missionaries, voyageurs, and fur trappers as early as the seventeenth century, though widespread European "new immigrant" and Yankee settlement in Wisconsin's northern interior forests did not begin until the late nineteenth century.[8] In Vilas County, this began in the 1880s.[9] This white settlement corresponded with waves of industrial exploitation. Most important in Vilas County, this involved iron mining on the Gogebic Range (to the northwest), and the logging of the white pine forests throughout the region. These stands of white pine were razed to the ground in the early twentieth century, leaving unsightly scablands of barren stumps and poor topsoil in their wake.[10] This land was parceled and homesteaded in forty-acre plots, a means to displace Native Americans through the creation of private agricultural property but unsuitable for prosperous farming. A few homesteaders eked out a living, but gradually the forest recolonized the region with secondary growth (with the help of the Civilian Conservation Corps and National Forest Reservation Commission) as part of a plan to help create a mixed economy of tourism and logging in the north.[11] Though the forest environment changed considerably during this time, the locals who stayed relied consistently on the wild foods the forest offered.

Some of these homesteads remained enmeshed in small-scale agriculture for a few generations, but many of these were abandoned, repossessed by the state, and transformed into federal and state forests. Some homesteads transformed into resorts as early as the late nineteenth century, catering especially to city-dwelling tourists from Milwaukee, Chicago, and the Twin Cities. These cities grew rapidly in the early twentieth century, fueled by a land shortage for a generation of farmers and an abundance of industrial work in automotive and harbor cities along the Great Lakes. This emergent middle-class lifestyle led to the desire for recreational opportunities away from the city. Many, a short generation or two away from their own rural roots, turned toward these northern expanses for their leisure.[12] At first, these northern resorts catered to wealthy tourists (including gangsters Al Capone and John Dillinger), who could take rail lines into the area, which were at first used to transport mineral ore and timber.[13] Later, with improvements to rural roads (which until the 1930s remained snowbound during the winter) and with the emergence of the automobile, such vacations became accessible for the emergent middle class beginning in the 1920s, and tourism intensified further following the Second World War.[14] Many outdoorsmen, laborers, and farmers put their knowledge of the outdoors to use for profit in the tourist industry.

Curiously, although subsistence practice was an essential means of food procurement and an aspect of everyday life at the time, relatively few hunting and fishing stories seem to have endured from these earliest days of tourism.[15] The reasons for their absence in oral histories could be many: these kinds of stories may fade quickly with the memory of a person; this generation is characterized more by conventional colonial founders' legends; hunting and fishing were too ordinary to narrativize; older fishing techniques (nets and set lines) produced food but not many memorable stories. Regardless, it's only after the emergence of tourism—and the increased awareness of outsiders and specialization of labor—that the context is created in which mid-twentieth-century guiding legends begin to thrive.

Between the 1930s and 1960s, wild foods served both as the basis for a tourist economy and as a vital food source for locals, most of whom lived on very modest incomes. Many locals say that in the 1950s between a third and a half of their diet was wild-harvested food. Until the 1960s, the only commercial food source in Manitowish Waters was one small, full-service grocery store that sold canned and dried goods from behind a counter. Even today, many still rely on the supplemental wild food they harvest, which can amount to hundreds of pounds of meat, fish, and edible plants a year. Depending on wild foods for sustenance shapes a community in profound ways. The year revolves around the feeding and spawning cycles of a dozen species of fish; the habits of deer, grouse, and waterfowl; berries and wild rice and the weather conditions that impact them. It creates profound awareness of the weather and natural cycles and how they affect dozens of different species. It creates complex relationships between the self, the foods we depend on, and the nourishment our own foods depend on. It shapes our sense of time, of place, and of our place in the world. It separates us from individuals who fished for "fun," for "bonding," or for "sport."

The popular image we have of noncommercial fishing today is actually the product of centuries of changing techniques, technologies, and legalities—largely driven by issues of class conflict, access to resources, and the transformation of a food source into a recreation. Many of our contemporary American perceptions of fishing ethics emerge during the resort era. In Wisconsin, between 1890 and 1915, a series of laws restricted the inland netting and seining of fish, banned the dynamiting of fish and the use of setlines, distinguished game fish from rough fish, and began limiting and banning the sale of inland game fish.[16] Though law enforcement was sparse in those days, the changes in harvesting technique gradually took hold as the norms. Fishing culture was changing rapidly during the 1940s and '50s as emerging technologies and markets for new recreational products impacted fishing practices. Boats were wooden, often homemade, and demanded that their owners have sufficient woodworking skills to maintain them.[17] There were, of course, no fish finders, and detailed lakebed maps did not yet exist. Rods were mostly made of split bamboo (though fiberglass rods were emerging), and baitcasting and spinning reels were displacing cane-pole fishing or simple centerpin reels in this region.[18] Angling itself was relatively new to the region, emerging in congruence with the tourist industry. This tool of "sport" fishing was purposed to make catching fish more challenging for the Western European gentry, who intentionally "handicapped themselves"[19] and generally held disdain for subsistence fishing and the use of nets and live bait.[20] For settlers, these "sporting" techniques were mandated to be the only legal way to subsist on game fish in the Northwoods.

Outboard motors were also just starting to be used, largely as status items, as the low horsepower made them only slightly more practical than rowing. Forrie Johnson tells of the first "large" outboard motor he saw:

> I still remember most motors were 3.5–4.5 horse at the resort in the earliest days here. And up comes [wealthy resort guest] Mr. Louie from Chicago. In his Cadillac. And he opens the trunk and he had a 25 horsepower Johnson. I almost fainted. I said, "I've never seen a motor that big." And I was strong, and he said, "Can you help me get it outta there?" I reached, and I looked at it, and it was a big new green 25. And I thought, "They don't even make outboards that big." And he had called ahead, and John [LaFave] had bought a new Thompson, a 16 foot, a nice boat just so it could carry that big a motor. Now they use them for trolling motors on canoes! Oh, 25 horsepower! And when we put it on we all went down to the dock to watch it. He cranked it up. No electric starter, just manual. He got it fired up and took off across the lake, and I thought, "Oh my god . . . I'd seen big inboards go, but I'd never seen an outboard of 25!" Now you see twin 350s on these big drum boats.[21]

The status accompanying new recreational technologies rapidly impacted fishing and boating in the north. According to the guide and boat restorer Dave Osborn, "When the wooden boat went out of favor in the '60s, when that miracle composite called fiberglass and aluminum took over the world, wooden boats fell out of favor at the time. In fact a lot of times that I've noticed in my boat restoration is that wooden boats—like in the '50s—would be painted aluminum color, just to look like one of those new aluminum boats that everybody was raving about."[22]

Some locals resisted the flashiness and allure of new extravagant technologies, which did not necessarily make for better fishing. According to Forrie Johnson, the local fishing guide (and my great uncle) Jake Nelson used to paint his aluminum boat, even though one crucial selling point of an aluminum boat was that it did not require painting and maintenance:

Do you remember that little MuralCraft he had there? He got it brand new from your mother and dad [John and Saima LaFave], and he flipped it upside down and he's painting the bottom of it a dull, flat green. Painted the whole bottom, right to the gunwale. And I says, "What are you doing? You don't have to paint an aluminum boat, Jake." And, "Oh yeah?" he says, "You realize what that looks like to a fish, under that big silver hull going by? Aluminum boat . . . ," he says, "You gotta flatten them out. They'll see that boat coming." And I've thought about that too, you think about a silver aluminum hull underneath like that. And he had a nice flat neutral dull green, not even enamel. Just flat. Like a big lily pad.[23]

For many outdoorsmen of that generation, like Nelson, invisibility, silence, and awareness are paramount to proper conduct while hunting and fishing. This conduct stands in stark contrast to the behavior of some tourists who fill the perceived emptiness of the wilderness with their own largess of ego, performing ritualized acts of conquest over nature,[24] shouting to hear the echo of their own magnitude in the "middle of nowhere" as they perform acts of colonial discovery and conquest in miniature.

We locals, however, knew the rules. These rules were the language we spoke with, and we carry them with us through our lives. Pay attention if you're leaving tracks in the woods. Don't spit if you don't want animals to know you've been there. Only speak in hushed tones if you're in the woods or on a lake. Feel every stone beneath your feet as you walk, and learn to bend your foot to fit those stones.[25] Listen and learn to be silent. Forrie explains how he was taught about the importance of silence while fishing:

> I fished a lot with George [Nelson] in the evenings on Allequash Lake. We used to fish it at night for bass and muskie. I caught some nice muskie with George in there. That's when I first learned that you don't knock your pipe on the gunwale of the boat when you're fishing for muskie. We had one of LaFave's boats in the back of the truck. And when I got done smoking, I'd knock knock knock knock on the gunnel, and knock the tobacco and crud out of my pipe. Did he chew me out! "You don't do that. We might as well go home. Fishing's over for the night if you knock on that. That carries for a mile underwater." It does.[26]

Tom Frandy explains how those unfamiliar with these customs would irk a late neighbor, Marie Kazmarek: "Marie used to always complain. She'd fish with some of, I don't know if it was Butch's kids, but they'd go up and they'd want to motor right up to the spot, then throw out the anchor, and then start fishing right away. And a few minutes later, motor someplace else, and stop right there."[27]

The behavior reflects the anthropocentrism that came to define outsiders, making unnecessary noise, rushing where patience is needed, not understanding in the least how their own behavior impacts that of the environment around them. There are artistry, creative expression, aesthetics, and values in socialized behavior, and these informal rules of conduct within these social nexuses came to distinguish locals from outsiders in terms of how one behaves, rather than simply where one is from.

"LIKE A FEATHER GOING THROUGH THE AIR": JAKE NELSON, ROW TROLLER

Though several of my relatives (all of whom died before I was born) "did some guiding" in the 1950s and 1960s, we had one exceptionally gifted angler in my family: my great-uncle Jake Nelson. Born to Finnish and Sámi immigrant parents in 1906 on a farm in Gogebic County, Michigan, Jake worked as a laborer and a logger, before serving in World War II. He returned to northern Wisconsin, where he lived a life of modest means, sharing a house with his sister Saima's family for most of his life, and passing away in the 1970s. In the summer, he guided guests at LaFave's resort. Forrie Johnson explains: "There was a salt-of-the-earth guy that one. A wonderful fisherman. If I were to rank guides in the world, up here, if I were to rank guides . . . You know they give Porter Dean all these accolades, and he was good, Porter, I've fished with him many times. But the best fisherman I've ever known was Jake. Absolutely."[28]

Jake's modesty and good-natured quietude set him apart from many other guides, even of his own era. If he caught a muskie (so notoriously difficult to catch, they are now called "the fish of 10,000 casts"), he wouldn't say a word unless someone forced it out of him at the end of the day.

Jake's presentation of lures was so realistic, he could get stubborn fish to strike, and on occasion even jump out of the water. Tom Frandy, my father, tells one of his favorite stories:

> Jake was quite a fisherman. One time he was out casting for muskies, and you know when you cast for a few hours, you kind of get into a routine of casting and reeling, casting and reeling, and your mind starts to wander. So as Jake's reeling one back, he pulls his lure straight out of the water

over his shoulder to cast again, and a nice muskie jumps out of the water and lands right in the boat! It must have been following his lure, and when the lure went flying out of the water, the muskie jumped for it.[29]

Tom explained that even though Jake was not one to make up tales, a nearby warden witnessed the event, prompting Jake to carefully lift up the muskie, which was not legally caught, and put it back in the water.

The convergence of limited netting rights, an emerging tourist industry, new rod-and-reel technology, and the lake-filled geography of the region made guides like Jake Nelson turn to row trolling, the dragging of lures behind a rowed boat to catch large and aggressive game fish. Relatively little is known about the spread of row trolling throughout the United States, but the technique is adapted from big-water fishing techniques using sails (and later motors). Most motor trolling on inland lakes was banned in Class A muskie waters in Wisconsin from 1923 to 2015.[30] In the Northwoods, trolling was seemingly uncommon before the 1940s, but the practice was established in Finland and Norway from at least the early 1800s in harvest of salmon.[31] Nelson was among the first established trollers in the area, and his technique demanded a mastery over his boat. Forrie Johnson notes: "He'd go out, when he was done guiding, he'd go out and row troll just by himself, just check the waters, and stuff like that. He was beyond outboard motors. He'd just use those oars."[32]

Admiring the grace with which Jake mastered his craft, Tom Frandy explains, "The oar would just clear the water on the way up, just like a feather going through the air." These sorts of aesthetics—simplicity, grace, mastery—came to define the conduct of the proper outdoorsman in the minds of the generations that followed these guides.

The aforementioned Bob Ellis learned row trolling from Jake, who lived across the lake and was instrumental in popularizing row trolling throughout the region. Forrie Johnson explains about the relationship between Jake and Bob Ellis:

I think Bob Ellis always wanted to emulate him. You know, Bob Ellis became famous because of Jake. Jake taught Bob Ellis how to row troll from a small lapstrake boat, and work the rock bars trolling with a rod locked under your foot, and rowing, and taking the bait over rock piles and weed beds and so on. And Bob Ellis became one of the best muskie fisherman. And I've seen him long after Jake was dead, row trolling all by himself all along the shore.

Sadly, he [Ellis] got killed up on Papoose Lake. I had seen him the week before row trolling on Trout Lake. It was late fall, and he loved the late fall. The following weekend he was up on Papoose Lake up over here. And he was row trolling along, and a huge speedboat didn't see him at all. They actually had started out from a bay. And the boat was up and ready to plane. And it came right down on top of him and killed him. Drowned him . . . killed him right in the water there.[33]

The popularity of row trolling faded for several decades for a variety of reasons, including increased use of outboard motors, improved casting technology, and the destruction of cabbage weed beds,[34] but it has enjoyed a modest resurgence in recent years among sport anglers, in part because of the Bob Ellis Classic row-trolling tournament, which began in 2003. For sportsmen, the rise of the silent sports movement, the reaction against expensive fish-finding technologies and continued commercialization of fishing, and a sense of nostalgia have doubtlessly contributed to this resurgence. Yet for many locals, trolling remained an effective, low-cost technique combining the best aspects of fishing: traversing and exploring and healthful living.

"MAKE A NOISE LIKE A WORM": TOURISM, CLASS TENSIONS, AND RESISTANCE

The resort era saw a heightened awareness of the differences between tourists and locals. Tourist economies thrive on economic and power imbalances between vacationers and locals. And these feelings often create complex and overlapping feelings of gratitude, patronization, dependency, and resentment. For instance, many from LaFave's resort still speak about the Louies, wealthy annual guests who worked as jewelers in Chicago. The following exchange illustrates the complex feelings the LaFaves had with their guests, who were "like family."

> **Forrie:** The guests in the old days, they became almost like family. The Louies. And the Gills. You could almost count on them coming for a given time. Louies were almost a pain in the rear when they'd come because they'd come early and stay right until almost fall.
> **Ollie:** And they'd eat breakfast at about 11. Of course by then . . . [implying it was a burden for her mother, Saima, who cooked]
> **Forrie:** They'd want the works then . . .

Tom: They were around so much that they kind of felt that they owned the place in a way . . . I think it would bother your mom [Saima] sometimes if they would just go into the till and make their own change. Get a couple candy bars, go into the register, and leave.

Forrie: *"Forrie, did you clean my boat today?"* "No, I filled it full of garbage." *"Did you get my boat bailed out yet?"* They'd be sitting on the big floating dock down there. Of course, they were good paying guests. And he'd always tip me when they left . . . bring me a Pfluger Supreme Reel or something for a gift when he came. And if he gave you a watch. . . . He was a jeweler from Chicago. He gave me a watch one time. It was a pretty nice watch. But for eight years after, he'd come up and remind me: *"How's your watch running? How's your watch, Forrie?"* "Wonderful, Mr. Louie. Look!"[35]

Tourist literature of the day further contributed to this culture of patronization, declaring this region a "four season recreational playground" that is "here for your enjoyment," rather than the home of living people. Locals were said to work as "custodians of this vast parkland" and were "here to serve you."[36] The experience was branded to erase local people and the network of socially accountable relationships that outsiders enter into as tourists. Even growing up there in the 1980s and '90s, I would hear tourists acting surprised that "people actually lived here," and that they were not a migrant labor force to serve their needs.

Tourists were frequently the subject of considerable frustration for locals. Many were thought to be disruptive, loud, and boisterous, and others were not familiar with rudimentary outdoors skills that locals take for granted. Jim Frandy tells one of his favorite stories: "It was legal to shoot the fish . . . more than one person shot a hole in the boat bringing a muskie in. Flop, flop, flop inside the boat and pow! Forrie tells a story about one person at the resort complaining that his boat leaked and wanted to get a different boat. And Forrie knew that he had shot a hole in it. What do you mean get another boat!? You shot a hole in this boat!"[37]

Locals, however, were not passive players in this relationship. In many instances, locals clapped back at guests. Jim Frandy tells:

I remember . . . Dad worked for the DNR, and they['d] have VIPs coming up, big shots from the DNR coming up. And Dad would guide them on some of the lakes that they used for rearing, like Trilby Lake. This Eschen-bach was another guy, [guiding] with Dad. And Eschenbach went out guiding with these VIPs in the other boat and one guy caught a muskie, and the VIP was reeling it in, and another VIP in the boats says, "Oh my god . . . is that a muskie?" Eschenbach says [in a gruff voice], "What the hell do you think it is, a chipmunk?" [laughter] That's the last time Eschenbach guided the VIPs.

The distaste for the ineptitude, the wealth and power, and the obsession with new gadgetry came to cement local identity in opposition to that of the outsiders. Though the backwoods aesthetic had roots, it was reinforced by means of a pro-cess of oppositional identity formation through these interactions with tourists.

Guides often had fun at the expense of the guests of the resort, playing with the etic perceptions of tourists. John LaFave used to tell a story—here recounted by Forrie Johnson—about one resort guide, Joe Ilg Sr.:

One early morning before the guests he was guiding got up for breakfast, Joe Ilg, Sr., saw some Indians go across a trail to a nearby lake. Traveling over this same trail with his guests later that day, Joe reached down to the ground, pulled up a pinch of grass, smelled it, then remarked, "I smell buckskin. Must be Indians around." Only a few minutes later, as they proceeded down the path with their fishing gear, there were some Indians at the end of the trail. Many such jokes were played on city guests, whom some guides called "city slickers."[38]

Jake Nelson was known for his one-liner quips that he'd deliver to tourists, that play with inversions of perspective. As Forrie Johnson tells: "Remember what Jake told Mrs. Louie, when she was waiting impatiently at the dock for the Louies to go fishing? Mrs. Louie spotted a robin there, and she wanted to get the robin's attention or something, and she said, 'Oh! I want to get a picture of me and this bird. How can I get the bird's attention over here?' And Jake's standing there, waiting patiently. And he says, 'Make a noise like a worm.'"[39]

Tom Frandy tells another, which pokes fun at tourists' inability to understand the most basic of fishing concepts: "Some of the guests had been talking about fishing, and he asked how things had been going. And [a guest] said, 'Well, I've been having a lot of problems because the fish are always striking short. They'd make a pass at it but they're always hitting short. They not getting the bait.' And [the guest] asked Jake if he had any suggestions, and he says, 'Well, put a longer leader on it.' [laughter] And the guy says, 'Yeah, that makes sense!'"[40]

Extending the leader, which attaches the lure to the line, essentially extends the line and would have no bearing on how fish strike a lure—creating something of an absurdist joke. The quip delineates insiders from outsiders, challenges the tourist's awareness of a fish's thinking and behavior, and helps establish a network of local values that tether local identity to ecological awareness and outdoors savvy. It's important to abandon anthropocentric thinking and see the world from the perspective of a fish.

"THE FIRST WHITE MEN EVER TO SET FOOT BACK HERE": EGO- AND ECOCENTRISM

My father used to tell me a story about Jake Nelson. One year, in the mid-1960s, they went fishing in Ontario. They pushed pretty far into the backcountry, trying to get into some less-accessible lakes. On a small portage trail, Jake said to my father, "Just think . . . we might be the first white men ever to set foot back here." Just as my father—a young man at the time—was starting to reflect on the magnitude of this achievement, he looked to the side of the trail, where he noticed a small old carving scratched into a tree: "Jake Nelson. George Nelson." My father always said that Jake never would have said another word about it, whether he had noticed the carving of not. That's just the kind of sense of humor he had, my father would say. For me, though, I understand the story as something that resists and mocks the colonial logics of discovery (after all, wherever you go, you're always in someone's backyard), and something that compels us to abandon the egocentric thinking that has permeated so many aspects of Western thought and embrace decentered and ecocentric ways of living and being.

Though subsistence fishing and hunting were always an important part of the Northwoods, their symbolic importance grew during the resort era, as tensions with outsiders helped define what it meant to be local. The connection to the land became how many locals understood themselves: as people *of* the land. Consequently, drawing boundaries between these groups led to a complex and tense relationship with many of the values that later came to define America in the postwar economy: consumerism, the rat race and keeping up with the Joneses, the rise of the nuclear family, and the culture of leisure. That wasn't us. We never vacationed, we lived sparingly, we could manage without work by harvesting our own food if we needed to, and we recognized kinship five generations back. This is the real world for us, and the rest remains mere artifice, like a foggy dream, even as we work and live within it. When we open our eyes, we live to rival Porter Dean's ability to endure the snow beneath his bare feet, to outwit Ray Kennedy's best pranks, and to row a lapstrake boat like Jake Nelson, who could make his oars glide intimately over the water like a song.

NOTES

1. Detloff, *Three Record Muskies in His Day*.
2. Abrahams, "Identity," 146–75.
3. Shuman, "Dismantling Local Culture," 345.
4. Lockwood, "A Fish Sandwich for All," 235–45.
5. Brady, "'The River's Like Our Back Yard,'" 146–47.
6. Bendix, "Tourism and Cultural Displays," 131–46.
7. Frandy, *Harvesting Tradition*.
8. Wisconsin Cartographers' Guild, *Wisconsin's Past and Present*, 4–5.
9. These north-central counties represented some of the latest incorporated counties in the state: Vilas and Iron (1893); Oneida and Forest (1885).
10. Wisconsin Cartographers' Guild, *Wisconsin's Past and Present*, 38–41.
11. Jensen, *Calling This Place Home*, 60–61.
12. Jensen, *Calling This Place Home*, 60–61.
13. Willging, *On the Hunt*, 71.
14. Wisconsin Cartographers' Guild, *Wisconsin's Past and Present*, 50–51; 60–61.
15. This observation comes from both growing up in the region and nearly fifteen years of professional work in the region with subsistence fishers and hunters.
16. Kline, Bruch, and Binkowski, *People of the Sturgeon*, 28–37; Wisconsin State Statutes, Chapter 307 (1893); Wisconsin State Statutes, Chapter 489 (1905).
17. Dave Osborn, interview with author.
18. Forrest Johnson and Olive Johnson, interview with author.
19. Nesper, "Ogitchida at Waswaaganing," 231.
20. Note, for example, Bilton, *Two Summers in Norway*, 144.
21. Forrest Johnson and Olive Johnson, interview with author.
22. Dave Osborn, interview with author.
23. Forrest Johnson and Olive Johnson, interview with author.
24. Harrison, *Forests*, 69.
25. I borrow this language from the Sámi poet Nils Aslak Valkeapää: "I walk on these stones / the rocky ground / my feet shaped by these stones." In Gaski, *In the Shadow of the Midnight Sun*, 115.
26. Forrest Johnson and Olive Johnson, interview with author.
27. Tom Frandy, interview with author.
28. Forrest Johnson and Olive Johnson, interview with author.
29. Tom Frandy, interview with author.

30. Wisconsin Department of Natural Resources, "Why Is Motor Trolling Not Allowed?"

31. Sirelius, *Suomalaisten Kalastus:I–III.*

32. Forrest Johnson and Olive Johnson, interview with author.

33. Forrest Johnson and Olive Johnson, interview with author.

34. Cabbage weed beds are important muskie habitat, as the fish often use them to ambush prey. The plant's broad leaves make it ideal for pulling a lure over the top of the bed.

35. Forrest Johnson and Olive Johnson, interview with author.

36. Vilas County Publicity Department, "Vilas County Wisconsin Map."

37. Jim Frandy, interview with author.

38. John (Jack) LaFave, *My Memories of Yesteryear.*

39. Forrest Johnson and Olive Johnson, interview with author.

40. Tom Frandy, interview with author.

BIBLIOGRAPHY

Abrahams, Roger D. "Identity." In *Eight Words for the Study of Expressive Culture*, ed. Bert Feintuch, 146–75. Urbana: University of Illinois Press, 2003.

Bendix, Regina. "Tourism and Cultural Displays: Inventing Traditions for Whom?" *Journal of American Folklore* 102, no. 404 (1989): 131–46.

Bilton, William. *Two Summers in Norway.* London: Saunders and Otley, 1840.

Brady, Erika. "'The River's Like Our Back Yard': Tourism and Cultural Identity in the Ozark National Scenic Riverways." In *Conserving Culture: A New Discourse on Heritage*, ed. Mary Hufford, 138–51. Urbana: University of Illinois Press, 1994.

Chippewa Valley Museum. *Changing Currents.* Museum exhibition. Eau Claire, Wisconsin, 2014.

———. *Harvesting Tradition.* Museum exhibition. Eau Claire, Wisconsin, 2017.

Detloff, John. *Three Record Muskies in His Day: The Life and Times of Louie Spray.* Couderay, WI: Trail's End, 2002.

Frandy, Jim. Interview with author, Manitowish Waters, Wisconsin, May 4, 2011. Archived at Chippewa Valley Museum, Eau Claire, Wisconsin.

Frandy, Tim W. *Harvesting Tradition: Subsistence and Meaning in the Northern Periphery.* PhD diss., University of Wisconsin, 2013.

Frandy, Tom. Interview with author, Manitowish Waters, Wisconsin, May 4, 2011. Archived at Chippewa Valley Museum, Eau Claire, Wisconsin.

———. Interview with author, Arbor Vitae, Wisconsin, November 15, 2006. Archived at Chippewa Valley Museum, Eau Claire, Wisconsin.

Harrison, Robert Pogue. *Forests: The Shadow of Civilization.* Chicago: University of Chicago Press, 1992.

Jensen, Joan M. *Calling This Place Home: Women on the Wisconsin Frontier, 1850–1925.* St. Paul: Minnesota State Historical Society Press, 2006.

Johnson, Forrest, and Olive Johnson. Interview with author, Manitowish Waters, Wisconsin, September 5, 2011. Archived at Chippewa Valley Museum, Eau Claire, Wisconsin.

Kline, Kathleen Schmitt, Ronald M. Bruch, and Frederick P. Binkowski. *People of the Sturgeon: Wisconsin's Love Affair with an Ancient Fish.* Madison: Wisconsin State Historical Society Press, 2009.

LaFave, John (Jack). *My Memories of Yesteryear: Life on Island Lake in the Early Days.* Collected and written by Forrie Johnson. Unpublished.

Lockwood, Yvonne. "A Fish Sandwich for All." In *Culture Work: Folklore for the Public Good*, eds. Tim Frandy and B. Marcus Cederström, 235–45. Madison: University of Wisconsin Press, 2022.

Nesper, Larry. "Ogitchida at Waswaaganing: Conflict in the Revitalization of Lac du Flambeau Anishinaabe Identity." In *Reassessing Revitalization Movements: Perspectives from North America and the Pacific Islands*, ed. Michael E. Harkin, 225–46. Lincoln: University of Nebraska Press, 2004.

Osborn, Dave. 2012. Interview with author, Manitowish Waters, Wisconsin, April 3, 2012. Archived at Chippewa Valley Museum, Eau Claire, Wisconsin.

Shuman, Amy. "Dismantling Local Culture." *Western Folklore* 52, no. 2/4 (1993): 345–64.

Sirelius, Uuno Taavi. *Suomalaisten Kalastus:I–III.* Helsinki: Suomalaisen Kirjallisuuden Seura, 2009.

Valkeapää, Nils Aslak. "Poem 141" In *In the Shadow of the Midnight Sun: Contemporary Sami Prose and Poetry*, ed. Harald Gaski, 115. Seattle: University of Washington Press, 1997.

Vilas County Publicity Department. "Vilas County Wisconsin Map." Tourist map. Park Falls, WI: MacGregor Litho, 1968.

Willging, Robert C. *On the Hunt: The History of Deer Hunting in Wisconsin.* Madison: Wisconsin Historical Society Press, 2008.

Wisconsin Cartographers' Guild. *Wisconsin's Past and Present: A Historical Atlas.* Madison: University of Wisconsin Press, 1998.

Wisconsin Department of Natural Resources. "Why Is Motor Trolling Not Allowed?" October 31, 2019. https://web.archive.org/web/20191031145308/https://dnr.wi.gov/topic/fishing/questions/trollhist.html. Accessed August 11, 2022.

Wisconsin State Statutes. Chapter 307 (1893), "An Act for the Protection of Fish in the Inland Waters, Lakes, and Streams of the State of Wisconsin." https://docs.legis.wisconsin.gov/1893/related/acts/307.pdf. Accessed June 10, 2020.

Wisconsin State Statutes. Chapter 489 (1905). "An Act to Amend Section 4560a of the Statutes of 1898 . . ." https://docs.legis.wisconsin.gov/1905/related/acts/489.pdf. Accessed June 10, 2020.

ADAM MERTZ

13

TOURISM, TREATY RIGHTS, AND WISCONSIN'S RURAL-URBAN POLITICAL DIVIDE, 1974–1994

From the mid-1980s through the early 1990s, federal court decisions recognizing Ojibwe nations' rights to hunt, fish, and gather off their reservations embroiled Wisconsin in controversy. The conflict grew especially confrontational and violent in the northern third of the state, where the Ojibwe exercised these rights. While some non–Native American Wisconsinites supported treaty rights as a civil rights issue, critics of treaty rights charged that these "special" rights for Native Americans undermined the state's increasingly significant tourism industry. Rural white residents in northern Wisconsin were particularly dependent on the tourism industry, and they worried that Native Americans' increased ability to exercise treaty rights—especially Ojibwe rights to spear walleyes in public lakes—would reduce the number of annual tourists, thereby threatening the livelihood of those involved in tourism. Because the state government and tourists from metropolitan areas had initially compelled northern Wisconsin to rely so heavily on tourism, northern Wisconsin residents already harbored hostility toward the more-populous southern part of the state. The treaty rights controversy, then, tapped a deep vein of animosity against state government agencies, especially the Wisconsin Department of Natural Resources (DNR), and combined those feelings with a sense that Native Americans had been unfairly granted an "elevated status" by federal courts. The treaty rights dispute therefore helped foment a rural-urban divide in Wisconsin politics.

FROM EXTRACTIVE INDUSTRY TO TOURISM

The treaty rights conflict grew in Wisconsin's "cutover" area, covering eighteen counties in roughly the northern third of Wisconsin. The region's name derives from its past in the lumber industry, from the late nineteenth century through the early twentieth century, when massive timber companies felled all the old-growth trees in the area. The cutover region includes five of Wisconsin's six bands of Ojibwe, often called "Chippewa," a Euro-American mispronunciation of "Ojibwe." The overwhelmingly rural, forested region hosts nearly innumerable vacation homes that surround the cutover's hundreds of beautiful lakes, and numerous vacation homes stand on non-lakefront property. Many year-round residents service this tourism industry by running area grocery stores, lodging for tourists who do not own vacation homes, gas stations, restaurants, equipment rentals, and landscape services. People who work at small-town businesses not directly related to tourism also populate the region. Many people in the cutover also work in extractive industries, mainly mining and logging. Access to abundant timber allowed many paper mills to spring up in the area, and these factories also employ cutover residents. The cutover lies north of the Corn Belt, and the cutover's northernmost areas are even above the Dairy Belt. Despite the area's shorter growing season, however, pockets of farming still persist.[1]

Originally, the Ojibwe occupied Wisconsin's cutover, along with the northern reaches of Minnesota and Michigan—and into Canada. The U.S. government acquired the land through treaties in 1837, 1842, and 1854; this land later came under federal court scrutiny as the "ceded territory." Shortly after these treaties were signed, the federal government enacted its allotment policies starting in the 1880s, which relegated the six Ojibwe bands to small, scattered reservations.[2] This series of forced displacements inaugurated the lumber boom of the 1890s through the 1910s in northern Wisconsin. Some parts of Wisconsin's cutover are on the periphery of the vast copper fields of Michigan's Upper Peninsula and northern Minnesota's iron range. In addition to the lumber boom, then, these immense mineral deposits also spurred Euro-American settlement of the Lake Superior region.[3]

As more timber fell, wealthy vacationers from large metropolitan areas, like Milwaukee and Chicago, used their political connections to press for conservation in northern Wisconsin, specifically conservation policies that would preserve their vacationland.[4] Once loggers cleared the land, timber companies sought to unload it. Lumber companies either sold their land directly to buyers or handed off the land to intermediaries, which offered these cleared tracts as farmland to settlers. The state of Wisconsin also assisted in the effort, using its Board of Immigration to actively recruit settlers to the cutover to establish yeoman farms, attempting to draw from neighboring states, especially their major cities. Immigrant settlers of various European ethnicities attempted to make the region into a collection of yeoman farm communities. The Board of Immigration worked with county agricultural agents to offer advice to the new settlers.[5]

As cutover settlement deviated from the architects' plans, however, most agricultural experts turned against yeoman farming in the cutover. Many of the settlers were often foreign born, mostly Finns, Czechs, and Poles. The Finns had a reputation for radical ideas, and the dedicated Catholicism of the latter two groups worried many state and county experts because they feared the settlers' religion would impede their "Americanization." These patterns worried many agricultural experts, especially after the first Red Scare began in 1919. And after the decline of agricultural prices beginning in the mid-1920s, the agricultural experts began to actively discourage farmer settlement, claiming it was no longer viable, and favored instead reforestation and an emphasis on tourism. The cutover's shorter growing season also confounded efforts to establish yeoman farms.[6]

As these efforts flagged, county and municipal governments, agricultural experts, conservationists, and some federal programs—like the New Deal Civilian Conservation Corps—encouraged the remaking of northern Wisconsin into a tourist haven. This reshaping limited the extraction year-round residents could perform themselves, which impeded independent economic activity for both Ojibwe residents and Euro-American settlers.[7] While these policies pushed out smaller yeoman farms, larger farms continued to operate and expanded in select areas, as did zones of logging and mining. Policymakers, however, had decisively steered the cutover toward tourism.[8]

To help in this effort, the state government established the Wisconsin Department of Conservation (WDC) in 1927, and the agency coordinated efforts at reforestation, stocking fish in lakes and rivers, and monitoring game to set hunting limits. As manufacturing boomed in the 1950s and 1960s in Wisconsin's larger cities—mainly in the southern and eastern parts of the state—industrial workers' incomes increased, and they clamored for more recreation opportunities, often in northern Wisconsin. The state government obliged by purchasing large swaths of land on which it expanded hiking trails and built various recreational facilities, like campgrounds and waysides.[9] The state further facilitated tourism by improving its highway system.

The cutover's private resort owners decried the expansion of the state park system because that program effectively used resort owners' state tax dollars to help undercut their own business. As one resort owner noted in the 1960s, because the state and county governments "use the tax payers['] money to build and . . . repair" public campgrounds, "we pay taxes to be pushed out of business." These sentiments extended beyond resort owners. In April 1969, the state held an advisory referendum on its mission to create more recreational facilities: the vote won in only twenty of Wisconsin's seventy-two counties but garnered 53 percent of the statewide vote. Most of the referendum's support, therefore, came from the state's populous counties, especially Madison's Dane County with 72 percent and 63 percent in Milwaukee County.[10]

Alongside the state's efforts to promote tourism, individual Wisconsinites and out-of-staters—mainly from metropolitan areas—built vacation homes in Wisconsin's rural areas. From 1960 to 1966 alone, the number of vacation homes increased from about 55,000 to over 96,000.[11] The construction of vacation homes inflated neighboring property values, which increased property taxes for nearby farmers and other year-round rural residents. The continued influx of retirees, who became year-round residents in their former vacation homes, exacerbated the problem. This form of recreation effected a rural gentrification that increased the cost of living for the permanent, year-round rural residents.[12]

All of these changes contributed to frustration with the WDC and its successor, the Department of Natural Resources (DNR). Many people who felt displaced or inconvenienced by rising land prices and property taxes disliked the DNR. After all, the DNR actually carried out most of the state's land purchases, on which the state built such enticing recreational facilities. Also, the DNR continued the WDC's role of enforcer for fishing, hunting, camping, and broader environmental regulations. And because tax dollars and fishing/hunting licenses paid DNR operating costs, many people resented having to fund the very agents who placed restrictions on them. Distaste for the state government, with special focus on the DNR, therefore ran deep in northern Wisconsin.

By the early 1980s, then, tourism represented an important economic activity for many residents in northern Wisconsin, especially for the area's white residents. These white rural residents worried that Native Americans' increased ability to exercise treaty rights—especially Ojibwe rights to spear walleyes in public lakes—would reduce the number of annual tourists, thereby threatening the livelihood of those involved in tourism. Because federal courts recognized these treaty rights, treaty rights opponents easily connected this new controversy to long-standing grievances about faraway government power.

DIRECT ACTION FOR TRIBAL SOVEREIGNTY

As tourism grew in Wisconsin's cutover, Native American peoples across the country and Wisconsin demanded equal rights and economic opportunity through self-determination, often by seeking effective recognition of treaty rights. The 1973 Wounded Knee occupation, in which Oglala Lakota American Indian Movement (AIM) activists occupied the Pine Ridge Indian Reservation in South Dakota, represents perhaps the most dramatic example of this struggle.

During the occupation, Victoria Gokee, chair of Wisconsin's Red Cliff Ojibwe band and Wisconsin Democratic governor Patrick Lucey's Indian Affairs coordinator, explained that "Wounded Knee is a manifestation of the frustrations that all American Indians feel as a result of the failure of government at all levels." Gokee warned that there "could be Wounded Knees in [the Wisconsin cities of] Milwaukee, Keshena, Hayward or Ashland at any time." Many Wisconsin Native Americans voiced grievances similar to those involved in Wounded Knee, including the discrimination experienced from law enforcement, in employment, from lack of access to sufficient credit, in receiving service from public utilities, and in being denied welfare benefits that "are extended to Whites without question." And in "school districts adjacent to Indian reservations," Gokee continued, Native Americans were subjected to excessive discipline, unjust tracking into low-achieving classes, and curricular materials that either "ignored or made fun of" Native American culture.[13]

On New Year's Day 1975, nearly two years after Gokee's warning, forty members of the Menominee Warriors Society, a small faction of Menominee Nation members, occupied the Catholic Alexian Brothers novitiate. While the Catholic order no longer staffed the 237-acre campus, they still retained title to the buildings and the land. Although the novitiate was located in neighboring Shawano County and therefore just outside the boundary of the Menominee Nation Reservation, the Warriors contested the treaties that created that arrangement, claiming that the novitiate actually stood on Menominee land. Because the Alexian order vacated the premises, the Warriors believed the novitiate buildings and campus should revert to Menominee control and be used as a healthcare and rehabilitation facility to supply services and jobs to the Menominee. Menominee tribal leaders criticized the occupation but sympathized with the sentiment that animated it. The occupation lasted for thirty-four days and precipitated confrontations between the local white residents, local and county law enforcement, and National Guard troops, whom Governor Patrick Lucey called in to maintain order.[14]

Native American occupations, like Wounded Knee and the Alexian Brothers, placed pressure on lawmakers to recognize treaty rights. As those rights went into effect through laws and court decisions in states like Washington, Oregon, and Wisconsin, state authorities and fishing and hunting groups protested those changes.[15] Washington State experienced a particularly fraught confrontation after 1974, when the Boldt decision guaranteed the indigenous nations of western Washington State the right to fish salmon as outlined under their earlier treaties.[16]

WISCONSIN'S *VOIGT* DECISION

Behind the more dramatic episodes of physical confrontations, a relatively minor incident in the 1970s produced a court decision in 1983 that shaped the struggle for treaty rights for the next decade: the momentous *Lac Court Oreilles Band of Chippewa Indians v. Lester P. Voigt, et al.* decision. The long-running court case arose from the 1974 arrest of two Lac Court Oreilles (LCO) Ojibwe, Frederick and Michael Tribble, who, emboldened by the 1974 Boldt decision in Washington State, engaged in ice fishing on public lands off an Ojibwe reservation. Frederick and Michael Tribble, backed up by the LCO band, claimed that under the most recent 1854 treaty, they could legally hunt and fish on any public land—even those off the reservation. In 1978, claiming the Ojibwe had forfeited their off-reservation rights in the 1854 treaty, federal district judge James Doyle ruled against the LCO interpretation after they brought their case to the court. The LCO appealed the case, and the Seventh Circuit Court of Appeals overturned Doyle's ruling, providing the 1983 *Voigt* decision. (Many referred to the case simply as *"Voigt,"* after the defendant Lester P. Voigt, who served as the first director of the DNR during the initial 1974 arrest that began the case.)[17]

In the *Voigt* decision, the court ruled that despite the establishment of the reservation system in the 1854 treaty, the approximately nine thousand Ojibwe— the LCO and Wisconsin's five other Ojibwe bands—retained rights to hunt and fish across all of the territory ceded in 1854, regardless of whether or not that land lay within current reservation boundaries. The Court of Appeals also tasked Judge Doyle with outlining a system of regulation for Ojibwe to hunt and fish off their reservations, an endeavor that proved quite lengthy. The U.S. Supreme Court refused to hear the state of Wisconsin's appeal, so the state government instead opted to block Ojibwe attempts to hunt and fish on private lands. But in 1985, the Seventh Circuit Court of Appeals again affirmed Ojibwe treaty rights, forcing the state of Wisconsin to lift its restrictions.[18]

The Ojibwe argued that the hunting and fishing could remedy the poverty and unemployment on the reservations. Ojibwe also pointed to the importance of these historical practices as markers of their cultural heritage and in reasserting their tribal sovereignty. Rather than continue to endure state regulation under the DNR, the state's Ojibwe bands formed the Great Lakes Indian Fish and Wildlife Commission in June 1984 to monitor and regulate hunting and fishing under their treaty rights. They modeled their commission on a similar one formed in Washington State after the 1974 Boldt decision.[19]

After the *Voigt* decision, an anti–treaty rights group, Equal Rights for Everyone (ERFE), sprang up in Hayward, a cutover village heavily dependent on the tourist industry. Hayward shared Sawyer County with the LCO Ojibwe reservation. By 1984, ERFE claimed four thousand members.[20] During the inaugural spearing season in spring 1985, the ERFE organized protests at the boat landings on the lakes on which some Ojibwe engaged in spearfishing walleyes.

The Ojibwe method of using a spear during the spring spawning season so obviously differed from the rod-and-reel method recognized by white anglers and state authorities. Some anti–treaty rights protest signs, in fact, called a spear a "lazy man's fishing pole," and another demanded that spearers "Fish the American way!"[21] Rod-and-reel fishing licenses, along with other state monies, funded the state government's program of stocking lakes with game fish. The state government had also built boat landings on more than one thousand lakes in the ceded territory as part of its efforts to foster public access to fishing and, more broadly, to promote tourism.[22] Treaty rights opponents, led by the ERFE, held racialized notions of the "proper" way to fish and worried about a reduction in tourism business, so they disdained the fact that their fishing licenses and tax dollars effectively subsidized the practice of spearing, such as with the creation of a separate agency for regulating spearfishing (the Great Lakes Indian Fish and Wildlife Commission). This confluence of concerns made the spearing issue incredibly contentious. And these protests at boat landings—sites that symbolized the cutover's recreational opportunities—proved the most public aspect of the *Voigt* decision.

After financial troubles and disagreement about the organization's direction, some ERFE leaders left in September 1985 to form a new organization, which they named Protect Americans' Rights and Resources (PARR). Larry Peterson, who had served as ERFE vice president, became board chair of PARR. Peterson, a forty-four-year-old self-described "redneck," lived near Park Falls, which lay between Hayward, an ERFE stronghold, and the PARR's most active area, Minocqua. In Park Falls, Peterson worked as a boiler operator at the Flambeau Paper Company.[23]

By the start of 1986, Peterson was editing and publishing the organization's newsletter, the *PARR Issue*. In the inaugural publication, the newsletter declared PARR a "grass roots, non-violent, non-profit, volunteer organization that has formed because of the Voigt Decision."[24] Peterson proclaimed that PARR was "not fighting the Indians," but was instead "fighting the Federal Government" for recognizing treaty rights.[25]

Minocqua, a cutover village of nearly 3,400 residents in Oneida County, sat near the reservation for the Lac du Flambeau band of Ojibwe. The reservation itself straddled Oneida County and Vilas County. Because the Lac du Flambeau engaged in more spearfishing than the other Ojibwe bands, most confrontations about spearfishing protests occurred in this area.[26]

Minocqua and the surrounding area relied heavily on tourism, especially in the summer. Every year, an estimated 1.2 million people fished and over 650,000 people hunted deer in northern Wisconsin. With the newly recognized treaty rights, the Ojibwe did not need to buy hunting or fishing licenses through the DNR, had a longer hunting season, and could potentially catch many more fish than non–Native American anglers.[27] Representatives from the Great Lakes Indian Fish and Wildlife Commission reassured tourists that spearfishing had not overharvested the lakes.[28] Those white residents who relied on the tourist trade, however, feared that the expanded treaty rights would deplete the fish and game and therefore reduce the influx of tourists.[29]

Because of these competing interests and repeated confrontations, treaty rights represented a contentious political issue, which often acquired a rural-urban polarization. PARR members pointed to a lack of political clout and expressed their frustration at the state government that resided in the faraway city of Madison, which lay in the southern part of Wisconsin. In fact, PARR pointed to past attempts by both northern Wisconsin and Michigan's Upper Peninsula—also covered under the ceded territory—to combine into the fifty-first state, which they planned to name "Superior," because both state legislatures ignored their respective northern reaches.[30] In 1985, however, the state of Michigan reached a settlement with the Ojibwe who lived there and with fishing groups and fishing charter associations.[31]

While in office, Democratic governor Anthony Earl proved relatively sympathetic to treaty rights, offering support for them as a civil rights issue. To study the conflicts and attempt to remedy them, Earl convened a special commission in 1984. He decided not to seat a PARR representative on the special governor's commission, yet he included representatives from each of Wisconsin's Native American nations. James Schlender of the Great Lakes Indian Fish and Wildlife Commission celebrated Earl's decision to deny PARR a seat on Governor Earl's special commission.[32]

But Earl's opponent for the 1986 gubernatorial election, Republican state assembly member Tommy Thompson, who hailed from rural western Wisconsin, told the PARR that he condemned Governor Earl's decision.[33] Because Governor Earl had the state investigate the treaty rights issue further, Thompson accused Governor Earl of having "drive[n] a wedge" between Native Americans and white residents in northern Wisconsin.[34] Thompson believed that treaty rights harmed the state's increasingly important tourism industry.[35] And on the campaign trail, Thompson attended a PARR event in Minocqua.[36] Thompson's opposition to treaty rights helped him win the 1986 gubernatorial election, and PARR members viewed Governor Thompson as an ally.[37]

The treaty rights dispute garnered attention outside northern Wisconsin, into the populous southeast corner of Wisconsin and beyond, where many tourists and vacation homeowners lived. Because vacation homeowners, along with hunters and anglers, were spread across the state and into neighboring states, by 1987 PARR had established some far-flung chapters.[38] A PARR supporter in Sheboygan pointed to the unfair arrangement that hunting and fishing licenses, along with taxes, paid "the salaries of all the wardens, deputies, and personnel involved to protect the spearers who are destroying the tourism of the area."[39]

Hearing concerns like these at PARR meetings, Peterson observed that many "Wisconsin and non-resident sportspeople are questioning their support of the Wisconsin DNR bureaucracy because of their part in allowing for the full implementation of Indian treaty rights."[40]

As the treaty rights issue spread, PARR hosted a national conference on treaty rights in Wausau, Wisconsin, in 1987.[41] PARR had its second national convention in Racine, Wisconsin, in 1988.[42] By hosting these conferences, PARR and other groups became leaders in the nationwide anti–treaty rights movement. Their 1988 conference, in fact, occurred in the same year as the publication of Ron Arnold's *Wise Use Agenda*.[43] Arnold's book inaugurated the "wise use" movement that opposed federal regulation and federal ownership of land and instead favored private ownership to promote stewardship of the land. The "wise use" movement cast rural residents, mainly white ones, as the victims of environmental regulations imposed by urban elites.[44] As the treaty rights issue spread, the conflicts in Wisconsin reached a crescendo in 1989.

THE 1989 CRESCENDO AND STATEWIDE POLARIZATION

Between 1984 and 1988, the Wisconsin state government and Ojibwe bands operated under a series of annual negotiated settlements while the courts, state officials, and Ojibwe representatives worked out a long-term solution.[45] In early 1989, the Mole Lake and Lac du Flambeau Ojibwe bands rejected the terms of a proposed ten-year settlement in which the state government attempted to reduce treaty rights in exchange for an end to boat-landing protests. After Judge Doyle's death, Judge Barbara Crabb took up Doyle's task. Judge Crabb created a judicial settlement by engineering the "safe harvest level" to prevent overfishing.[46] Though this decision placed clear limits on the number of fish Ojibwe could harvest, it also provided legal sanction to spearfishing, thereby securing its status.

Northern Wisconsin resort owners worried that the DNR would reduce the catch limit for rod-and-reel fishers because they believed spearfishers would catch too many walleyes earlier in the season. Resort owners therefore feared reduced clientele for the season.[47] In April 1989, five hundred anti–treaty rights protesters, mostly representing the northern Wisconsin tourist industry, marched at the state Capitol. The protesters implored state government officials to reach a favorable solution because, as one resort owner explained, "You've got our lives in your hands."[48] Because of the court decision and the worries it inspired, 1989 proved to be the worst year for boat-landing protests.[49]

Treaty rights supporters highlighted the racial elements of those who opposed treaty rights. The protests often displayed plentiful hauls of racial stereotypes. A sign at a boat-landing protest, for example, read "The North Woods is for timber wolves not timber niggers."[50] And a treaty rights supporter, who attended a PARR protest gathering, described the scene with disgust: "U.S. flags flew everywhere, blaze orange costumes, . . . an Indian effigy hung on a spear, a beery crowd, mistruths, and broad, unsubstantiated statements like 'every Indian is a drunk riding the welfare system.'" Because of this scene, the observer "felt like I was at a Nazi rally against Jews."[51]

Treaty rights supporters also tried to dispel the tax-exempt myths attached to Native Americans. James Jannetta, attorney for the Lac du Flambeau Ojibwe, explained that the Ojibwe paid both federal and state income taxes. They only received exemption from the state sales tax for their purchases made on the reservation and from the state income tax for any on-reservation employment.[52]

Treaty rights opponents refuted the charges of racism these "outside" activists heaped on them. A treaty rights opponent from Gordon, for example, "deeply resent[ed] being called a [r]acist," when they were in fact "striving for equal rights and equal opportunity for everyone—not through violence but by talking, circulating petitions, writing letters and protesting peaceably [sic]!"[53] And Peterson found it detestable to "label people racist who merely have a difference of opinion from you." Peterson, on behalf of himself and PARR, denounced racist bumper stickers about the issue—and pointed to "T-shirts being worn by some Indian tribal members with obscene, racial remarks" printed on them about white people.[54] In fact, Peterson received a defaced PARR membership application that called PARR members the "Assholes/Rednecks of Am[erica]," along with many other vulgar comments.[55]

As the treaty rights controversy dragged on, treaty rights supporters drove to the boat-landing protests to serve as witnesses in an attempt to mitigate violent confrontations.[56] A Merrill public school teacher who supported PARR called these treaty rights advocates "bleeding heart liberals" who had a "formidable propaganda network (media, churches, academics, etc.)" at their disposal.[57] A Neenah PARR member criticized Tom Maulson, leader of the Lac du Flambeau Ojibwe band, for going to the notoriously liberal University of Wisconsin–Madison to "drum up support from the liberal college students."[58] And Peterson scolded DNR head George Meyer for inviting "southern [Wisconsin] pro-treaty groups to come north."[59] Peterson indicted those "guilt ridden Americans," like many "well educated Urban Elites, Academics, News Writers, Church Leaders,

Government Officials, Tribal Spokespersons , and the like," who used "their titles and influence to promote" treaty rights.[60] Although anti–treaty rights groups certainly had their own allies outside northern Wisconsin, the constituency of treaty rights supporters fueled the narrative of a rural-urban political divide.

Cutover residents had long understood that people from big cities to the south—the agricultural experts (educated at UW-Madison) who turned the cutover away from yeoman farming; government regulators empowered by politicians in Madison; and tourists from metropolitan Madison, Milwaukee, and Chicago—held excessive sway over their lives. These same faraway people who had compelled cutover residents to focus on tourism now seemed to have bestowed upon Native Americans the means to potentially undermine the cutover's tourism-based livelihoods. Treaty rights opponents' newer scorn about "special" rights for Native Americans, therefore, easily grafted onto their long-standing grievances.

THE TOURISM DILEMMA

For Governor Thompson, the treaty rights controversy presented an especially acute affliction because he had consistently stoked sentiments against treaty rights, citing threats to the state's tourism industry. Indeed, the conflict helped him win office in 1986. Thompson's opposition to treaty rights had emboldened groups like PARR, which exacerbated boat-landing demonstrations. These confrontations endangered participants, thereby scaring away prospective tourists. Moreover, the intensity of the 1989 boat-landing protests exhausted law enforcement resources and even alienated some PARR members.[61] And the federal government refused to intervene in the treaty rights dispute in Wisconsin.[62] Thompson's stance on treaty rights therefore threatened tourism, an increasingly important part of the state's economy, which Thompson had vowed to protect. By late 1989, then, Thompson needed to settle the treaty rights dispute to save the tourism sector.[63]

Many state politicians also recognized the need to resolve the dispute to save the state tourism industry.[64] And after the terrible boat-landing protests in spring 1989, the Wisconsin Tourism Federation pressed for a settlement to the treaty rights issue to protect the state's tourism industry.[65] In 1990, before the start of the year's spearfishing season, ten cutover chambers of commerce, led by the villages of Minocqua, Lac du Flambeau, and Boulder Junction, decided to cooperate with bands of Ojibwe to end the disputes in hopes of not discouraging tourists. Lac du Flambeau Ojibwe leaders promised to spear fewer walleyes to avoid reducing the fishing limits for people using rod-and-reel poles.[66]

Many reformers, who looked to the longer term, proposed new state public school curricular standards to educate the state's public school students about the history of Native American treaty rights. Treaty rights supporters formulated these new curricular standards and pushed for their passage in the late 1980s. Convinced of the need for a resolution to the long-running conflict, Governor Tommy Thompson signed the new law, called Act 31, requiring Wisconsin public schools to teach Native American history. He signed it shortly after the close of the especially contentious 1989 spring spearfishing season.[67] To express their disgust for Thompson's signing of Act 31, PARR leaders called Thompson "One Term Tommy" and vowed to continue their opposition efforts.[68]

In February 1991, the Lac du Flambeau Ojibwe band filed suit against another anti–treaty rights group, Stop Treaty Abuse. Judge Barbara Crabb granted the Lac du Flambeau's injunction. Yet Judge Crabb weighed the possibility of still allowing anti–treaty rights protests while requiring law enforcement to maintain a significant "buffer zone" between the protesters and the Lac du Flambeau spearfishers. After deciding the buffer zone option was untenable, Judge Crabb made permanent the injunction against treaty rights opponents. Crabb's decision destroyed the credibility of the Stop Treaty Abuse group and, by extension, PARR's credibility. Politicians who had expressed sympathy with anti–treaty rights organizations, including Governor Thompson himself, abandoned the cause.[69]

Despite the severity of the conflict, rod-and-reel fishing groups did not merely oppose treaty rights. As the treaty rights controversy subsided, in fact, an alliance of Ojibwe bands, environmental groups, and some sportsfishing groups began to coalesce to oppose mining in northern Wisconsin. This brought them into conflict with the Thompson administration, which supported expansion of mining and logging as forms of economic development. One member of Governor Thompson's cabinet, James Klauser, worked as a mining lobbyist, so Klauser dutifully supported the expansion of mining and logging as well.[70] Despite this friction, though, Thompson successfully exploited the rural-urban political divide by casting his Democratic opponents in both the 1994 and 1998 gubernatorial elections as "Madison liberal[s]." This political epithet combined the elements that anti-treaty groups used to express their opposition: liberalism confined to Wisconsin's cities, especially its college-town capital of Madison.

Using this label, Thompson won unprecedented third and fourth terms as governor.

CONCLUSION

Because of the growing importance of tourism in Wisconsin's economy, disputes over treaty rights brought many issues to the fore. Most Democratic leaders offered only tepid support for treaty rights, but their stance proved quite robust compared to Republican governor Tommy Thompson's vigorous opposition that stoked racial animosity. Because the conflict persisted so long and touched on so many related issues, the treaty rights dispute also helped racialize taxes, regulations, and government spending.

The Native American treaty rights controversy served as a lightning rod that attracted racially charged concerns about Native Americans receiving disproportionately large shares of welfare and gaining "special" exemption from taxation. Although treaty rights opponents recognized some of their allies outside northern Wisconsin, most treaty rights opponents disdained southern Wisconsin, where the state's large cities lay. For treaty rights opponents, these cities were the source of unhelpful politicians, allies of Native Americans, government officials who imposed regulations, and the vacation homeowners who had increased property taxes on the year-round northern Wisconsin residents. The treaty rights issue, then, helps explain the development of a rural-urban divide in state politics. This political formation is especially acute in the Great Lakes borderlands, an overwhelmingly rural region where many Native Americans live and where tourism is such an important economic activity.

NOTES

1. Robert Gough, *Farming the Cutover: A Social History of Northern Wisconsin, 1900–1940* (Lawrence: University of Kansas Press, 1997), 11 and 220–27.

2. Chantal Norrgard, *Seasons of Change: Labor, Treaty Rights, and Ojibwe Nationhood* (Chapel Hill: University of North Carolina Press, 2014), 108–13; Gough, *Farming the Cutover,* 27.

3. Larry Lankton, *Cradle to Grave: Life, Work, and Death at the Lake Superior Copper Mines* (New York and Oxford: Oxford University Press, 1991).

4. Norrgard, *Seasons of Change,* 108–13.

5. Gough, *Farming the Cutover,* 27–28, 34–37, 94–99, and 107–14.

6. Gough, *Farming the Cutover,* 94–99, 107–14, 126–27.

7. Norrgard, *Seasons of Change,* 108–13; Gough, *Farming the Cutover,* 166–78.

8. Gough, *Farming the Cutover,* 166–79 and 219.

9. William F. Thompson, *The History of Wisconsin: Continuity and Change, 1940–1965* (Madison: Wisconsin Historical Society Press, 2014), 6:273, 275, 277, 288–304.

10. Thompson, *The History of Wisconsin*, 6:288–93, 295, 299–304; quote on page 302.

11. Thompson, *The History of Wisconsin*, 6:288–93, 295, 299–304.

12. Gough, *Farming the Cutover*, 226–27.

13. Victoria Gokee to Patrick Lucey, March 15, 1973, Folder 18—Indian Affairs (Briefings) 1973–74, Box 6, Lucey Records (Series 2419), Wisconsin Historical Society (hereafter cited as WHS).

14. Libby R. Tronnes, "'Where Is John Wayne?': The Menominee Warriors Society, Indian Militancy, and Social Unrest during the Alexian Brothers Novitiate Takeover," *American Indian Quarterly* 26, no. 4 (Fall 2002): 526–58.

15. "Indians, Wildlife Group at Impasse," *Wisconsin State Journal* (hereafter cited as *WSJ*), March 16, 1975, section 1, page 10. See also Jim Klahn, "Legal Spiderweb Surrounds Salmon Fishing Dispute," *WSJ*, August 2, 1981, section 8, page 1.

16. Zoltán Grossman, *Unlikely Alliances: Native Nations and White Communities Join to Defend Rural Lands* (Seattle: University of Washington Press, 2017), 37–45 and 211.

17. Grossman, *Unlikely Alliances*, 209–12; "Ojibwe Treaty Rights," Milwaukee Public Museum, https://www.mpm.edu/educators/wirp/nations/ojibwe/treaty-rights.

18. "Ojibwe Treaty Rights," Milwaukee Public Museum. Wisconsin's Native Americans also often experienced harassment even from DNR officials when Native Americans attempted to exercise their hunting and fishing rights guaranteed by treaties. Victoria Gokee to Patrick Lucey, March 15, 1973, Folder 18—Indian Affairs [Briefings] 1973–74, Box 6, Lucey Records [Series 2419], WHS; Tim Franklin, "Indian Hunting, Fishing Rights Rankle Firms," *WSJ*, January 3, 1984, section 3, page 1.

19. James W. Oberly, "GLIFWC: The Founding and Early Years of the Great Lakes Indian Fish and Wildlife Commission," in *Indigenous Perspectives of North America: A Collection of Studies*, eds. Enikő Sepsi, Judit Nagy, Miklós Vassányi (Newcastle upon Tyne: Cambridge Scholars Publishing, 2014), 32–50; Sharon Cohen, "Chippewas Assert Rights, Go to Court," *WSJ*, December 9, 1985, section 1, pages 1 and 4.

20. Cohen, "Chippewas Assert Rights, Go to Court." See also the finding aid for the Larry Peterson Papers (hereafter cited as LPP), University of Wisconsin–Madison Librairies, https://search.library.wisc.edu/catalog/9911125155802121.

21. "A Look at the 1987 PARR Rally, March," *PARR Issue*, June 1987, 17, and "Butternut Lake Protest," *PARR Issue,* October 1987, 5, respectively.

22. Oberly, "GLIFWC," 37 and 44; PARR, "Chippewa Treaty Rights," unknown date between 1989 and 1991, Reel 3, Frame 544, LPP, WHS.

23. Richard Eggleston, "Northwoods Their Concern, but Similarities End There," *WSJ*, October 18, 1984, section 4, page 1. See also Edward Windorff Jr. to Larry Peterson, November 8, 1985, Reel 1, Frame 574, LPP, WHS; the finding aid for the LPP, https://search.library.wisc.edu/catalog/9911125155802121.

24. "Who and What Is PARR?," *PARR Issue* 1, no. 1 (Spring 1986): 1.

25. "PARR Protest Rally and March," *PARR Issue* 1, no. 2 (Summer 1986): 1.

26. Oberly, "*GLIFWC*," 44–45; Maryann Mrowca, "Spearfishing Off to 'Low-Key' Start," *WSJ*, April 14, 1988, 2C.

27. Cohen, "Chippewas Assert Rights, Go to Court."

28. James H. Schlender to Wisconsin legislators, July 23, 1986, Folder 15—Indian Treaty Rights, 1984–1986, Box 25, Esther K. Walling Papers (hereafter cited as EWP), University of Wisconsin—Oshkosh Area Research Center (hereafter cited as UWO).

29. Franklin, "Indian Hunting, Fishing Rights Rankle Firms."

30. Vicki Miazga, "Treaty Rights Opponents Brew Treaty Beer," *PARR Issue* 1, no. 5 (June 1987): 16.

31. Department of the Interior, "Major Fisheries Dispute Settled," press release, March 28, 1985, Folder 1—Hunting and Fishing Proposals, 1983–1990, Box 14, EWP, UWO.

32. JP Leary, "Act 31: Issues & Origins," *Mazina'igan* (Spring/Summer 2013): 11–14; "Governor's Commission," *PARR Issue* 1, no. 3 (Fall 1986): 2; Larry Peterson, "Statement on Governor Earl's Treaties Study Commission," press statement, July 11, 1986, Reel 3, Frames 1047–1049, LPP, WHS; James H. Schlender to Wisconsin legislators, July 23, 1986, Folder 15—Indian Treaty Rights, 1984–1986, Box 25, EWP, UWO; Paul DeMain, "Reason Can End 'War in Woods,'" *Wausau Sunday Herald*, April 14, 1985, page unknown, Folder 1—Hunting and Fishing Proposals, 1983–1990, Box 14, EWP, UWO.

33. Tommy Thompson to Larry Peterson, July 10, 1986, Reel 1, Frame 624, LPP, WHS.

34. Doug Mell, "Thompson, Earl Spar," *WSJ*, October 24, 1986, section 1, page 1.

35. "Thompson Criticizes Welfare 'Explosion,'" *CT*, October 1, 1986, 24.

36. "Governor Hopefuls Criticize Spearing, Indian Treaty Rights," *WSJ*, June 20, 1986, section 1, page 6.

37. "Governor Thompson Handed List of Possible Proposals," *PARR Issue* 1, no. 5 (1987): 10.

38. "PARR Chapter Chairmen and Representatives," *PARR Issue* 1, no. 5 (1987): 12.

39. Syd Herman, "Sparks from the Campfire," *Lakeshore Chronicle,* May 1987, unknown page, Reel 3, Frame 369, LPP, WHS.

40. Larry Peterson, "Wisconsin DNR Short $4.35 Million in 1989," January 17, 1989, Reel 3, Frame 508, LPP, WHS.

41. Larry Peterson, untitled cartoon, *PARR Issue* 1, no. 5 (June 1987): 10.

42. "2nd PARR National Convention Set," *PARR Issue* 2, no. 1 (Winter 1988): 1.

43. Ron Arnold, *The Wise Use Agenda: The Citizen's Policy Guide to Environmental Resource Issues* (Bellevue, WA: Free Enterprise Press, 1989).

44. Grossman, *Unlikely Alliances*, 43 and 212–13.

45. Thomas Busiahn, Neil Kmiecik, Jim Thannum, and Jim Zorn, *1989 Chippewa Spearing Season—Separating Myth From Fact* (Odanah, WI: Great Lakes Indian Fish and Wildlife Commission), Folder 18—Indian Treaty Rights, 1989–1990, Box 25, EWP, UWO.

46. Grossman, *Unlikely Alliances*, 221; Oberly, "GLIFWC," 45–46; "Ojibwe Treaty Rights," Milwaukee Public Museum.

47. Ron Seely, "Resorts Predict Doom if Limits Cut," *WSJ*, April 27, 1989, 1B.

48. Ron Seely, "Spearing Anger Hits Capitol," *WSJ*, April 27, 1989, 1B and 2B. See also Grossman, *Unlikely Alliances*, 216–17.

49. Doug Mell and Jeff Mayers, "Rejection May Haunt Thompson," *WSJ*, October 27, 1989, 2B.

50. Ron Seely, "Myths, Racism Often Hide the Facts about Indians," *WSJ*, May 10, 1989, 1C and 2C.

51. Anonymous, "Public Dialogue Must Continue," letter to the editor, *Daily News*, December 24, 1989, Reel 1, Frame 954, LPP, WHS.

52. Seely, "Myths, Racism Often Hide the Facts about Indians."

53. Sherryl M. Reinolt, open letter "To all people concerned about the treaty-rights situation in Northern Wisconsin," unknown date in 1989 (but after June 21, 1989), Reel 1, Frames 964–966, LPP, WHS.

54. Tim Kehl and Larry Peterson, "Pastor, PARR Executive Director Square Off," *PARR Issue* 2, no. 1 (Winter 1988): 17.

55. Anonymous, defaced PARR membership application form, unknown date in 1989, Reel 1, Frame 957, LPP, WHS.

56. Ron Seely, "Spearfishing Is Hot Issue," *WSJ*, April 16, 1989, 1B and 6B.

57. Ray Cherka to Larry Peterson, September 10, 1990, Reel 1, Frames 1096–1101, LPP, WHS.

58. John Seefeldt to Larry Peterson, February 1990, Reel 1, Frame 1021, LPP, WHS.

59. Larry Peterson, remarks to PARR/STA Solidarity Rally in Minocqua, April 15, 1989, Reel 3, Frames 1126–1129, LPP, WHS; quote from Frame 1128.

60. Larry Peterson, "When Myth Prevails, Can Rights Be Wrong? (Truth Half-Told Is Truth Withheld)," unknown date between 1987 and 1990, Reel 3, Frames 1199–1201, LPP, WHS.

61. John R. LeGautt to Larry Peterson, May 31, 1989, Reel 1, Frames 848–850 and Charles E. Crofoot, Oneida County Sheriff, press release, May 5, 1989, Reel 1, Frame 833, both in LPP, WHS.

62. Joe Beck, "U.S. Official Turns Down Role in Treaty-Rights Feud," *WSJ*, June 3, 1989, 1A.

63. Busiahn, Kmiecik, Thannum, and Zorn, *1989 Chippewa Spearing Season*.

64. Assembly Republican Caucus, "Chippewa Treaty Rights," undated, Folder 17—Indian Treaty Rights, 1989, Box 25, EWP, UWO.

65. Tom Coenen, Lobbyist for the Wisconsin Tourism Federation, to members of the Legislature, "Re: Chippewa Indian Settlement," October 24, 1989, Folder 17—Indian Treaty Rights, 1989, Box 25, EWP, UWO.

66. "Chambers to Urge End to Dispute," *WSJ*, February 13, 1993, 3C; "Recall Candidate Differs with Chambers' Views," *WSJ*, February 24, 1990, 3B.

67. Leary, "Act 31"; "Indian Education for All Kids Urged," *Green Bay Press-Gazette*, June 9, 1989, B-1.

68. Cartoon, no author or date listed, Reel 3, Frame 38, LPP, WHS.

69. Brian L. Pierson, "The Spearfishing Civil Rights Case: Lac Du Flambeau Band v. Stop Treaty Abuse-Wisconsin" (Great Lakes Indian Fish & Wildlife Commission, 2009); Oberly, "GLIFWC," 48.

70. Grossman, *Unlikely Alliances*, 221, 225–38, 336n114.

CONTRIBUTORS

RAY E. BOOMHOWER is senior editor at the Indiana Historical Society Press, where he serves as editor of the quarterly popular history magazine *Traces of Indiana and Midwestern History*. The recipient of the 2010 Indiana Authors Award for his contributions to the state's literary heritage, Boomhower has written numerous books and articles about the Hoosier State. His books include biographies of Ernie Pyle, Gus Grissom, May Wright Sewall, Jim Jontz, John Bartlow Martin, John Bushemi, and Juliet Strauss. Boomhower's 2008 book, *Robert F. Kennedy and the 1968 Indiana Primary*, received the Indiana Center for the Book's Best Book of Indiana Award in the nonfiction historical/biographical category.

JACOB BRUGGEMAN is a graduate of Miami University (B.A., M.A. '19) and the University of Cambridge, Darwin College (M.Phil. '20), where he studied economic and social history. Bruggeman is now a PhD student in American History at Johns Hopkins University. He is the coauthor, with Eric Rhodes, of the book chapter "From Crass Materialists to Missionaries of Culture: A Regional History of Cultural Ascendance and Economic Decline through the Cleveland Orchestra," forthcoming in *Where East Meets (Mid)West: Exploring an American Regional Divide,* a Kent State University Press collection edited by Jon Lauck. Additionally, Bruggeman is an editor of the *Cleveland Review of Books* and has written columns or criticism for the *Wall Street Journal, USA TODAY, Washington Times, Detroit News, Cincinnati Enquirer, Columbus Dispatch,* and *BELT Magazine.*

PETER J. DECARLO is a public historian at the Minnesota Historical Society. In his position, he produces scholarship on regional history and works on public exhibits, interpretive programs, web content, and digital and print publications. He is the author of *Fort Snelling at Bdote,* a decolonizing narrative focused on placemaking that reframes Minnesota's premier National Historic Landmark. DeCarlo's research interests include settler colonialism and colonial borderlands, Native American studies, the nineteenth-century Upper Midwest, and memory studies. His current research project focuses on Minnesota and the Northern Plains as a site of imperial struggle. A public servant, DeCarlo's main ambition is using history to support community dialogues and projects aimed at building a better future. DeCarlo grew up in the Twin Cities and holds a master's in history from the University of Wisconsin, Eau Claire. He is also the author of "Loyalty Within Racism: The Segregated Sixteenth Battalion of the Minnesota Home Guard During World War I," *Minnesota History* 65, no. 6 (Summer 2017).

TIM FRANDY was born and raised in the Northwoods of northern Wisconsin and is an assistant professor of Nordic Studies at the University of British Columbia. His research centers around Indigenous peoples and ethnic minorities, subsistence traditions and cultural worldview, and the environmental humanities. He is the editor and translator of *Inari Sámi Folklore: Stories from Aanaar,* the first multivoiced anthology of Sámi oral tradition published in English, and coeditor with B. Marcus Cederström of a volume on public folklore and the public humanities titled *Culture Work: Folklore for the Public Good.*

ZACHARY MICHAEL JACK is the author of many award-winning books on the culture and history of the Midwest and a member of the board of directors of the Midwestern History Association (MHA). A seventh-generation Iowan, Jack is a professor of English and a faculty member in the Chicago Area Studies (CAS) program at North Central College in northern Illinois.

THEODORE J. KARAMANSKI is professor of history and director of the Public History Program at Loyola University Chicago. He has worked as a heritage consultant for numerous state and federal agencies as well as for *National Geographic,* the National Trust for Historic Preservation, and the *Travel Channel.* He is the author of ten books on Midwestern and Canadian history, including *Fur Trade and Exploration* (1983), *Deep Woods Frontier: A History of Logging in Northern Michigan* (1989), *Ethics and Public History* (1990), *Rally 'Round the Flag: Chicago and the Civil War* (1993), *Schooner Passage: Sailing Ships and the Lake Michigan Frontier* (2000), *North Woods River* (with Eileen McMahon, 2009), *Blackbird's Song: Andrew J. Blackbird and the Odawa People* (2012), and, most recently, *Mastering the Inland Seas: How Lighthouses, Navigational Aids, and Harbors Transformed the Great Lakes and America* (2020). His current research is on the environmental history of Lake Michigan.

KEVIN KOCH is the author of three books that explore the sense of place through nature, history, and personal connection to the landscape: *Skiing at Midnight: A Nature Journal from Dubuque County, Iowa* (2002); *The Driftless Land: Spirit of Place in the Upper Mississippi Valley* (2010); and *The Thin Places: A Celtic Landscape from Ireland to the Driftless*. His essays have appeared in the *North American Review, Big Muddy,* and numerous other magazines, journals, and newspapers. He is a professor of English at Loras College in Dubuque, Iowa, where he teaches courses such as Nature Writing, Writing the Midwest Landscape, The Midwest Driftless Area, and Mississippi River Lore and Legacy. When not teaching or writing, he can be found bicycling, kayaking, or hiking throughout the Driftless Area.

JON K. LAUCK is the author of several books, including *Prairie Republic: The Political Culture of Dakota Territory, 1879–1889* (University of Oklahoma Press, 2010); *The Lost Region: Toward a Revival of Midwestern History* (University of Iowa Press, 2013); *From Warm Center to Ragged Edge: The Erosion of Midwestern Regionalism, 1920–1965* (University of Iowa Press, 2017); and *The Good Country: A History of the American Midwest, 1800–1900* (University of Oklahoma Press, 2022). He has edited several collections, including *The Midwestern Moment: The Forgotten World of Early-Twentieth-Century Midwestern Regionalism, 1880–1940* (Hastings College Press, 2017); *Finding a New Midwestern History* (University of Nebraska Press, 2017); *The Interior Borderlands: Regional Identity in the Midwest and Great Plains* (Center for Western Studies, 2019); *The Conservative Heartland: A Political History of the Postwar American Midwest* (University Press of Kansas, 2020); *The Making of the Midwest: Essays on the Formation of Midwestern Identity, 1787–1900* (Hastings College Press, 2020); *Heartland River: A Cultural and Environmental History of the Big Sioux River Valley* (Center for Western Studies, 2022); and four volumes of *The Plains Political Tradition: Essays on South Dakota Political Culture* (2011, 2014, 2018, 2022). Lauck has worked for several years as a full-time professor, a part-time professor, U.S.

Senate staffer, and a lawyer and is currently serving as an adjunct professor of history and political science at the University of South Dakota and as editor-in-chief of *Middle West Review.*

HENDRIK (HANK) MEIJER was a reporter and editor before joining the family retail business in Grand Rapids, Michigan, where he is executive chairman. He is the author most recently of *Arthur Vandenberg: The Man in the Middle of the American Century* (University of Chicago Press, 2017). His first book, *Thrifty Years: The Life of Hendrik Meijer* (William B. Eerdmans Publishing, 1984), was a biography of his grandfather. He is vice-chair of both the Gerald R. Ford Presidential Foundation and the National Constitution Center, a trustee of the Kettering Foundation and The Henry Ford, and a fellow of the Hauenstein Center for Presidential Studies at Grand Valley State University.

ADAM MERTZ earned his PhD in U.S. labor history from the University of Illinois at Chicago. Adam's dissertation, "Growing Realignment," explores Wisconsin's history since the 1960s—mainly its tax policies and politicians' efforts to spur economic development—to explore how suburban sprawl from metropolitan areas and recreational areas shaped the rural-urban divide in politics. Adam teaches classes at Waubonsee Community College in Aurora, Illinois.

GREGORY S. ROSE is dean and director of The Ohio State University at Marion and associate professor of geography. His bachelor's degrees in geography and history are from Valparaiso University in Indiana, and he earned his master's and doctorate degrees in geography at Michigan State University. His research area is the nineteenth-century Midwest. He has conducted research and published on the birthplace origins and previous residences of immigrant populations using U.S. Census nativity data and genealogical records; the cultural impacts of these populations on the Midwestern landscape; the historical economic development of the region; and the definition of the Midwest as a region according to cultural elements, vernacular perceptions, agricultural areas, and the physical environment.

HILARY-JOY VIRTANEN is an associate professor of Finnish and Nordic Studies at Finlandia University in Hancock, Michigan. A folklorist by training, Virtanen researches numerous aspects of Finnish ethnic and Upper Midwestern folklife, including festivals, traditional arts, and laborlore. She has previously published on the Finnish American folklore characters Heikki Lunta and St. Urho, as well as on issues of orality and literacy in storytelling, Finnish American leftist music and social history, and World War I draft resistance. Much of her work has a public orientation, and she has presented her research in the form of museum exhibits, public lectures, websites, and films as part of her interest in sharing humanities and social sciences works with the communities she researches. She is the 2019 recipient of the Finlandia University Board of Trustees Distinguished Faculty Award.

CHRISTOPHER VONDRACEK is a reporter covering rural Minnesota and agriculture for the *Minneapolis Star Tribune*. A native of Wells, Minnesota, he graduated with degrees in literature and journalism from the University of South Dakota and a degree in creative writing from Hamline University in St. Paul. His debut book of poetry, *Rattlesnake Summer: 66 Poems for 66 South Dakota Counties* (IPSO Gallery, Badger Clark Publishing) was published in 2020.

GLEAVES WHITNEY is the author or editor of numerous books. He became the executive director of the Gerald R. Ford Presidential Foundation in 2020. Before that, he directed the Hauenstein Center for Presidential Studies at Grand Valley State University from 2003 to 2020. Prior to that, he served as a speechwriter for Michigan governor John Engler from 1992 to 2003. Educated at the University of Michigan, he was named the first senior fellow of the Russell Kirk Center for Cultural Renewal in 1995.

INDEX

References to illustrations appear in italic type.

Printed in the USA
CPSIA information can be obtained
at www.ICGtesting.com
CBHW030335080324
5104CB00001B/57